Theatre History Studies

2012 VOLUME 32

Edited by

RHONA JUSTICE-MALLOY

PUBLISHED BY THE MID-AMERICA THEATRE CONFERENCE
AND THE UNIVERSITY OF ALABAMA PRESS

Designed by Todd Lape / Lape Designs
Typeface: Minion
Articles appearing in this journal are abstracted and indexed in *Historical Abstracts* and *America: History and Life.*

∞

The paper on which this book is printed meets the minimum requirements of American National Standard for Information Sciences-Permanence of Paper for Printed Library Materials, ANSI Z39.48-1984.

MEMBER
CELJ
Council of Editors of Learned Journals

Cover: Toby scores a hit with the audience. Courtesy of Theatre Museum, Midwest Old Threshers, Mount Pleasant, Iowa.

Theater History Studies is an official journal of the Mid-America Theatre Conference, Inc. (MATC). The conference encompasses the states of Illinois, Indiana, Iowa, Kansas, Michigan, Minnesota, Missouri, Nebraska, North Dakota, South Dakota, and Wisconsin. Its purposes are to unite people and organizations within this region and elsewhere who have an interest in theatre and to promote the growth and development of all forms of theatre.

Theatre History Studies is devoted to research in all areas of theatre history. Manuscripts should be prepared in conformity with the guidelines established in the *Chicago Manual of Style,* and emailed to mullener@muohio.edu, or submitted in duplicate, and sent to Elizabeth Reitz Mullenix, PhD, Professor and Chair, Miami University Department of Theatre, Center for the Performing Arts, Rm. 121, Oxford OH, 45056. Consulting editors review the manuscripts, a process that takes approximately four months. The journal does not normally accept studies of dramatic literature unless there is a focus on actual production and performance. Authors whose manuscripts are accepted must provide the editor with an electronic file, using Microsoft Word. Illustrations (preferably high-quality originals or black-and-white glossies) are welcomed. Manuscripts will be returned only if accompanied by a stamped, self-addressed envelope bearing sufficient postage.

This publication is issued annually by the Mid-America Theatre Conference and The University of Alabama Press.

Subscription rates for 2012 are $15 for individuals, $30 for institutions, and an additional $8 for foreign delivery. Back issues are $29.95 each. Subscription orders and changes of address should be directed to Allie Harper, The University of Alabama Press, Box 870380, Tuscaloosa, AL 35487 (205-348-1564 phone, 205-348-9201 fax).

Theatre History Studies is indexed in *Humanities Index, Humanities Abstracts, Book Review Index, MLA International Bibliography, International Bibliography of Theatre, Arts & Humanities Citation Index, IBZ International Bibliography of Periodical Literature,* and *IBR International Bibliography of Book Reviews,* the database of *International Index to the Performing Arts.* Full texts of essays appear in the databases of both *Humanities Abstracts Full Text* and *SIRS.* The journal has published its own index, *The Twenty Year Index, 1981–2000.* It is available for $10 for individuals and $15 for libraries from Elizabeth Reitz Mullenix, PhD, Professor and Chair, Miami University Department of Theatre, Center for the Performing Arts, Rm. 121, Oxford OH, 45056; (513) 529-3053.

CONTENTS

CONTENTS

BOOK REVIEWS

CONTENTS

ILLUSTRATIONS

Company

Keynote Speech from the Thirty-second Mid-America Theatre Conference

—BILL RAUCH

I'm a company man.

I grew up in a very hospitable family. When I was a child, a lovely and quite crazy woman who went to our church came to stay for a few days and ended up living with our family for a good six months. That was more typical than unusual. My family moved a lot when I was growing up, on average once every two years. My father was a company man in a solid corporate mold, his career confirming the truth in the joke that IBM actually stands for "I've Been Moved." Wherever his work took us, though, my parents opened their home to new acquaintances that quickly became friends.

In my early twenties, when my peers and I started our own theatre, we would gather at my parents' house. Everyone would fly into the local airport, and as many as fifteen of us would crash in sleeping bags in the basement. The next morning, we'd take turns showering and making breakfast before piling into our big blue van and hitting the road for our next residency in some far-flung corner of the United States.

I now live with my husband and our two sons in southern Oregon, and the example that my parents set is alive and well in my life. This is our first home with a spare bedroom. Because Ashland is a great place to visit, our guest room is filled nonstop from late May through early October every year. Sometimes we have so many guests at once that they spread out onto the couch or the floors of other rooms as well. I especially love flipping pancakes in the morning or grilling burgers on a summer night to feed a house full of people I love.

What can I say? I'm a company man.

In the summer before my senior year of college, I had my first experience as an audience member at a Wooster Group show. My heart started to pound much faster than it ever had before in a theatre. My artistic life was forever changed. My encounter with one of our nation's leading experimental troupes did not make me rededicate myself to pursuing radical aesthetic forms. The lesson that I took away from my Wooster Group encounter was that exceptional work of any kind comes out of company. In response, I devoted the last semester of my senior year of college to launching the Kronauer Group, a twenty-person ensemble that would work together on multiple projects. No one auditioned; I just invited fellow student actors who I respected to come play. We performed in the basement of my dorm, as well as multiple corners of our campus, and did dozens of projects, some for a day and others for several weeks at a time.

Most of the founding members of Cornerstone Theater Company were part of that senior-year experiment in company. After graduation, I had worked as a word processor at a tombstone company (that's the subject of another talk) and then at the Kennedy Center as an assistant director to the stage and opera director Peter Sellars. When I told my father about my desire to cofound a community-based theatre company, he was concerned, if not outraged, that I'd leave a good job at a major cultural palace, the Kennedy Center, to "run around the country with my friends from school."

How could he not understand? I'm a company man.

Twenty years later, I finally reached a period in my career when I was a full-time freelance artist. I was excited to spread my wings, to focus exclusively on working as a director without the burden of institutional responsibility. From my last day as Cornerstone's artistic director until the day I was appointed artistic director of the Oregon Shakespeare Festival (OSF), there were a total of four months. Four months is the sum total of my life as an exclusively independent artist.

I should have known better. I'm a company man.

I promise to move on from this endless refrain with its unfortunate emphasis on my gender, but I do really want to hammer home the point that my life has been devoted to company, which has made the thought of addressing you on this topic a fairly daunting proposition. Before I go any further, I want to thank you for the honor of inviting me and for listening to whatever I might share. My colleague John Fletcher tells me that the Mid-America Theatre Conference is for "artists who think and scholars who make art." As a big believer in border crossing and boundary erasing, this description made me very excited to be in a room with all of you.

I want to share some stories today from the two companies that have shaped my life so far: Cornerstone Theater Company, where even as a founding artistic director I was one member of a small consensus-run ensemble; and the Oregon Shakespeare Festival, where I am, no matter how uncomfortable it makes me to say it, the head of a 550-person company.

Given my upbringing and my college experiments, it's not a huge surprise that at the age of twenty-three, I, along with my colleague Alison Carey, co-founded a theatre company.

Cornerstone started in 1986, but its genesis was a few years earlier when some of my friends and I heard a dreadful statistic—that 98 percent of Americans didn't go to professional theatre on anything approaching a regular basis. In the process, a professor of ours told us that theatre was a dead art form. Of course we loved the theatre and we hoped to prove the learned professor wrong. The easiest way, it seemed, to find out why people didn't feel that theatre was an important part of their lives was to get to know them. And hey, what better way to get to know someone than to do a show with them?

So the eleven of us who were founding ensemble members of Cornerstone bought a big blue van and hit the road, moving into tiny rural towns—usually with populations between two hundred and two thousand—that had no active tradition of live theatre. We spent five years living for two to four months at a time in communities across the United States—from Virginia to North Dakota to Maine to Florida to Texas, and plenty of places in between—mounting plays with first-time actors of all ages for an audience of their families and neighbors. We turned a welding shop, a city hall basement, an abandoned high school gymnasium, and a cattle-auction barn into theatres where we would perform. We also lived in unusual places, because we raised the cash costs of our projects ourselves, only asking the community to provide performance space and housing in what we called "otherwise unoccupied facilities." In practice that meant everything from some smelly trailers in the leaf of a highway clover to an abandoned fast-food restaurant to that vacant high school where we would cook in the home ec room, shower in the locker rooms, and roller-skate through the hallways in the wee hours of the morning. Great stuff for exorcising your high school demons!

After five years of work with rural communities, we eventually chose to settle down in Los Angeles because of its remarkably diverse communities—it's like you're within driving distance of the whole world—and what started as a two-year urban residency became a home. Cornerstone Theater is now in its twenty-fifth year of working with urban and rural communities, continuing to thrive under the artistic leadership of Michael John Garces.

Over the years, the way we defined company at Cornerstone shifted and grew, but our commitment to the concept of company never wavered. I want to relate some of the lessons we learned along the way.

We learned that what we did always succeeded, even amidst occasional spectacular failure. People were always willing to come together across huge divisions in order to create art, whether they were African Americans and European Americans who had been locked in a two-decade long economic boycott in a Mississippi town, fundamentalist Christians and atheists debating the true nature of morality in a timber town in the Pacific Northwest, or neighbors in a South Los Angeles neighborhood who feared crossing a block to be in a show because of rival gangs. Surprisingly courageous individuals again and again crossed lines to form a company and make something beautiful.

We learned that everyone has a story to tell and that everyone has something to bring to the table. We did an adaptation of Molière's *Tartuffe* in a Great Plains farming town of 250 people at the height of the late-1980s family farm crisis; as we worked alongside farmers to adapt the play to their realities, Molière's play about religious hypocrisy became a story of the disintegration of the family farm. Our desire to be relevant with an exposé of televangelism quickly faded into irrelevance. As professional artists, we had to pose some of the questions—but we did not hold all, or even many, of the answers.

We learned that it's not always easy to build company. We learned about perseverance, about eating lunch with the tribal elders on a Paiute Native American reservation in Nevada for thirty days in a row until an elder finally agreed to be in our adaptation of the Greek tragic trilogy *The Oresteia*. We learned to bartend so that the bartender and his wife in a small town could play Horatio and Gertrude in a Wild West version of Hamlet. That was our first-ever community-based adaptation, and it was motivated by a Sunday-school teacher threatening to quit, which in turn launched a community-wide investigation into Shakespeare's blasphemy and our—I now quote a rancher who hit the nail on the head—"smart-ass college kid rewrites." We learned to listen harder in order to make better art. We learned to follow the community's lead in times of crisis, too. Eleven-year-old Tiffany Dozier was killed by gang gunfire in front of our performance site after a dance in the LA neighborhood of Pacoima, just weeks before our opening night. We wondered if it was responsible to have another nighttime event at the same facility so soon after this tragic murder. The cast, including friends and relatives of Tiffany, told us that the play had to go on because of Tiffany's death.

We learned to move out of our comfort zone in order to expand who was in the room. We learned to seek source texts outside the Western canon and to do passages of plays in Spanish, Mandarin, Korean, Tagalog, and American Sign Language to create access through language. We learned again and again to find the courage to talk to the person in the room with whom you are certain you have the least in common and who makes you the most afraid. For me, it was usually guys with gun racks in the back of their pickups, some of whom went on to become my friends and colleagues.

We learned to assume that everything is possible. In Mississippi we cast as Romeo a high school senior, Edret Brinston, who had failed the state literacy test twice. Soon after mastering his leading role, he passed the test with flying colors and graduated from high school. In an LA neighborhood we undertook a three-play cycle. In the first show, we cast a young woman named Stephanie Escobar. In the second production, Stephanie's mother joined as an assistant stage manager and her brother Andrew ran the soundboard; by the third production, her sister Laura was on the backstage crew and their father, a bus driver by day, was playing in the show band. We learned that the arts are one of the few activities in which multiple generations of a single family can participate together—and we became determined to be an arts organization that created more of those opportunities for families.

We learned that to build something worthwhile, we had to take the time to engage deeply. We did our original projects in six weeks. By late in my time at Cornerstone, we devoted over four and a half years to a faith-based cycle of plays, creating individual projects with distinct Buddhist, Christian, Hindu, Jewish, Muslim, and other religious communities—including a community of lesbian, gay, bisexual, and transgendered people of multiple faiths—and then bringing together members of all of those faith-based communities into what we called a Bridge Show. The character of a gay Muslim in this culminating project led to huge dissension and division—all of the straight Muslim cast members eventually quit—but there were hours and hours of deeply painful and meaningful conversations that opened many of our hearts and minds. Today, Cornerstone doesn't conceive of working in a community without being part of a larger, longer-term cycle of community projects that will culminate in a Bridge Show.

We learned that we should cross lines, too. As a professional arts organization, we had a responsibility to help found or strengthen local resources that would exist long after our residency ended. After playing a lead in a Cornerstone production, Ron Temple, a farmer who stands six feet, nine inches tall, founded an arts organization in his rural Kansas community of Norcatur; years later a state tourism brochure cited the town as "being known far and wide for its arts and culture." During his Cornerstone show, Ron turned his farm over to his sons-in-law and spent fourteen hours a day rehearsing and trying to learn his lines. "This acting thing," Ron said to a camera crew from CBS Evening News, "is a lot like sex. Everybody knows a little bit about it, but it's the technique that counts."

Guillermo Aviles was a high school senior who planned to enlist in the military after graduation. When he was cast in a leading part in a Cornerstone production in the San Miguel neighborhood of the LA community of Watts, the director persuaded the talented young man to apply to college to study theatre. Guillermo not only became the first in his family to achieve higher education, but he received his master's degree as well. With a portion of box-office proceeds from the Cornerstone project in Watts, Guillermo helped to found the Watts Village Theatre Company, which is still creating work under his leadership seventeen years later.

We learned that you often can't know the ripples of the work and that you have to maintain faith. Three years after our hugely controversial and successful biracial *Romeo and Juliet* in Port Gibson, Mississippi, the community had created only one biracial show on its own. I'll confess to you now that I felt ashamed: I feared that we had failed these folks in the long haul. When revisiting the community as part of a national tour, at least twenty people told us the same story: Port Gibson became part of Main Street USA, a federally funded program for small towns to revitalize their Main Streets. The community had recently been honored for having the most racially integrated board in the United States. "It was because of the play," was the constant refrain. "We all met and learned to trust each other through the play." Talk about the power of company! The results of artistic work that strengthens community cannot be measured solely through an artistic lens.

In the 1980s when we started our company, we were constantly asked whether what we were doing was art or social work, as if no one could conceive of art as being something that is central to community identity. Cornerstone doesn't get asked that question anymore, because the way people perceive art has changed. In fact, many of you have been at the vanguard of participatory art-making, and I'm optimistic enough to believe that the rest of our society is starting to catch up with what you all know so well.

As I mentioned earlier, Cornerstone's company makes major policy and programming decisions by consensus. This means that a decision is not reached until everyone can agree to it and that any one individual can block a decision from being made. True consensus decision making, as those of you who practice it know, is insanely time consuming and very trying. It can also result in a much wiser decision than would have been made by any individual, no matter how inspired.

One of many examples of this involved our first grant from the National Endowment for the Arts (NEA). After banging on the door of the NEA for two years—at that time, to us, an eternity—we received the stamp of approval of our first federal grant the same year that Jesse Helms authored the obscenity clause. Any organization receiving federal funds would have to sign an oath promising, in essence, to not do anything obscene, including but not limited to depictions of homoeroticism—a linguistic turn that I remember vividly two decades later. At that time, I was terrified of turning down the grant: as a young company, we had fought so hard to win it. Moreover, Theatre Communications Group, of which we were a brand-new member, took the official position that it was necessary to sign the oath, albeit under protest, in order to not prove to conservative legislators that the endowment was no longer needed—a pretty darned compelling argument to me at the time. It was only through the rigors of consensus decision making that I finally saw the group's wisdom and changed my position. If Cornerstone were to be footnoted someday as the final nail in the coffin of the NEA, my colleagues' argument went, then we'd wear that label with pride and not with shame. I was saved from my own fear through a consensus process.

Nevertheless, I eventually reached a point in my personal journey where I needed to be free to make my own mistakes as a leader, and the consensus model no longer worked for me. This was absolutely a factor in my decision to leave Cornerstone after twenty years. Now I am free to make all sorts of my own mistakes at OSF, and believe me, I do. On the other hand, along with three of my former Cornerstone colleagues that I begged to join me in Ashland, there is a marked increase in transparent communication and open decision making in the halls of the OSF.

When I began thinking about the possibility of landing in Ashland, I had a moment of panic: was I giving up my life's commitment to ensemble and a personal mission of community-based art? The festival is a very different company from Cornerstone—with an operating budget of over $29 million, over 410,000 audience members, most of whom come from hundreds of miles away, and the largest acting company in the United States performing 822 performances of twelve plays in rotating repertory, it operates on a different scale (to say the least) and with a different focus than I was used to.

But the panic passed when I remembered again what had drawn me to the OSF. Okay, a somewhat embarrassing but revealing story. In 2002, I directed my first show in Ashland as a guest director. The artistic director at the time, Libby

Appel, took me out to dinner and asked what I'd like to be doing in five years. Without thinking, I blurted out, "I'd like to be in your job." "My job is not available" was the stern response! I stammered that I knew that, and that I planned to stay at Cornerstone my whole life anyway.

But upon further reflection, I realized that my unedited response revealed that I had fallen in love with a new company. And it was just that that drew me: company, not only the acting company of one of twelve productions, not only the full acting company of over one hundred men, women and children, but all 550 employees of the festival, a dynamic group of artists, artisans, administrative and support staff that prides itself on its company affiliation.

Of course you know what my blurted comment led to: five years later, almost to the day, was the beginning of my full-time tenure as artistic director of the OSF. Be careful how you answer questions about your future, right?

In the intervening years, as I've become simply the artistic director and not the "new" artistic director, we have been working actively to expand our definition of company in many ways.

We have added community partners to expand the circle of stakeholders in our work. As one example, we produced the world premiere of *Welcome Home, Jenny Sutter*, a play about a female Marine returning from Iraq. In a first for the festival, we enlisted our local VFW branch to partner with us. Through the VFW we met Iraq War vet Melissa Steinman, who played an essential role in advising us, building a panel of vets who met with the cast, and helping us to organize an initiative in which all veterans, active-duty military personnel, and reservists would receive two free tickets throughout the run. We also erected a remembrance tree in the lobby for audience members to honor loved ones who have served our country. By the show's closing, the tree hit the ceiling at eighteen feet in height, covered in notes that were overwhelmingly moving, and we had given away over fifteen hundred free tickets to vets. After the opening performance, an audience member grabbed me in the lobby and said, "I'm a wounded Marine vet. You people nailed it and I thank you." He began to cry, and of course I began to cry. And this was not just an access issue: by inviting vets to come for free, we were also sending a very deliberate message to the wider audience that this play was one that needed to be seen by everyone, regardless of one's position on the war in Iraq.

We've launched American Revolutions: the United States History Cycle, in which we're commissioning up to thirty-seven new plays—the magic number believed to be the total in the Shakespeare canon—to help establish some shared vocabulary about our national identity. William Shakespeare lived in an age of anxiety, especially on the question of who was going to replace the childless monarch Elizabeth, and in response he wrote history plays that examined the transfer of power in his country's past. Inspired by the spirit and scale of Shakespeare's work, we want to build a canon of plays that helps us learn from our country's past in order to illuminate the best paths for the future. Under the thematic umbrella of American Revolutions, the plays will all look at a moment of change in U.S. history; we're collaborating not only with playwrights but also with historians and other academics, as well as museums, to create the most vibrant possible body of work. To name a few examples, we've got a writer working on a play about LBJ and the passage of civil rights legislation (produced in 2012); a writer working on America's relationship to the Philippines; and a writer/director team, which happens to include the son of George Moscone, writing a play about an adult son's delayed response to his father's political assassination that will run in repertory this season with Shakespeare's *Julius Caesar*. (This is *Ghost Light*, which opened in July 2011). Alison Carey, who cofounded Cornerstone with me and who is now in Ashland running the History Cycle, likes to say that American Revolutions is a lot like Cornerstone, except the community we're working with is the entire United States.

Our Green Show provides preshow entertainment, free of charge, from early June to early October. For almost fifty years, the Green Show stage hosted Renaissance dancers and Elizabethan music. In a move that was most directly inspired by my Cornerstone years, we opened up the Green Show to include an ever-rotating bill of fare that would include artists from our local community and artists from as far away as Mexico City or New York, performers who were community youth and performers who were professionals working at the peak of their craft. Each night the programming changes from, say, classical violinists to hip-hop dancers who specialize in a form called crumping. (I'm really interested in the intersection of classical theatre and hip-hop as a contemporary form that combines street slang and elevated poetry, much like William Shakespeare, but that, too, is a topic for another talk.) For a theatre that relies heavily on tourists as audience, the Green Show has become a gift to our local community; wildly popular with local audiences, by the use of local performers it also allows the community to literally become part of the company.

I believe in resident companies of actors. Actors with shared history, who work together over one or several seasons of rigorous rotating repertory, create better productions. The higher the number of shared seasons, the more shorthand and trust that develops, and the better the work has the potential to be. I passionately believe that it's why the great works of dramatic literature, for many centuries, have come out of acting companies. Shakespeare was not a lone genius writing in isolation. He was a company man. He wrote masterpieces of dramatic literature in collaboration with a resident acting company that worked in rotating repertory. Molière, Lorca, Brecht, Chekhov—most of the great dramatists in Western dramatic literature—created their work in collaboration with companies. And dramatic traditions from outside the Western world are also usually company-based, if not community-based.

At most theatres in our country, with the blessed exception of small ensembles, we have dismantled resident acting companies at a startling rate, even companies with "Company" or "Repertory" in their names. After all, you can save money by not having actors sit around if you don't need them in a certain show. And, with a Hollywood-style mentality, you can always find the actor who fits the role if you're willing, if I may paraphrase Mike Daisey's wonderfully effective image, to FedEx actors into your community, freeze-dried, from New York or LA, and ship them back when the show closes. But this cost-effective, typecast-driven mentality is destroying the quality of work in our field. It is thoroughly shortsighted. Ashland's resident acting company is a huge part of why I'm in my current job.

The acting company is also why we're pouring considerable resources and energy into commissioning new work, new work that is created with and for a resident company of actors. It's why we've put a company of actors at the center of new play development by launching what we call the Black Swan Lab for New Work. I believe it's the primary reason why audiences are flocking to Ashland in record numbers: to see the same company of actors tackle a huge variety of styles of work in three wildly different spaces.

At the same time, a company should never be static. Artists need to be continually challenged, to have our assumptions undermined and to be filled with new ideas and energies, so that we can then surprise ourselves, surprise each other and our audiences with our choices. One of the most potent ways to wake ourselves up is to welcome new collaborators who bring us fresh perspectives. At OSF, I have been very open about my desire to rotate actors in and out of the company, for everyone's growth, as well as to bring new directors and designers to work with us, to continually challenge and expand our notion of what is possible.

Entitlement is rarely a healthy emotional dynamic. Ideally, company members don't work together season after season because of a sense of duty, of obligation. In my ideal company, I work with colleagues season after season because there is no one else I can imagine in whatever season is coming next, and because there is no other place on earth where those colleagues want to be creating work and to be growing as an artist right now. Through this work we create bonds that are constantly replenished with each new project.

One of the most challenging episodes in Cornerstone's existence came about five years before I left the company, when we decided to eliminate lifetime tenure for ensemble members. There was a beauty, never mind an appealing sentimentality, to the notion that once in, you were in for life. The problem was that it began to paralyze all of us. As an artistic director, I was not alone in being terrified of adding ensemble members—the notion of a lifetime commitment was too high a hurdle, one that perhaps none of us founding members would ever have made it over. Conversely, there were inactive ensemble members whose lives had moved into new directions but who were terrified to give up their role in the ensemble because the lifetime stakes were so high. After a year of emotionally draining meetings, the ensemble courageously re-formed the rules of ensemble membership. Members would rotate through three-year stints; at the end of each three-year period, we would be encouraged to reflect on whether or not we were still growing and wanted to remain. A committee of ensemble members who were not up for renewal would then make decisions about who to renew and what new members to add. Of course this was a complex system that created new challenges, but the positive effect was palpable: you could feel the company, individually and collectively, breathe again. And ever since, Cornerstone's ensemble has both lost and gained members almost every year in a way that has absolutely contributed to the organization's artistic vitality.

Of course, any acting company is not just the sum of its great individual performances. A company can and should grow through shared training as well. A few years ago I appointed a director of company development, Scott Kaiser, whose job is not only to help find new company members but also to maximize opportunities for growth of the current company. We have weekly ateliers, skill-building workshops, that are open to all company members. We have physical trainers on staff, a Feldenkrais teacher, and a singing coach. We are always looking for new ways to deepen our collective skill set and to keep our company's craft firm and fresh. I am also thrilled that some of our actors have asked to grow in new directions by helping to direct or to choreograph—it's been eye-opening for everyone involved to have members of the acting company sit on the other side of the rehearsal room table.

Both at Cornerstone and in Ashland, as we wrestle with company, we inevitably wrestle with questions of diversity and inclusion. In bad moments, moments where the fear takes over, I find myself witnessing or even participating in arguments about a hierarchy of oppression. So here are some truths that I've observed.

It's sometimes hard to be black in this field.

It's sometimes hard to be white in this field.

It's sometimes hard to be Latino, to be Asian, or to be mixed race in this field.

It's sometimes hard to be differently abled in this field.

It's sometimes hard to be a young practitioner, sensing that you have to prove yourself before you're given opportunities and yet fearing that you may never get the opportunities to really prove yourself.

It's sometimes hard to be a more mature practitioner, fearing that your opportunities might be eroding.

And for every single one of us, it's always hard to be reduced to only one aspect of your identity, especially if you're not making the choice about which part of your infinitely complex self you want to bring forward in a given moment.

I trust that you are getting my point here. Something that I constantly stress to the festival company is that there is privilege and challenge associated with longevity and there is privilege and challenge associated with newness; there is privilege and challenge associated with everyone's race and ethnicity that cuts in every possible direction; there is privilege and challenge that comes with every aspect of our diversity.

Last season we held two forums on white privilege that generated huge controversy. For some company members, the very title was a racist affront; as one staff member wrote me, "I have a strong feeling that the Festival would like me to wear a button that says 'I'm sorry I'm white.'" For others, white privilege is not an accusation but a neutral term of fact, acknowledging an unlevel playing field. Issues of class reverberate strongly in Ashland as well, both in terms of privileges that come based on proximity to the work onstage and simple dollars and cents.

The great equalizer is the work, the work that demands our talent, our skill, and our passion. What brings us together is the work.

Do I think we all need to have the same political perspective? The same aesthetic point of view? The same beliefs in terms of how we approach our diversity? Do I think we should put all our energy into trying to eliminate every possible interpersonal conflict? No, absolutely not.

But I do believe that our work will be stronger if there are safe spaces for us to increase our trust. Our work will be stronger if we can learn to speak without fear and with trust about difficult issues. Our art demands that we explore with openness and candor some of the toughest questions that have faced and continue to face humankind. How can we do that if there is an environment of fear or a lack of trust? I have devoted my life to the theatre because I believe that it is a rehearsal for changing the world, "not to resolve the contradictions," as the theatre artist Robbie McCauley once put it, "but to house the contradictions."

It's healthy to have conflict of ideas, which is different than personal conflict. We don't want to avoid conversations because they're uncomfortable. It's challenging to make the distinction clear between conflict of ideas and conflict of relationships, but it's essential that we try. If you find your blood pressure rising when someone is speaking, instead of shutting down or shutting doors, try getting curious and open. Can you imagine how mighty the energy would be if we all started our new relationships in any new endeavor by assuming trust instead of waiting for it to be earned?

I have had the privilege of guest teaching a lot, and teaching ongoing courses in various academic settings. In only one of those many theatre departments did I actually feel a true spirit of company. It was radically different and better when my colleagues and I were genuinely cheering each other's successes and trying to help each other solve problems. What we modeled to our students as a group of colleagues was far more profound and long lasting than any bit of wisdom any of us might share in our individual classrooms.

After opening our 2011 season in Ashland, within one forty-eight-hour stretch we opened four productions, three of them in rep in the same space. There are always themes that cut across the plays that end up surprising me. This year, a shared theme that kind of knocked the wind out of me was . . . translation. In every production, from the Spanish dialogue and lyrics in a 1970s urban *Measure for Measure* to a new play that is about trying to capture dying languages, translation was in the Ashland air.

All of this has gotten me thinking: in order to create a play in the first place, we each have to collaborate across our various individual areas of expertise. We have to translate from each other's languages into our own and then back into the languages of our colleagues again every single day. It's a miracle, when you really think about it. Reflecting on the theme of your conference, and in many ways the theme of my entire career, translation becomes a really useful metaphor. I'd go so far as to say that a surprising number of our field's triumphs, and our trials too, come from our attempts to translate. Good translation is needed for company to flourish.

So how can we become more keenly aware of both parties in a conversation—ourselves and our listeners? How can we recognize that our language, so familiar to us, may in fact be completely foreign to our listener? Can we assume goodwill? Ask clarifying questions? Operate on facts, not myths, and climb down that old "ladder of inference" that we race up based on our assumptions and prejudices? And when spoken or written language isn't working anymore, can we resort to a kind of charades, putting our tension into laughter instead of expressions of anger? Let's save our righteous anger for those special moments when we see that we can really change the world—or at least our own workplace—for the better. Life is short, to borrow from the Buddhist saying, and quarrels exist because we forget that fact. Let's create more and more empathy everywhere we work. One definition of empathy is the capacity for participating in, experiencing, and understanding another's feelings or ideas. Together we can reveal the truth of what Rollo May says: "Communication leads to community, that is: to understanding, intimacy and mutual valuing."

There will always be gaps between ideas and language, gaps between your perceptions and my perceptions, gaps between your feelings and my feelings. But here's the cool part: We are in the business of navigating those un-traversable gaps. And we know as theatre makers that it is in the gaps, in what is seemingly untranslatable, that the drama often happens.

Speaking again of translation, the 2011 season marked the tenth OSF production to include American Sign Language. The number of deaf and hard-of-hearing audience members has skyrocketed because of deaf actor Howie Seago's presence in our acting company. It's such potent proof of the power of representation. As plays teach me again and again, there is nothing quite like the power of seeing your story or yourself on a stage.

Ben Cameron, program director for the arts at the Doris Duke Charitable Foundation, has visionary perspective on these issues. He persuasively argues that organizations need to think outside familiar paradigms in order to thrive. "The most successful work," says Ben, "involves diverse groups of individuals focused on a common problem—diverse in generation, profession, tenure with the organization, culture and more." Diverse groups of individuals focused on a common problem—that's as good a definition of company as I can imagine.

Okay, a quick personal story from Cornerstone, eleven years ago.

We were doing a large-scale Bridge Project that brought together members of each of the fourteen communities in greater Los Angeles with which we had worked to date. As I greeted the cast at the first rehearsal, I realized that a good half of the people in the circle knew that I was a gay man, while those community members from projects in our earlier years did not, because I had not yet been comfortable in those days to share that part of my identity. At that moment, my husband, Chris, an actor in the company, wheeled in a stroller with our newborn son, Liam. I realized that this was not a moment for internalized homophobia, that, in fact, it was a real moment of truth in my life. I quickly introduced Chris as my partner and our new son, Liam. My pride in my family mixed with a toxic anxiety about how certain community participants would respond; my fears focused like a laser beam on one particular woman, a middle-aged African-American born-again Christian from the low-income neighborhood of Watts, of whom I was particularly fond. My own cultural biases kicked in as I imagined her reaction to my announcement, the painful comments that would accompany her immediately quitting the show. I'm ashamed to tell you that I couldn't even look her in the eye as I addressed the group. I wasn't sure whether I could have her in my company, but I knew as a fact that there was no room for me in her company. At the first rehearsal break, she leapt from her chair and raced across the room toward me. "Oh boy," I thought, "here it comes."

"Where's that baby?" she shouted. "That baby is the luckiest baby in the whole world to have two such wonderful dads. Let me hold him."

Again and again, my life has been filled with such moments of grace. My work at Cornerstone and now in Ashland brings me in contact with people who re-teach me what it's so easy to forget: the astonishing beauty of each and every single human being. It always surprises me anew in the way that the deepest truths do, truths whose power you've somehow forgotten, like dear old friends that you get to reconnect with once a year at an event like this.

Theatre is collaborative to its core. One could argue that all the performing arts are, but there is something about the way our discipline samples from and combines so many other disciplines that makes it feel uber-collaborative. It's one of the reasons that I most love it, and I suspect the same is true for many of you.

We work in a chronically underfunded field, and it has only gotten worse in the Great Recession. But there is a resource that is more powerfully self-renewing than money, and it lies in the hands of everyone in this room: our power to create company. It's said that organizations grow into the questions they ask. What questions can we pose of ourselves and of one another in the coming year that will shape our field? How will we communicate with our colleagues and our students? What kind of work-life balance will we achieve as we try to practice our notoriously workaholic profession?

So as we leave this conference and go back into our individual spheres of influence, as we all try to make a difference in our own individual ways while practicing our collective, company-based art form, let's carry questions from these days together back with us. Questions that we might ask others and especially ask ourselves:

How do we treat the guests in our artistic home?

How do we behave as a guest when we're in others' homes?

Who are we keeping company with? And why?

Who are we not keeping company with? And why?

Yes, I am a company man, and I'm grateful that today I get to be in your company. Thank you so much.

Cut the Cow, Cut the Queen

Problems of Cultural Translation

—VIRGINIA SCOTT

Playwright Constance Congdon once remarked to me that she was pleased that her play *Tales of the Lost Formicans* had had a successful production in Egypt. When the censor came to call, almost everything was approved—even adultery and some very objectionable language—except an exchange between Cathy and Judy about cows: "You're not a cow." "I don't want to be a cow." "You don't have to be a cow." That little moment had to go, although Congdon had no idea why. Clearly, some cultural dissonance was operative.

By and large, when a new play is written and produced, the writer, the actors, and the members of the production team believe they understand the verbal and cultural codes by which their intended audience is informed, moved, and entertained, or offended or bored. When a play is produced elsewhere than its place of origin it is normally translated, sometimes linguistically (when the original language is not that of the new intended audience), but almost always culturally. The production mediates between the text and what Hans Robert Jauss calls the audience's "horizon of expectations."[1] Or as director Peter Brook, whose Broadway production of Maurice Valency's adaptation of Friedrich Dürrenmatt's *The Visit* was a success in 1958, put it at the time, "all forms of theatre are related to specific social and cultural conditions."[2] This assumption seems to have bestowed on Brook and on various other Broadway directors, producers, and adapters of the day almost total freedom to revise texts in order to recode productions.

This study undertakes a case history of one such recoding: the 1954 New York production of Jean Giraudoux's *Ondine*, adapted by Columbia professor Maurice Valency, produced by Roger L. Stevens for the Playwrights' Company, directed by Alfred Lunt, and starring Audrey Hepburn and Mel Ferrer. It considers not only the verbal translation of the play from French to American English but also its transplantation from a semi-institutionalized Paris venue, Louis Jouvet's Théâtre Athénée, to a commercial Broadway house. *Ondine* is available for such a study because two rehearsal manuscripts of Valency's adaptation are included in his papers at Columbia University; three published versions also exist.[3] In addition, the producer's records are held at the Wisconsin Historical Society. I was also able to interview a member of the original cast, Marian Seldes, who played Bertha, Ondine's rival for the love of the knight, Hans. It is not my intention to either condemn or defend the production of *Ondine* that reached Broadway on February 18, 1954, but rather to try to discover the circumstances, the assumptions, and the reasoning that guided the choices made by the producer, the director, and the adapter, and to speculate briefly about what was gained and what was lost in translation.

Jean Giraudoux, probably the greatest French playwright of the first half of the twentieth century, was allied with Louis Jouvet. Jouvet was one of Paris's most important and influential actor-directors, and his Théâtre Athénée was both "commercial," in that it sought to make a profit, and what adapter Maurice Valency called "an enduring organization."[4] Jouvet was its producer, director, and star actor from 1935 to 1939 and from 1945 until his death in 1951. *Ondine* had been written as a vehicle by Giraudoux for Jouvet and his mistress and star, Madeleine Ozeray, who specialized in *tendres ingenues.*[5] It opened at the Théâtre Athénée on May 4, 1939, after months of preparation, to general enthusiasm from the public and the critics, ran until the end of June, and was unusually successful, so much so that Jouvet wired Giraudoux in New York to crow about the box-office receipts. Unfortunately, the successful run was interrupted by the outbreak of World War II.

Ondine is what the French call a *féerie,* which implies not only a fairy tale but also a play that requires a spectacular and magical visual production. The plot concerns Ondine, a water spirit or, in Giraudoux's words, a water monster, who falls utterly and passionately in love with a human and chooses to become his wife. Unlike Hans Christian Andersen's little mermaid, Ondine does not bear the physical pain of her choice, but her sufferings are nonetheless great, as the all-too-human husband discovers the impossibility of loving her as she loves him. Filled, as are all of Giraudoux's plays, with wit and irony, images and artifice, *Ondine* presents enormous verbal challenges to a translator.

The Broadway production was organized in the conventional way as the "Playwrights-Ondine Company," financially and legally a singular entity. Unlike the Paris production, the New York production was a hurried affair. It got under way in mid-November 1953, when director Alfred Lunt signed his contract and began to discuss designers.[6] Rehearsals began on December 26, and the production opened in New York on February 18, 1954, after a two-week tryout in Boston. What it shared with its Paris predecessor was status as a star vehicle, although in this case stardom was recent and based on motion pictures. Both Audrey Hepburn, who played Ondine, and Mel Ferrer, who played Hans, had just had their first important film roles, Hepburn in *Roman Holiday* and Ferrer in *Lili.* A month into the play's run, on March 25, Hepburn won the Oscar for best actress. Although *Ondine*'s reviews were generally good and Miss Hepburn's were ecstatic, and although Hepburn, director Lunt, and designer Peter Larkin all won Tony awards, the play closed on July 3 after a run of fewer than six months and only a month after it had paid off its production costs and begun to make a profit. Officially, the reason for the closure was the exhaustion of the young female star; in fact, Miss Hepburn's and Mr. Ferrer's contracts expired at the end of the 1953–54 season, and the management was unable to negotiate an extension with them or replace them with comparable stars.[7]

Negotiations for a New York production had first begun in March 1952, when the *New York Times* reported that Roger L. Stevens, "under the banner of the Playwrights' Company," was negotiating with the Giraudoux estate and with Maurice Valency. A contract was signed March 22 with Giraudoux's wife and son and on March 26 with Valency; however, production was delayed for nearly two years when Schuyler Watts, a sometime producer and playwright, who had also translated the play, claimed to have exclusive English-language rights to it.[8] After months of acrimonious negotiations, detailed in the files of the Playwrights' Company, an agreement was reached on November 13, 1953, that obliged Stevens to listen to a tape recording of Watts's adaptation, although he retained the absolute right to decide which version he would produce.[9] Unsurprisingly, Stevens chose the Valency adaptation, which he already owned. He announced his decision to Watts in a letter that makes his criteria clear: he had concluded that "regardless of the merits of your script, it would not be practical to do this version [which] would be over the heads of the general public that has to view the play in order to keep it going. After all, without the attendance of ten thousand people a week, it is impossible to keep a play going in these days of high-cost Broadway productions, and I feel that the Valency version is much more commercial than yours. . . . I feel it is necessary to try to do this beautiful play in as commercial a fashion as possible."[10] Watts eventually agreed to a compromise that granted him program credit ("Produced by arrangement with Schuyler Watts") and a share in the royalties.

Would Watts's version, presumably more faithful to the original, have succeeded on Broadway? Possibly, although Stevens and his collaborators might well have been justified in thinking that such a translation would be too long and too dense and too poetic to appeal to those ten thousand people a week. Unfortunately, I have not been able to find a copy of Watts's version,[11] but examples included in the two letters—one of ten pages, one of twenty—that Watts wrote to Stevens suggest what was probably a more accurate and certainly more poetic translation.[12] On the other hand, the letters also are evidence of a translator who would have been unendurable at rehearsals.

Pasted onto the bottom of page 22 of Watts's December 13 letter to Stevens is a clipping from an unidentified source: "There's no question that orthodox business methods and thinking do kill art." In this instance, Broadway commercial orthodoxy did result in a production that was much shorter and far less exuberantly theatrical than the Paris original. In Paris, for instance, the Illusioniste established his credentials by magically bringing forth a comet, the tree of Judea, the pyramids, the city of Ys, the Trojan horse, and a naked Venus.[13] In New York the Illusionist was restricted to producing thunder and lightning, a shower of flowers, and Venus rising from a trap.[14] Other changes were made so that the New York production could employ fewer actors. In Paris, thirty-three actors played forty-six roles;[15] in New York, twenty-two actors played twenty-nine roles.[16] While there was a considerable diminution in ondines, courtiers, and servants, even important characters were cut, including the Poet, who was conflated with Bertram, and Queen Yseult, a selection of whose lines was given to King Hercules.

The multiple Valency manuscripts and published texts make it possible to document various states of the play in rehearsal and performance. The date of Valency's original copyright was 1951.[17] The earliest extant manuscript, however, is annotated by its author as "My revised script: Dec. 1953. First rehearsals." This is probably the script he was required by the agreement of November 13 to recopyright on December 15. Presumably Valency—who had considerable experience as an adapter for Broadway—had made many textual changes on his own and in collaboration with the producers, who would have been concerned not only with the play's commercial possibilities but with its cast size and production costs. Cuts and changes made during rehearsal can be tracked via handwritten notes in the first manuscript as well as the second manuscript, also annotated. In 1956 there appeared a Samuel French acting edition that—according to Lawrence Harbison, a senior editor at French—should reproduce the stage manager's prompt script and thus be the most reliable evidence of what was actually spoken and performed onstage.[18] Two versions under Valency's control appeared in *Theatre Arts* in December 1954 and in a Hill and Wang Dramabook edition in 1958. The Samuel French version is the most changed from the first manuscript; the *Theatre Arts* version restores some and the Hill and Wang edition restores still more of the cuts and changes made throughout the rehearsal process. Such restorations suggest modifications made probably not at the instance of Valency.

Not that Valency was a purist. He was definitely an adapter, not a translator, although he seems to have believed, as he says in a brief essay that accompanies the *Theatre Arts* text, that "the changes in *Ondine* were trifling."[19] Most of us would probably not agree. His attitude toward adapting for Broadway is clear, however, when he adds: "Even the dialogue, in many places, has a marked similarity to the original text, as much, at any rate, as a Broadway audience might be expected to tolerate, and my own natural inability to play follow-the-master would permit." His view of a text that the Broadway audience might tolerate, similar to the one expressed by Roger Stevens, becomes clear as one compares his version to Giraudoux's original; his primary task, as he saw it, was to bring the text into conformity with what he believed to be the Broadway audience's theatrical expectations, moral values, and ability to handle complex material.[20]

A small but telling example of how the text was clarified for that audience is the treatment of a character who appears in the original as the Roi des Ondines in act 1, the Illusioniste in act 2, and an Homme du Peuple in act 3. Valency seems to have been deeply concerned that the audience might not know that all these incarnations were the same character, so he named him the Old One throughout. In MS 1 (1–15) Ondine's "mysterious friend" is not named. The sequence reads:

HANS: In spite of what your mysterious friend just told you? about men?
ONDINE: I learned nothing that I didn't know.
HANS: Naturally not. You asked the questions. You gave the answers.
ONDINE: Don't joke. He's very near. And he's very dangerous.

This is reasonably close to the French. But then Valency made several handwritten changes:

HANS: In spite of what your mysterious friend outside just told you?
ONDINE: I learned nothing from him that I didn't already know.
HANS: Naturally not. You asked the questions. You gave the answers.
ONDINE: Don't joke. He's very near. And he's very dangerous.
HANS: Who?
ONDINE: The Old One. The King of the Sea.
HANS: The King of the Sea.
ONDINE: I'm afraid, Hans.

In MS 2 (1–15) the character name is repeated:

ONDINE: Don't joke. He's very near. And he's very dangerous.
HANS: Who?
ONDINE: The Old One.
HANS: The old one?
ONDINE: The King of the Sea. I'm afraid, Hans.

Valency noted on the title page of MS 2 that the "Old One must be recognized each time," and elsewhere that the "old one should be recognized only by his voice and face—not costume." But it seems that voice and face were still not enough. In the French original, and in MSS 1 and 2, the character first appears as the head of an old man with a crown and a beard at the window and says, "Too late, Auguste" (1–3); in the Samuel French edition, he recites, "No lock so strong, no bar so stout, will serve to keep the Old One out" (8).[21] There is even a letter in the producer's archive from Ninon Tallon, who represented the Giraudoux estate, to Roger Stevens dated January 31, 1954, just before the Boston opening. She takes up the issue again on behalf of herself and Valency: "If . . . the Old One could always have his own special lighting, he would be recognized more easily which is very important for the understanding of the storyline."[22] The key concern in all of this is the importance of "storyline," of making sure the audience understands the threat the Old One represents to the union of Hans and Ondine.

The issue of "storyline" is not negligible. As critic William Becker pointed out in the *Hudson Review:* "In the peculiar, abstract, and somewhat dehumanized dramatic world which Giraudoux's plays express, it is largely the nobility and power of the language which make the action vital and give it an empathic reality. Subtract that quality of language, and (in *Ondine* at any rate) a good many technical faults of craftsmanship press into view."[23] If Becker is right, then perhaps Valency was justified in trying to edge the script toward conformity with prevailing Broadway structural conventions.

Another example of a plot issue is Giraudoux's introduction of an imaginary aria from the opera *Salammbo.* This has always puzzled critics, although it would appear to be part of a thematic structure involving mythical lovers. The Broadway team, also puzzled, decided to leave *Salammbo* in but use it differently. In the French original, the singers only appear in the interlude at the end of act 2. In MS 2, however, Valency has devised a running gag for the *Salammbo* singers: they would appear early in the act and begin to sing each time the opera is mentioned. In the Samuel French text the singers enter once, ready to sing, and then exit when the Lord Chamberlain decides against the opera. They make another brief and puzzling appearance at the end of the act. In this instance it seems fair to say that the solution was no solution, although Valency must have liked his running gag; it is restored in the Hill and Wang edition.

Yet another structural problem—along the lines of Chekhov's gun on the mantelpiece—is the Lord Chamberlain's use of the King's wart as an example of what Ondine must never mention. When she does mention it—as of course she must—the moment is not memorable in the original, since the King does not react. Valency, on the other hand, uses Ondine's faux pas to clear the stage and invents several follow-up lines for the beginning of the private interview between the two—a more or less standard bit of well-made playwriting, which does seem to smooth over a bumpy place that would be difficult to stage.

Other changes appear to be less justified. Assuming a midcentury American audience's distaste for sex and religion onstage, Valency responds by censoring the play. The French Ondine is sexually aware; her love for Hans is both physical and spiritual. In the original act 2, for instance, after she learns that Hans has a fiancée, Bertha, Ondine accuses him to her parents of having been sexually aggressive: "So it's true what 'L'autre' told me about men. They trick you onto their knees, they crush your mouth with kisses, they rub their hands all over your body" (1.6).[24] She then bites her own arm and accuses Hans of having done it. The bite is left in, the roving hands are cut, as is her vision of Bertha: "I can see her from here, the dark angel, with her shadowy moustache. I see her naked, the dark angel, all hairy. That sort of dark angel has a little tail curled up in the hollow of her back. It's well known" (1.6).[25] All other overt sexual references are also cut, including La Première Ondine's effort to seduce Hans: "Would you like me naked, beautiful knight? Should I lie on my back? Should I lie on my side?" (1.8).[26] Obviously, what the French call "la fameuse pudeur Americaine" was in play.

Blasphemy also seems to have been a concern. In the original, Hans testifies at Ondine's trial that she had deified him, "pushed love to blasphemy" (3.4). He was her bread, her wine, her god. She knelt before his image, kissed the hem of his garments, prayed in his name. "The saints were me. The holy days were me. On Palm Sunday, entering into Jerusalem on his ass, his feet dragging on the ground, who did you see?" And Ondine answers, "You."[27] This sequence—shortened to "Who were your saints, Ondine?" "You." "Who were your angels? Whose face did you see in the holy pictures in your Book of Hours?" "Yours"—also includes a disclaimer added by Valency, who has the First Judge point out that "These creatures are not Christian. They cannot blaspheme."[28]

Finally, of course, many of the cuts made by Valency or by Valency in consultation with the producers and the director remove cultural references, philosophical digressions, and metaphorical passages, much of what characterizes Giraudoux's work and makes it unique. It would be tedious to report all of the cuts here, but act 2, scene 11, originally between Ondine and Queen Yseult, can serve as an example. According to Colette Weil, this long duet is the central scene of the French play.[29] It was certainly one of the most difficult and problematic for Giraudoux; at least seventeen versions of it have survived. The final version of what finally became act 2, scene 11, is roughly two thousand words and plays in twelve and one-half minutes. In the American acting edition, the scene, which takes place between the King and Ondine, is roughly nine hundred words and plays in five minutes.

In the Broadway version, the scene concentrates on plot. Ondine reveals the pact she made with the Old One, that Hans would die if he ever deceived her, and then decides to attempt to triumph over the growing relationship between Hans and Bertha with the principle that familiarity breeds contempt. Only a few lines remain of the part of the scene that defines what Ondine is and why Hans, a human being, matters to her. The King still says: "[Hans] is not for you. His soul is small. Human souls are tiny. There is no man whose soul is great enough for you." But Ondine no longer answers "I have no soul." In fact, throughout his adaptation Valency has made Ondine less strange, less otherworldly, more human, no longer "un monstre aquatique" or "just like the ondine raised in a swimming pool in Nuremberg who mated with a seal."[30] Valency did restore "I have no soul" in the Hill and Wang edition.

Along with what he seems to have considered boring or unnecessary or potentially offensive, Valency was also alert to any assumed knowledge. As a result, most cultural references are gone. The King's name remains Hercules, and the setting is the "Hall of Hercules," but the satire implicit in the pedantry and errors made by the King and the Chamberlain is cut, as is Queen Iseult. Curiously, in the French original, Ondine, who knows so little of human culture, upon hearing the Queen's name, asks, "Tristan? Where is Tristan?" Judging by some of the scene variants, Giraudoux must have thought that placing Hans and Ondine in the context of the most famous tragic lovers of medieval legend was important. Nonetheless, in New York the reference was gone. As was the character Alcuin, a famous Latinist at the court of Charlemagne, whom Giraudoux has moved to the court of King Hercules. As was even a reference to Hamlet's contemplation of Yorick's skull.

As rehearsals continued, pressures of time and money also continued to shape the choices made for Broadway, and many of the more complex scenes were simplified after the play went into production. One notable example is the "interlude" or musical entertainment in act 2. Originally, the banks of the lake near Auguste's thatched cottage were to be discovered behind a scrim. While a troupe of ondines and their king enacted the kidnapping of the infant Bertha, two opera singers were to launch into the imaginary duet from *Salammbo.* The song of the ondines and the duet were perfectly coordinated, leading to the revelation that Bertha was the daughter of Auguste and Eugénie. In Valency's manuscripts, while the same setting is indicated, the two singers, who interrupt the ondines after their first verse, are magically silenced by the Illusionist, and the ondines finish their remaining four verses unimpeded. In the Samuel French script there is no lakeside setting; three ondines arise out of a fountain already onstage, the *Salammbo* singers are dismissed by the Illusionist after one couplet, and the song of the ondines is much shortened and rewritten. Given that the manuscripts do not indicate these changes, it seems likely that at some point the lakeside setting and its scrim were deemed unnecessary or too expensive. What mattered was that the plot point, that Bertha was the child of Auguste and Eugénie, was made. Again, Valency returned to his original version in the Hill and Wang edition. (I did wonder if this cut was made for purposes of amateur performance, something that has been known to happen in Samuel French acting editions. However, Miss Marian Seldes, who played Bertha and who was kind enough to let me interview her about the production, is sure that no lakeside setting ever existed on Broadway.)[31]

Some changes also may have been made either to feature one of the stars or because one of the stars put pressure on the director and the adapter. Examples of the first include the removal of Bertha from the end of act 3 so her presence would not distract from Ondine and the addition of Ondine to a scene in act 2, overhearing an encounter between Bertha and Hans. Although this is recorded in a photograph published in *Theatre Arts,*[32] it seemed possible that this was a publicity shot, but Miss Seldes was certain that it was a production photo.

Contracts with the two stars demonstrate how important their presence was to the success of the enterprise.[33] Both had substantial "points," that is, shares in the box-office receipts. Mr. Ferrer was to receive "seven and one-half percent of the gross weekly box office receipts, but in no event less than Fifteen Hundred Dollars," while Miss Hepburn was to receive, in addition to a weekly salary, "ten percent of all weekly box-office receipts in excess of Fifteen Hundred Dollars." Both were also to receive daily box-office reports. Both were given director approval. Miss Hepburn approved of both Alfred Lunt and Robert Lewis, Mr. Ferrer only of Mr. Lunt. Miss Hepburn's appearance was contingent upon Mr. Ferrer's; she had the right to withdraw from the contract without liability if he did not appear in the play. He agreed to accept second position in the costar billing, but only if "the actress receiving the first star position shall be Audrey Hepburn."

According to Miss Seldes, Audrey Hepburn was "a perfect star," and no evidence suggests that she used her status to influence the text or the production. Her costar, on the other hand, seems to have tried to influence both. One obvious textual change that well may have been made at the prompting of Mr. Ferrer is the deletion almost every time it occurs of the word "stupid" when applied to the Knight Hans. The French Ondine calls Hans beautiful but stupid many times. In Valency's version "stupid" appears only once, at the very end,[34] and in the scene between Ondine and King Hercules, a whole complicated discussion of Hans's character is severely truncated, including Ondine's confession that she chose the stupidest of all the knights so he would never realize that she was an ondine.

Ferrer may also have tried to undermine Alfred Lunt's authority, although the evidence does not permit any speculation about what effect his behavior might have had on the text. A letter of February 2, 1954, from Victor Samrock to Mel Ferrer, care of Audrey Wood, is blunt to the point of rudeness, suggesting a contretemps of some duration. It reads:

> Dear Sir:
>
> We have been notified of a telegram sent by you to Miss Audrey Wood in which you make certain peremptory demands in connection with our production of "Ondine." We wish to advise you that the primary artistic decisions on this production are being made, and will continue to be made, by Mr. Maurice Valency, Mr. Alfred Lunt and ourselves.
>
> With respect to the staging of "Ondine," this letter will also serve to confirm in writing what has heretofore been stated to you orally,—that Mr. Alfred Lunt is in complete charge of this department. The Management expects all members of the cast to perform their services to the best of their ability in accordance with Mr. Lunt's directions.[35]

The notion that Ferrer was actually responsible for "packaging" the New York production of *Ondine* for Audrey Hepburn has considerable currency in fan biographies and on the Internet,[36] although nothing in the files of the Playwrights' Company confirms that claim. Indeed, it would seem to have been Roger Stevens who began looking for support for a production in early 1952. A telegram dated March 24 from Robert E. Sherwood to Victor Samrock reads, "Please tell Roger I am deeply impressed with Ondine and hope he has obtained rights," and an article in the *New York Times* of the same date noting that Stevens holds a ten-day option makes no mention of Ferrer, who had not met Audrey

Hepburn at that point.[37] Nonetheless, it seems clear that Mel Ferrer believed that he had the right to influence and even interfere with the play's production, perhaps because he believed that he had sufficient influence with Miss Hepburn to control her continued presence in the company.

None of this—that writers and producers may think that Broadway audiences are limited and that French plays are much too philosophical and talky for them, or that actors will try to assert power in situations where they are legally powerless—should come as a surprise. It's all pretty much business as usual. More to the point, however, are some basic issues of adaptation and translation suggested by this case study.

When Maurice Valency decided to adapt *Ondine* in 1950, the academic discipline of translation studies was barely nascent. Without much thought for what has now become, both practically and theoretically, a contested issue, Valency the adapter became someone responsible, with the director and producer, for "the primary artistic decisions" of the production.[38] He seems to have seen himself not as a representative of the original author, Jean Giraudoux, but as the creator of a new original.

Oddly, for someone whose adaptations for Broadway were so well known, Valency has had very little to say about the art or craft of translating and/or adapting. But his claim that "*Ondine* in English is substantially the same play that Giraudoux wrote in French," qualified by what the "Broadway audience might be expected to tolerate, and *my own natural inability to play follow-the-master would permit*" (my emphasis), is a clue to how he thought about both the art of translation and the translator's role in production.[39] In other words, added to some unchallenged assumptions about the Broadway audience was the adapter's own distaste for the often thankless subordinate role of translator.

In the introduction to his *Jean Giraudoux: Four Plays,* Valency's remarks on translation are limited to a single paragraph in which he claims that "these adaptations . . . come as close to the original as in the circumstances it was possible to make them. . . . All were made with a definite end in view, that is, production on the American stage, and for this purpose a line-by-line translation would be of little use."[40]

Russell Graves, reviewing *Four Plays* in the *Educational Theatre Journal,* recognizes the sophistry of Valency's argument that one can either translate a foreign play line by line (which no rational translator would ever do) or assume perfect freedom to do as one likes, given the "Broadway audience." Graves proposes that a literate audience exists and that it is this audience which is "cheated by the way in which translations become available to it. A New York producer decides upon a foreign play as his next project; he employs a translator who works closely with the production; the play is translated, adapted, and twisted to provide Broadway fare. And when all the hullabaloo is over, the book appears, the 'actors' edition. . . . The script has been fixed in its American version for time immemorial."[41] Although not strictly true in this instance—Valency did provide a final version that superseded the acting edition—what is probable is that most productions of the play, especially in schools and universities, have used the Samuel French text.

What Graves wants is "a definitive translation," but without considering if a definitive translation of *Ondine* would provide a useful performance script. A later, more accurate translation of *Ondine* by Roger Gellert was published in 1967.[42] Critic Gerald Weales, reviewing the book and comparing Gellert's translations to Valency's, does not, however, "want to hail Gellert as the Englished Giraudoux." His ear is faulty, his English is awkward, and "he fails to catch the verbal quality of Giraudoux."[43] But at least he tries to serve the play, unlike Valency, who "seems to alter things just because he likes his version better."[44]

Is a verbal and cultural translation of a play like *Ondine* possible, one that respects, though not slavishly, the original? The further history of the play in the United States reveals no examples. While not a standard of the American repertory, it is occasionally produced professionally, usually by small theatres. In recent years there have been professional productions in Seattle, in Austin, in Ottawa, and off-off-Broadway. The off-off-Broadway production used Gellert's translation, which may have been partly responsible for a review describing the play as too long, tedious, and with dated language.[45] The other productions used original adaptations, possibly in defiance of copyrights. Just how far adaptation can go is suggested by a line from a review of the Coda Theatre Project production at the Blue Theatre in Austin in July 2005: "The production most often succeeds when the actors tell the story through movement. While no credit is given in the program for choreography, the energetic, dynamic, well-executed dancing, most often performed by Moore [as Ondine] and Andrea Broussard, Hallie Martin, and Collier as, respectively, the spirits of Fire, Wind, and Earth, is highly entertaining."[46] Entertaining? Perhaps. Related to Giraudoux's play? Only tangentially.

Perhaps some degree of cultural transformation is the only way that plays like *Ondine* can be produced today in North America. Or perhaps that is cultural arrogance speaking. After all, Valency's adaptation of Dürrenmatt's *The Old Lady Pays a Visit* has been superseded by other, more faithful translations, and Brecht's plays are available in multiple versions, some reasonably close to the original. But were someone to want to reprise *Ondine* on Broadway in 2012, unlikely though that is, the probable course of events would be to hire a translator to provide a "literal translation" and a well-known playwright to adapt that "literal translation" into a production script heavily affected by the physical and financial limitations of the contemporary professional theatre as well as by assumptions about the present-day Broadway audience.[47] *Plus ça change, plus c'est la même chose.* Of course, present-day Broadway's solution to the problems of translating plays like *Ondine* is simply to avoid producing them. A cast packed with stars might manage a limited run of a play by Molière, the most skillfully and successfully translated of classical French playwrights, and the social comedies of French playwright Yasmina Reza, in verbal and cultural translations by Christopher Hampton, have been successful.[48] But while Reza may be the "heir of Jean Anouilh," she is an heir who can create a tight dramatic structure where three or four characters, speaking short, witty dialogue and inhabiting a single set, keep an audience entertained for ninety minutes—a perfect, modern, commercial play. Her plays are, then, translatable in the context of the contemporary anglophone professional theatre. But are Giraudoux's? And if so, is there a middle ground between line-by-line translation, which often produces a text that is neither speakable nor playable, and the sort of imaginative reinvention that barely resembles the original? Of course there is, but in that middle ground the eventually staged text of a translated or adapted play will certainly have been influenced by some or all of the factors discussed in this study.

Patrice Pavis defines two possible ways of thinking about translation for the stage. In the first instance, there are translators who "jealously guard their autonomy and who often think of their work as publishable as its stands." The translation is not attached to any particular mise-en-scène, nor does it determine a mise-en-scène. Pavis here quotes Jean-Marie Deprats, who argues that "translating for the stage does not mean twisting the text to suit what one has to show, or how or who will perform. It does not mean jumping the gun, predicting or proposing a *mise en scène.*" In the second instance is what François Regnault calls the "translation destined to be performed in a particular *mise en scène* and linked to a particular stage production . . . , the text . . . subordinated to theatre."[49] Although both types certainly exist in the contemporary American theatre, especially if one includes regional and university theatres, the first is more usually found in published academic texts while the second is the norm in the professional theatre. The typical process by which such texts are developed is not unlike that by which *Ondine* was adapted and produced in 1954.

Valency did, indeed, take unnecessary liberties with the original text; he practiced what James Campbell calls "creative misreading."[50] His Ondine is sixteen instead of almost fifteen, she can survive underwater for fifteen minutes instead of ten, she has spent two months perfecting meringues instead of pie crust. A more fastidious adapter might have granted Giraudoux his specific details. Nonetheless, the 1954 production of *Ondine* represents a solution to the dilemma of translation in the theatre. The text of a play is necessarily transformed to meet production conventions and specifics, as well as assumptions about the new audience. Whether that transformation succeeds or fails, the original remains. It is not damaged or changed by any single translation/adaptation; and—at least once it joins the public domain—it is available for alternative versions. While it is true that Valency's *Ondine* once was, as Russell Graves pronounced, the only *Ondine* Americans knew, the play can now be known differently. This does not mean, however, that a different translation or adaptation or version will somehow magically override the verbal and cultural gaps between 1939 Paris and 2012 New York while "staying true" to Giraudoux's play.

In a recent issue of the *Times Literary Supplement,* Ruth Morse writes, apropos of several productions of Shakespeare in France where "Shakespeare [was] in the service of directors' passions," that the plays were absorbed "into something culturally more recognizable by domesticating the strange."[51] Although she means this as adverse criticism, it might also be taken as an axiom for theatrical translators. Without a certain amount of "domestication," a play as specific to its time and place as *Ondine* would have little opportunity for a sustained theatrical life.

Notes

1. Quoted by Susan Bennett, *Theatre Audiences: A Theory of Production and Reception,* 2nd ed. (London: Routledge, 1997), 48.
2. "Directing *The Visit:* An Interview with Peter Brook," in Randolph Goodman, *Drama on Stage,* 2nd ed. (New York: Holt Rinehart and Winston, 1978), 569.
3. *Ondine* in *Theatre Arts,* December 1954, 34–63; *Ondine: A Romantic Fantasy in Three Acts,* adapted by Maurice Valency (New York: Samuel French, 1956); *Ondine* in *Jean Giraudoux: Four Plays,* adapted and with an introduction by Maurice Valency (New York: Hill and Wang, 1958). Although some stage managers' scripts are included in the files of the Playwrights' Company held at the Wisconsin Historical Society, the stage manager's script from *Ondine* is not included.
4. Maurice Valency, introduction, *Jean Giraudoux: Four Plays* (New York: Hill and Wang, 1958), xvii.
5. She may be best known outside France from Fritz Lang's film of *Liliom,* in which she played Julie opposite Charles Boyer.
6. Contract of November 18, 1953, between Alfred Lunt and the Playwrights-Ondine Com-

pany, Box 42, Folder 18, Papers of the Playwrights' Company, Wisconsin Historical Society, Madison. A letter from Robert E. Sherwood to John C. Wilson of November 16 notes that "You have convinced Alfred of the quality of the fellow who designed 'Teahouse of the August Moon' and, as the Lunts probably told you, they would like to have him go out to Genessee Depot and map out the physical production with them." The "fellow" was Peter Larkin. Ondine Correspondence, Box 42, Folder 18, Papers of the Playwrights' Company. Although Mrs. Lunt, the actress Lynn Fontanne, had no official connection to the production, she apparently did attend rehearsals and collaborated with her husband.

7. As early as February 10, 1954, a replacement was being sought for Hepburn (Letter from Dick Killin to Roger L. Stevens.) See Ondine Correspondence, Box 42, Folder 18, Papers of the Playwrights' Company. Among the possible replacements for Hepburn: ZiZi Jeanmaire, Mai Zetterling, Dorothy Tutin.
8. Apparently, he did. An Agreement of November 13, 1953, just before rehearsals began, reveals that "in 1941 WATTS received from Giraudoux himself the right to adapt the French play 'ONDINE' into English (in which its title, the common and proper French noun 'ondine' translates into 'UNDINE,' as which the adaptation and translation was copyrighted by Watts in the same year), and the rights to which were later duly exercised by WATTS and the deceased French author's revenue therefrom was collected in 1950 by L. Arnold Weissberger, as attorney-in-fact for the GIRAUDOUX ESTATE, all of which is of record with the Authors League of America, Inc. and the Dramatists Guild thereof." The Giraudoux Estate, represented by Ninon Tallon, in 1951 gave Valency the right to make an English version of the same play, which Valency copyrighted as *Ondine* in the same year. Tallon declared that the rights were "free, clear, and unencumbered." Agreement between MAURICE J. VALENCY and W. J. SCHUYLER WATTS and the ESTATE OF JEAN GIRAUDOUX . . . and ROGER L. STEVENS, November 13, 1954, Box 42, Folder 16, Papers of the Playwrights' Company. Watts had earlier locked horns with the actress Elisabeth Bergner, who also claimed to have the rights and wanted to produce a translation by Giraudoux's son, Jean-Pierre Giraudoux.
9. Agreement of November 13, 1953, 3.
10. Ondine Correspondence, Box 42, Folder 19, Papers of the Playwrights' Company.
11. Two copies have been sold on e-Bay in recent years (2008 and 2010) by a dealer who assumed they were the text of the Broadway production. See www.worthpoint.com/worthopedia.
12. December 9 and December 13, 1953, Box 42, Folder 18, Papers of the Playwright's Company.
13. Jouvet's notes, "Decoration d'*Ondine*," *Cahiers Jean Giraudoux* 2–3 (1973–74): 25.
14. *Ondine* (Samuel French), 38–40.
15. Jean Giraudoux, *Ondine*, in *Théâtre complète* (Paris: Livre de Poche, 1991), 759–60.
16. *Ondine* (Samuel French), 4.
17. Agreement of November 13, 1953, 2.
18. Telephone interview, July 19, 2006. Mr. Harbison noted that further cuts might have been made for the amateur market but that only Mr. Valency could have done so.
19. Maurice Valency, "Some Facts about a Myth," *Theatre Arts*, December 1954, 33.
20. A study conducted by the Twentieth Century Fund from 1963 to 1965 (William J. Baumol and William G. Bowen, *Performing Arts—The Economic Dilemma: A Study of Problems Common to Theatre, Opera, Music and Dance* [New York: Twentieth Century Fund, 1966]) characterized the Broadway audience: it was 57.6 percent male and had a median

age of thirty-nine years. Of the men, 80.5 percent were professionals or managers and the median educational level of all the men was graduate school. Nearly 60 percent of the women were also professionals, and the median educational level of all the women was four years of college. Average income was $14,000 a year, and the average number of Broadway performances attended was 8.1.

21. All the references to the Old One are retained in the Hill and Wang edition, indicating that Valency perceived these changes to be constructive.
22. Letter from Ninon Tallon to Roger Stevens, Ondine Correspondence, Box 43, Folder 1, Papers of the Playwrights' Company.
23. William Becker, "Classics and Imports," *Hudson Review* 7, no. 2 (1954): 266.
24. Giraudoux, *Ondine* in *Théâtre complète,* 776. "Ainsi, c'est vrai ce que l'autre m'a dit des hommes! Ils vous attirent par mille pièges, sur leurs genoux, ils vous embrassent à vous écraser la bouche, ils passent sur vous leur main partout."
25. Ibid., 777. "Je le vois d'ici, l'ange noir, avec son ombre de moustache. Je le vois tout nu, l'ange noir, avec ses franges en poil. Ce genre d'ange noir a une queue frisée au creux des reins. C'est bien connu."
26. Ibid., 782. "Faut-il me mettre toute nue, beau chevalier? Faut-il m'étendre sur le dos? Faut-il m'étendre sur le flanc?"
27. Ibid., 839. "Tu t'agenouilles devant mon image, n'est-ce-pas, Ondine? Tu baisais l'étoffe de mes vêtements! Tu faisais tes prières en mon nom! . . . Les saints, c'était moi. Les fêtes, c'était moi. Pour les Rameaux, qui voyais-tu, entrant dans Jérusalem sur son âne, les pieds traînant à terre?"
28. A colleague, Richard Trousdell, who was kind enough to read this essay, has suggested that all the Christian references would have been accessible to the French audience, most of them at least nominally Roman Catholic, but not necessarily to the New York audience, which included many Jews.
29. Colette Weil, "Genèse et versions primitives d'*Ondine,*" *Cahiers Jean Giraudoux* 8 (1979): 62.
30. Giraudoux, *Ondine* in *Théâtre complète,* 835. "Elle est tête et gorge comme celle de Nuremberg, qu'on élevait dans la piscine. On lui avait mis un phoque . . . Ils on même eu des enfants."
31. By phone, July 24, 2006, in answer to a letter.
32. *Ondine* in *Theatre Arts,* 42.
33. Contract between the Playwrights' Company and Audrey Hepburn, November 11, 1953, and Contract between the Playwrights' Company and Mel Ferrer, November 18, 1953, Box 42, Folder 15, Papers of the Playwrights' Company.
34. In the French text, Ondine says in act 1, shortly after meeting Hans: "Vous est une bête." *Bête* is a rather complex word that means both "beast" or "animal" or "fool" or "stupid person." In MS 1, Valency translates this: "You're not very bright, are you? No. You're stupid," but "very" and "You're stupid" have been crossed out. In MS 2, the line reads, "You're not very bright, are you? No." This translation remains in the Samuel French edition, but the translation that included "stupid" is included in both the *Theatre Arts* version and the Hill and Wang edition.
35. Victor Samrock to Mel Ferrer, February 2, 1954, Ondine Correspondence, Box 43, Folder 1, Papers of the Playwrights' Company.
36. See, for instance, Alexander Weber, *Audrey: Her Real Story* (New York: St. Martin's Press, 1994), 95. For a popular account of the Hepburn-Ferrer-Lunt relationship during

Ondine, see Donald Spoto, *Enchantment: The Life of Audrey Hepburn* (New York: Harmony Books, 2006), 115–30.

37. Ondine Correspondence, Box 42, Folder 16, Papers of the Playwrights' Company; *New York Times*, March 14, 1952, 20.
38. Victor Samrock to Mel Ferrer, February 2, 1954.
39. Valency, "Some Facts about a Myth," 33.
40. Valency, introduction, *Jean Giraudoux: Four Plays*, xxi.
41. Russell Graves, "Books in Review," *Educational Theatre Journal* 10, no. 4 (1958): 362–63.
42. Jean Giraudoux, *Plays: Amphitryon, Intermezzo, Ondine*, trans. Roger Gellert (Oxford: Oxford University Press, 1967).
43. Gerald Weales, "Dressing Giraudoux for Market," *Kenyon Review* 29, no. 5 (1967): 698–704.
44. Ibid., 701–2.
45. Jenny Sandman, "Review of *Ondine*," *Curtain Up: The Internet Théâtre Magazine*, http://www.curtainup.com/ondine.html.
46. Barry Pineo, "Arts Review: *Ondine*," http://www.austin-chronicle.com/arts/2005-07-08/278475.
47. For a discussion of how translations and adaptations are generated in the contemporary theatre, see Roger Baines and Manuela Perteghella, "Interview with Christopher Hampton," in *Staging and Performing Translation: Text and Theatre Practice*, ed. Robert Baines, Cristina Marinetti, and Manuela Perteghella (Houndsmill: Palgrave Macmillan, 2011), 173–86. A sign of the times: the three editors are described as lecturer in French and translation studies, assistant professor in translation studies, and senior lecturer in translation studies, academic titles that did not exist a generation ago.
48. Ibid., 181. Hampton, who works closely with Reza, says: "we do two versions of the plays. We do the English version and then, when it's done in New York, we do an American version. . . . and if you compare the English version and the American version you'll see a considerable number of changes."
49. Patrice Pavis, "Problems of Translation for the Stage: Interculturalism and Post-modern Theatre," trans. Lauren Kruger, in *The Play Out of Context: Transferring Plays from Culture to Culture*, ed. Hanna Scolnicov and Peter Holland (Cambridge: Cambridge University Press, 1989), 32.
50. James Campbell, "Creative Misreading," *New York Time Book Review*, June 12, 2011, 35.
51. Ruth Morse, "In the Name of the *Farceur*," *TLS*, May 13, 2011, 18.

Companies to Keep

Air-Raid Dramas and International Ethical Responsibility in America, 1936–1939

—LISA JACKSON-SCHEBETTA

On October 27, 1938, Columbia Broadcasting System (CBS) aired Archibald MacLeish's *Air Raid,* a thirty-minute radio drama and mock newscast in which the announcer "transported" listeners to a small, unnamed village in southeastern Europe. Only women, the elderly, and children populate the village. It is the morning, and the men have left for a battlefield, located far outside the town. When a breathless soldier arrives in the town square and urges the women to seek cover from sighted airplanes, the women scold him. War does not want women, they declare, nor their sleepy town. The women are wrong; the planes come and pitilessly strafe the villagers in the square. MacLeish composed the piece in response to Picasso's 1937 mural *Guernica,* the black-and-white, eleven-by twenty-five-foot representation of the bombing of the defenseless Basque town of the same name. On his first viewing of the painting, MacLeish wrote that he *heard* it more than saw it.[1]

Air Raid was named one of the best radio plays of 1938. Three days after its broadcast, Orson Welles and the Mercury Theatre on Air presented *The War of the Worlds,* Welles's radio-drama adaptation of H. G. Wells's 1898 novel. Americans were harangued into believing the United States was under aerial attack by hostile alien forces. Welles's broadcast terrified listeners for a number of reasons. Welles used recognizable place-names, such as Jersey City and Hoboken Hall, and mimicked the conventions of radio emergency broadcasting. Welles's project exploited general fears about the rise of fascism as well as specific anxiety about what many people felt had been a narrowly averted world war during

September's Munich Crisis, when live reports repeatedly interrupted regularly scheduled radio programming. I contend that Welles's broadcast also capitalized on a particular conceptualization of aerial warfare engendered by the documentation and representation of the Spanish Civil War, including the bombing of Guernica, a process in which *Air Raid* and its creative team figured.

During the Spanish Civil War, two technologies combined to affect how the public imagined warfare and themselves in relation to it: radio and the airplane. Beginning during World War I, through Italy's invasion of Ethiopia, and into the Spanish Civil War, the development of aerial warfare strategies changed ideas about the legitimacy of warfare, those who waged it, and how it was waged, including what and who counted as acceptable targets. The number of radios in American homes increased rapidly in the 1920s and 1930s. Through sound—through the air—hundreds of thousands of disparate listeners, ensconced in the privacy of their own homes, could be included in and joined to a national, even a global, listening public. The interplay of the two technologies reached a synergistic culmination during the Spanish Civil War. The composition, broadcast, and reception of *Air Raid* is an example of that synergy.

In response to the Mid-America Theatre Conference's 2010 theme of "Company," I have taken the term *company* as a collective, not an intentionally formed or officially regulated group, but a coalescence of individuals related through shared concerns, ideas, experiences. In this essay I explore the synergy between two such companies (one, radio broadcasters and play authors; two, their auditors) in relation to the formation of a third company: *U.S.* citizens transformed into *global* citizens through the effect and affect of aerial warfare and air-raid radio dramas on corporeal identity and ethical awareness.

Aerial Technology, Radio, and Global Violence

"The sun rose today on a city whose tallest tower lay scattered in crumbled bits of stone," read the first line of the *New York Herald* report. "Hordes of people on foot, working their way slowly and painfully up the island . . . always they looked fearfully upward at the sky."[2] The date of the article was July 30, 1921. The *Herald* was not reporting events that had actually happened. The newspaper was completing a scenario of what *could have happened*. The day before, Brigadier General William Mitchell had carried out a mock air raid on New York City. At noon on July 29, Mitchell's U.S. bombers, playing the role of enemy planes, flew twice over the lower portion of New York City at elevations of eight thousand and five thousand feet. They theoretically unloaded "twenty-one tons of gas, flame and fragmentation bombs," the effects of which, reported the *New York Times* (also documenting possible rather than actual outcomes), were felt up to Times Square.[3]

The simulated air attack on New York City functioned partially as a publicity stunt. Mitchell, spurred by his flying experiences in World War I, had been aggressively agitating for increased investment in American aerial war power for years. Mitchell and the military crafted a charged backstory for their July 1921 performance: war had been declared on the Blue Nation (the United States) by the Red Nation (a name reflecting the anti-Communist campaigns in the United States). American ground forces, the story went, were engaged with foreign invaders on U.S. soil, and the enemy quickly issued orders to attack from the air. The American military was unprepared to meet the challenge, and New York was left in ruins. Further attacks, continued the story, were planned for Philadelphia and Washington, D.C.

Michel de Certeau writes that stories are spatial practices. In their telling, they "carry out a labor that constantly transforms."[4] Through description and performance, stories create, in the imagination and through lived daily actions, places and spaces that did not exist before. Mitchell's air raid on New York, a hybrid of materiality (real planes flying low) and invention (bombs dropped from enemy attackers), functioned to imaginatively change New York City. New York-the-place was not literally destroyed, but it was transformed into New York-the-target, a different kind of space in the public imagination. Mitchell adamantly proclaimed air power the future of warfare. Although he was eventually court-martialed and demoted for his renegade stunts, he was not alone in his thinking.

Over the next fifteen years, interest in and anxiety over rapidly developing aircraft technologies—including increased flying distances, lighter and more agile bodies, and larger loads of explosives—continued to grow. In 1927, Charles Lindbergh's solo flight across the Atlantic catapulted him to the status of a national hero, a master of a technologically complex future. Yet as international tensions increased event by event from 1929 onward, aerial technology became strongly linked in global, public imaginations not with heroics but with a second major war. In 1936, in an attempt to assuage international discontent over the Berlin Olympic Games, Germany invited Lindbergh to their country as an honored guest. Lindbergh was particularly impressed with the German Luftwaffe, the same fleet that would help destroy Guernica in 1937.[5] Air power, and wonder over how and when it might be used, saturated public consciousness.

Throughout the 1920s and into the 1930s, nations around Europe prepared their populations for air-raid attacks—and offensives. Bomb shelters were built and sirens tested; governments set aside money to requisition gas masks for every citizen. China hurried to increase anti-aircraft artillery. Americans, too, began to feel the darker implications of airpower. In the United States in August 1936, one month after the outbreak of the Spanish Civil War, the largest mock war maneuvers since World War I took place in the Midwest, iterating on a grander scale Mitchell's 1921 performance. In 1936 the military was interested in testing and demonstrating long-range air raids, those that could penetrate beyond a nation's borders and into its heartland. At Fort Knox, a mock air raid ensued in which the Blue forces attempted to defend key territory from the Red invaders. The Reds, however, were joined this time by a Brown nation, marking the sky with a color constellation that represented two threats to American democracy: communism and fascism.

Lidell Hart, identified as a "British military critic," observed in February 1936 that "wings of terror" shadowed Europe. "However different may be the angles from which the peoples of Europe view the possibility of war," Hart wrote, "there is a common slant in the view they take of its nature. Their thoughts instinctively fly upwards—and their imagination flies faster."[6] Hart's article ultimately cautioned against civilian panic over the effectiveness of air raids in war, claiming the fear of air raids was not proportionate to the number of aircraft held by any country, the aircrafts' technological capabilities, or the damage they could inflict. Countering Hart's February 1936 argument were Italy's air raids over Ethiopia in 1935 and 1936, in which hospitals, interior villages far from the front, and market squares were regularly bombed and strafed. After thirty planes unloaded approximately one thousand projectiles onto the unfortified town of Dessye, Emperor Haile Selassie wired the League of Nations in Geneva. Italy, Selassie explained, had "adopted a policy of destroying our people, not by the use of its own troops, but solely by mechanical means."[7]

Hart's admonishments to quell panic might have been justified in terms of his technical expertise, but Ethiopia proved to citizens of the world that even if contemporary aircraft were not the super-machines of their imaginations, in certain hands they were capable of wreaking destruction and havoc behind the battlefront and among civilians. In the summer and fall of 1936, events in Spain provided further evidence. In the Spanish Civil War, as during Italy's attacks on Ethiopia, non-military populations (villages with no ostensible strategic significance and undefended towns) were targeted from the air.[8]

From the first months of the Spanish Civil War, both sides relied on air raids. Entire cities became battlefronts, and aircraft preceded, followed, or maintained offensives. Although strategic bombing had been used during World War I, it was the front, the terrible stalemate of trench warfare, and not urban and civilian damage that dominated the memories of that war. During World War

I, aerial warfare was touted as a cleaner method of conducting war. Dogfights, high above the ground, might neatly decide the outcome of battles and avoid scores of injured troops.[9] As technology advanced and nations began building up their aerial battlements, it soon became clear that the attraction of the dogfight, its potential to render a front obsolete, translated to a very scary proposition indeed: the possibility of a war conducted in large part, or even entirely, through strategic bombing. In her study of French and British newspaper coverage of the Spanish Civil War, Caroline Brothers documents a rapt fascination in the public imagination with the urban quality and civilian casualties of the conflict. American newspapers, too, exhibited keen interest in urban warfare. William Carney, a *New York Times* correspondent in Madrid, reported one of the first large-scale descriptions from Spain in December 1936. A third of the city, Carney estimated, had been destroyed by air raids. Refugees lived in subway tunnels. Sniper battles were carried out across city squares. In the center of Carney's article figured a map of Madrid, with indications of where bombs had destroyed parts of the city.[10]

Americans were able to see aerial warfare and its effect on urban and rural civilian populations in new and increasingly disturbing ways through photographic journalism centered on images of urban warfare and air-raid victims. They were also able to *hear* it, for the first time, through their radios. H. V. Kaltenborn presented the first live battle report from Spain in 1936. Radio listeners were suddenly given access to an aural iconography they had only imagined, heard reproduced or recorded, or experienced at a front themselves. Geography was radically eclipsed through sound, and with this collapse of distance, corporeal and ethical awareness of global violence was reconfigured.

Aural Iconographies

H. V. Kaltenborn, one of the stars of radio in 1937, along with Fred Astaire, Bing Crosby, and Helen Hayes, was working in France as a correspondent for CBS when fighting between Spanish Nationalists and Loyalists erupted in July 1936.[11] Although Kaltenborn gained acceptance from the military on both sides of the conflict by showing a circular in which one photograph depicted him with Hitler and another with a Soviet commissar, he could not broadcast from Spain without censorship. Based in Hendaye, France, Kaltenborn was fortuitously positioned when the Nationalists attacked Irún. He was able to place himself, with a series of patched wires and a portable microphone, on a small corner of French territory that jutted into Spain. His position was literally in the middle of a battle, as the Nationalists and Loyalists fired at each other across his location.[12] Working by telephone to Paris, London, and Rugby, and then by shortwave to New York, Kaltenborn huddled in an abandoned farmhouse, or sometimes in a haystack, so close to the action he could kick at freshly spent bullets around his feet.[13]

In his transcripts, broadcast live from July to September 1936 and published in 1937, Kaltenborn oriented his listeners to the conflict, discussed the political causes behind it, and described what he witnessed. He also made an effort to initiate the auditor into the sounds of war. "In a moment or two," he spoke on September 3, "when the machine gun, which has been barking intermittently all evening, sounds again, I will stop talking for a moment so that you may get something of the sound of this Civil War." Noted in the transcript are "sounds of machine guns" and "sound of firing" and "plane motor."[14] "One soon gets to be an expert," Kaltenborn reported from his haystack, nearly a month after his first broadcasts, "in distinguishing between the high shriek of an air bomb, the skyrocket-like whiz of a shell and the sharp whistle of rifle and machine gun bullets."[15] After a month of listening to Kaltenborn, radio audiences must have been gaining some expertise themselves, not only in the identification of sounds but the damage that resulted from them. Kaltenborn's broadcasts were listened to intently. The ratings prompted CBS to send fourteen staff to Europe for live reporting on events, including the Munich Crisis of September 1938, Kaltenborn's next star news turn.[16]

By the time Japan attacked Pearl Harbor, 90 percent of Americans had at least one radio in their homes, and the average American listened for four hours a day.[17] Listeners felt a particular affinity toward radio announcers. George Burglehaus, from Sumner, Washington, for example, wrote to Kaltenborn on June 20, 1930, in response to one of Kaltenborn's news commentaries. In a lengthy letter, Burglehaus "outlin[ed] his own views on the news. He closed by inviting the commentator to drop by for a visit."[18] That Burglehaus invited Kaltenborn to "drop by for a visit" indicates a perceptive collapse of both interpersonal and geographic distance. The voices that came through the radio were closer, in time and space, to the listener; by extension, events and places became closer as well.

In the United States, the medium of radio intrigued not only newscasters but also hopeful and established playwrights and poets. The Columbia Workshop, created by writer Irving Reis for CBS in 1936 as a "showcase" for new and experimental drama, received thousands of script submissions, eventually reaching seven thousand in one year.[19] The conventions of the news broadcast—on-the-spot reporting, authentic soundscapes, and the relationship between the listener and the radio persona—proved particularly seductive to and effective for writers. By mimicking the newscast conventions, dramatists brought urgency, authenticity, and intimacy to their dramatizations. When Orson Welles broadcast his production of *Julius Caesar* for the Mercury Theatre on Air in 1938, he "recruited" none other than the increasingly celebrated Kaltenborn to "report" the play using selections from Plutarch.[20] History and fiction, past and present, were thus fused through Kaltenborn, whose vocal presence—a sound listeners were accustomed to hearing report the most crucial developments in the rise of fascist power—immediately colored Welles's broadcast with contemporary relevancy and legitimacy for a vast public.

"In the radio announcer," Bruce Lenthall writes, "writer-directors had a trusted figure, one that Americans routinely turned to for information and guidance."[21] Whereas Welles's *Julius Caesar* broadcast was a hybrid formed from a mimetic newscast and the dramatic canon, the slippery relationship between truth and fiction that the structure of radio news broadcasts could facilitate inspired new works as well, many of which prioritized a soundscape. The radio productions demanded innovative recording techniques to achieve the authenticity listeners expected and the dramatic effect and affect writers, as well as their creative teams, hoped for.[22]

Similarly, "on-the-spot reporting" transported listeners to the sites where events were happening, often at the side of a trusted newscaster. A studio announcer would begin his report by establishing a technical and verbal connection to a reporter in the field: "New York, this is Berlin. Come in Berlin." The reporters and announcers seemed to embody the cities from and for which they spoke.[23] In the age of radio, distance shifted, not in terms of literal but of imagined geography. Lidell's argument that planes were not capable of flying long distances was a hard sell to listeners who, through sound, experienced a closeness to the damage the planes inflicted. Archibald MacLeish would capitalize on these developments in *Air Raid.*

Air Raids and Radio Dramas

Radio artists, including Archibald MacLeish, Norman Corwin, Abe Oboler, Irving Reis, and Orson Welles, were interested in taking listeners on *journeys* through sound and, often, using these narratives to impart their own views on the political exigencies of the moment. Such was the case with MacLeish's *Air Raid.* CBS broadcast *Air Raid* on October 27, 1938; the program garnered a wide listenership. Max Wylie named it one of the best broadcasts of 1938–39. The dramatization was widely reviewed, in the *New York Times,* the *One Act Play*

Magazine, the *Christian Century*, and *Time* magazine.[24] As reported by the *New York Times* in April 1939, the *Saturday Review of Literature*'s poll of reviewers and literary managers considered its quality worthy of a Pulitzer Prize nomination.[25]

In MacLeish's play, a defenseless village in "southeastern Europe" is bombed two hours past dawn, at the height of the day's activities. *Air Raid* aired from 10:00 to 10:30 P.M. eastern standard time, but MacLeish introduced the piece through a station announcement that informed listeners the time was "ten seconds past 2 A.M."[26] From the outset, auditors were inducted into a collaboration in the experience about to unfold. They would be expected to play along as listeners, to suspend their disbelief and inhabit partial "roles" along with the actors. Perhaps the time announcement caught their attention, perhaps it disoriented them, but it was necessary that listeners feel they were existing simultaneously with the action of the play in order to re-create the on-the-spot broadcasting experience. If it was 2:00 A.M. on the East Coast of the United States, it was around 8:00 A.M. in southeastern Europe. Immediately after the time announcement, the studio director greeted listeners.

> STUDIO DIRECTOR:
> Ladies and gentleman:
> You have only one thought tonight all of you
> . . . .
> you have one thought tonight and only one:
> Will there be war? Has war come?
> Is Europe burning from the Tiber to the Somme?
> You think you hear the sudden double thudding of the drum
> You don't though . . .
> Not now . . .
> But what your ears will hear within the hour
> No one living in the world would try to tell you.
> We take you there to wait it for yourselves.[27]

In his opening lines, the studio director created anticipation over what was about to be broadcast. He also, by describing listeners to themselves, subtly oriented them to the roles they were about to play. Listeners' imaginations were actively engaged through a heightened self-awareness. From the image of a burning Europe, the director moved to the audibility of the drums of war. Those sounds were presumably, as the listeners had not yet been "taken" anywhere, on American soil. The implication was that war in Europe would mean war in the United States.

The studio director continues, mimicking the technical difficulties of a live broadcast and adopting the momentum of an "event-in-progress."

> We take you there to wait it for your selves.
> Stand by: we'll try to take you through
> *(The station cuts out: there is a moment's delay: it cuts in again)*
> One moment now: we'll try to take you.
> The ultimatum you remember was for sunrise by their clock:
> Midnight by ours. Now ours is long past midnight.[28]

The studio director establishes contact with the radio announcer, on site. From that moment on, a waiting game, of which the announcer and at-home audience are aware and the villagers willfully ignorant, ensues.

MacLeish sets one narrative, the activities of the villagers and their reaction to the air raid, within the frame of a radio announcer who witnesses all. The announcer describes events on the ground and narrates the action of the sky. From his vantage point atop a tenement building, situated between earth and air, he can see both. The villagers indicate no awareness of his presence. The radio audience, who has been "brought" to the announcer through the airwaves, "sits" with him on the roof. The announcer brings listeners up to date:

> We have seen nothing and heard nothing:
> Before dawn we thought we heard them:
> It was wind we heard in the valley cedars.[29]

For the next four pages, the announcer is largely silent as the village goes about its life.

When the air-raid siren wails, the women and villagers do nothing. Even when a male sergeant breathlessly tries to herd them to shelter, the women laugh him off. War, the women declare, is men's business. Women do not have time for it, quite literally. The sirens have sounded before and will sound again, but war is for men. While the women argue with the sergeant, the announcer breaks in, letting his listeners know six minutes have passed, and only four remain until the planes arrive. The sergeant, exasperated, shouts at the women: "This enemy kills women!" Even as explosions are heard, and even as the radio announcer urges his audience to "Listen," explaining that he cannot see but can only hear the sounds, still the women remain adamant that the planes will not come for them.[30]

The planes relentlessly draw closer and closer, their "roar" increasing "moment to moment." Breathlessly, the announcer attempts to describe the planes and actions to his listeners.

> ANNOUNCER:
> There are many. Hard to guess how many . . .
> (Rapidly)
> We've got them now: we see them:
> They're out of the dazzle: they're flying
> Fighting formation in column
> Squadron following squadron
> Ten—fifteen squadrons
> Bombing models mostly
> Big ones: three motors. . . .[31]

Both he and his listeners have been waiting for this, for only a short time, approximately twenty minutes airtime, but that brief twenty minutes seems languorous compared to the hysterical rapidity with which the planes appear and proceed to destroy the village, dropping bombs and gunfire into the square. Yet, still, the women refuse to believe. They run into the streets shouting to one another: "Show it our skirts in the street; it won't hurt us! Show it our softness! Show it our weakness! Show it our womanhood! Into the street! All of us!" In response, the stage directions indicate "a crazy stammering of machine guns hammer above the rising roar" of the motors. The women shriek: "It's us do you see? It's us don't you see?" The announcer remains silent. The radio listeners hear the next moments of story in pure sound: "For an instant the shrieking voices of the women, the shattering noise of the guns and the huge scream of the planes are mingled, then the voices are gone and the guns are gone and the scream of the planes closes to a deep sustained note level and long as silence."[32] The radio announcer and studio director never speak again. The planes silence the world, fulfilling the sergeant's prophecy that this enemy does not adhere to the boundaries of battlefronts. This enemy kills civilization.

In his recollections, MacLeish described *Air Raid* as a "journalistic operation."[33] He wrote the play, he remembered, after "Guernica had happened and it was quite natural to try and imagine a city which was going to undergo that kind of attack."[34] Guernica, a small town in the Basque region of northern Spain with no military significance, had been destroyed by Nationalist forces in April 1937. Despite Nationalist protestations of innocence and their subsequent attempts to lay blame to the Republicans, or claim the Basques burned their own city, the attack on Guernica was seen, as Phillip Knightly points out, as an "indiscriminate bombing of a civilian target as a deliberate experiment in terror."[35] Guernica was a "watershed" in the war. After Guernica, *Time, Newsweek,* and *Life* went pro-Republic. Guernica, aided by Picasso's mural commissioned for the Paris Exhibition of 1937, came to symbolize the horror of fascism. MacLeish began writing his play in response to Picasso's painting. "I no longer remember where or how," MacLeish wrote in 1980, "I first came face to face with *Guernica*—probably that same year in a reproduction in a newspaper. I only know that when I saw it first, I *heard* it—began to hear it."[36] MacLeish sought to bring the aural iconography of his imagination to American radio audiences.

Although MacLeish received criticism through the 1920s and 1930s from various facets of the Left for not being radical, political or communist enough, he became an active and vocal supporter of the Republic when the Spanish Civil War broke out.[37] Like many of his colleagues, MacLeish's pacifist and antiwar stances turned to anti-fascism when the Spanish Civil War began. Speaking at the Second Congress of the League of American Writers, he expressed his convictions that there was no other choice: "In that war, that Spanish war on Spanish earth, we, writers who contend for freedom, are ourselves, and whether we wish so or not, engaged."[38] *Air Raid,* however, is not so much a cry for intervention in Spain—the situation there was looking quite bad by the fall of 1938—but more a visceral warning to Americans that what was happening in Spain would in no way be isolated from the United States. That the United States was safe because of its oceans, or protected because German planes could not fly such great distances, were false assurances. MacLeish's inspiration for *Air Raid* was Guernica and Picasso's painting, but the ultimate effect of the play was a mapping of Guernica, as an unprepared victim of fascism, onto the towns and homes of his listeners. Spain, thus, was mapped onto America, a move that served to undermine arguments that America could remain aloof from the powder keg Europe was becoming. "This enemy," as MacLeish's play showed, was indiscriminate, hindered neither by qualms for civilian life nor, as MacLeish demonstrated through the manipulation of structure and sound effects, by any distance, actual or imagined.

In *Air Raid,* MacLeish did not just present the story of bombed civilians. He also manipulated structure and sound by melding the two in startling and disorienting ways, the first of which created a triangular interaction between radio announcer, audience member, and soundscape. MacLeish understood that sound could affect the listener viscerally, that it could be felt before it was heard, and that the images it could conjure in the mind's eye could be worse than any visual could accurately render. "The sound of the air raid," MacLeish said, "must be *kinetic* at first rather than *audible* to create an effect few in America have ever heard. The ominous hums of the planes strikes horror."[39] The auditory effects of

Air Raid were intentionally engineered to be as real as possible. William Robson, who had worked with MacLeish on the crowd scene for *The Fall of City*, remembered how the scripted planes were realized:

> We had . . . German fighter bombers coming in from a great distance over a small town in northeastern Spain. . . . I wanted the effects of the plane [coming] before you see them, before you really hear them. There's this kind of strange sound that develops into the sound of an airplane. So I said to the sound effects man, "I want the effects of these planes coming in to start under sixteen cycles per second." The guy looked at me and said "you're crazy! That's the threshold of hearing." I said, "Yeah, I want it to start at twelve." He said "But nobody will hear it. But by God, it started from nowhere."[40]

The play text veered away from verisimilitude through its poetry and its early, brief voyeuristic views into homes, but the news broadcast, in combination with the piece's soundscape, anchored the listeners' experience in a terrifying auditory reality.[41] Kaltenborn's broadcast from Irún was the first time many American radio listeners heard the sounds of live battle. MacLeish's play was the first time most Americans heard an air-raid siren, or bombing planes, in their own home. Air raids in Spain were enacted in America. Through sound, the distance between the two countries was rendered irrelevant.

"The radio announcer," MacLeish pointed out in an interview three days after the play's broadcast, "has become a dramatic device far beyond expectations as revealed by the European crisis, and chiefly by those announcers who went on the air at Prague."[42] *Time* magazine deemed the radio announcer "the most accepted public spokesman in 20th Century life."[43] MacLeish thought of him as a Greek chorus, able to explain and legitimate action, capable of connecting and implicating listeners. "These [announcers]," held MacLeish, "have a function; they are recognized by large audiences of nonliterary people as being proper participants."[44] MacLeish's radio announcer created a participatory frame for American listeners in *Air Raid.* He and his listeners share ears, but, perched atop a tenement building, he serves as their eyes. The auditors depend on him and, by having to rely on his sight, establish an intimate connection with him, a kind of shared body across time and space. The announcer situated in a foreign land is not a foreigner to the radio listeners. He is familiar, he is one of them, linked by nationality. He observes the actions around him as a stranger, much as his listeners might were they in his position.

The final moments of *Air Raid,* as noted above, are sound only. The radio announcer frantically describes the approaching planes, but his voice is drowned out by "the shrieking voices of the women, the shattering noise of the guns and the huge scream of the planes."[45] The voice of the announcer never resurfaces, suggesting, perhaps, that his perch has been destroyed along with the rest of the village. The studio director never intrudes again either. The last sound the radio audience hears is a single woman's wail and the droning departure of the planes fading to silence. The audience receives closure to the story of the village, but the narrative frame in which it was set, and in which they were playing roles and participating, is left without an ending. No authoritative voice reemerges to sum up or describe the scene. The audience is not, within the frame of the play, transported back to their living rooms. They are left at the site of the village, figuratively, without their trusted narrator. The play absents complete catharsis. Listeners are abandoned, disturbed, haunted by the visuals they imagine accompany such a soundscape. Listeners also experience loss: the trusted *American* spokesman is gone. This enemy kills women and children in foreign lands. This enemy also kills Americans.

Air Raid was an attempt to document the horrors of the Spanish Civil War, but it also suggested that such horrors brought immediate and dire implications for the rest of the world, including the United States. MacLeish collapsed imagined distance between America and Spain by bringing the sound of aerial warfare—its approach and departure, as well as its attack—into American homes and by leaving Americans in the unnamed southeastern European town with their dead, or at least wounded, radio announcer. Both of these moves transformed Americans from protected observers into potential casualties, imprinting on their minds and ears the possibility of air strikes in their towns and upon their loved ones.

MacLeish never named the village of his play, nor did he explicitly indicate that he was documenting Spain in the text. Certain references gave his locale away. The women were all dressed in shawls and skirts, a popular way to represent Spanish women in the United States. The enemy was described as "he who gets his picture made at the big parades . . . with his fist out"—an allusion to Hitler. Still, MacLeish maintained a blanket of ambiguity within the text of the play, so much so that a listener might have at times forgotten where the report was coming from. MacLeish was interested in informing his listeners of what the events of his play, drawn from events in Spain but not specified as located there, portended for them. MacLeish was politically pro-Republic, but he also understood the threat of rising fascism and the consequences of aerial warfare on personal levels as well. His brother had been shot down flying planes in World War I; the machines were deadly and becoming deadlier. MacLeish also penned a dedication to *Air Raid* : "For my wife, my Mother, my Sister, and my

Daughter who do not need—not yet—to fear the sky."[46] The waiting game his radio announcer recounted to the home audience was not contained in Spain or Europe; it had already begun in the United States.

In April 1937, MacLeish and his creative team explored innovative sound effects for *Fall of the City,* another radio piece inspired by rising fascism but not based in war. They hired dozens of extras and recorded in the New York City armory, hoping to amplify crowd noise in an authentic way. William Robson and Irving Reis, both of whom would participate in the *Air Raid* broadcast, were involved with *Fall of the City.* Orson Welles played the studio announcer. Welles was not in the *Air Raid* cast; he had his hands full, no doubt, preparing his rushed *War of the Worlds* project. One of his Mercury Theatre actors, Ray Collins, took the role of the studio announcer. Welles and MacLeish were moving in the same political and creative circles; they were also carrying out similar experiments with radio drama, its soundscape, form, and content. When Welles presented his *War of the Worlds,* three days after *Air Raid,* radio listeners were primed to trust a news broadcaster. The addition of specific American place-names as targets of an aerial attack coalesced a collection of puzzles pieces (live sounds of battle, images and representations of material annihilation and civilian casualties) floating in the public imagination and snapped them into a cohesive picture.

Corporeal and Ethical Identities

Bernd Huppauf wrote that World War I, the "first modern technological war," was a "threshold in the crisis of representation of modern warfare." How war was conducted, documented, and understood changed radically. Narrative strategies as well as visual modes of documentation wrestled with an "experience of absurdity in a seemingly never-ending war, a war which appeared to have emancipated itself from human control."[47] As machines featured more prominently, the slow agony of trench warfare could potentially, it was understood, be eclipsed, but at what cost? The massive loss of life in World War I, and the scores of living, yet extremely injured, soldier bodies left behind, attested unequivocally to the cost of warfare. The machines of war, and the airplane in particular, continued to loom as shadowy unknowns. They were subject to human control but also beyond it, capable of damage far more awesome than a brigade of human militia could ever dream. Would the use of these machines decrease or multiply the possible injuries and losses of another world war?

In the decades after World War I, the human mind struggled to imagine what the next war would look like, how the aircraft of World War I had evolved, and what it would mean for military personnel and civilians alike. On the floor of Parliament in 1932, Hanson W. Baldwin warned his fellows that the airplane, as an "instrument" of war, could irrevocably change the face of civilization, literally and imaginatively: "If the conscious of the young men should ever come to feel . . . with regard to this one instrument, that it is evil and should go, the thing will be done. But if they do not feel like that, well, as I say, the future will be in their hands. But when the next plane comes and European civilization is wiped out, as it will be and by no force more than by that force, then do not let them lay blame on the old men: let them remember that they principally, or they alone, are responsible for the terrors that have fallen upon the earth."[48] Six years earlier, Billy Mitchell had expressed similar convictions, with the aim of convincing Americans to lobby for more U.S. air power. In the next war, Mitchell proclaimed in the May 1926 *Collier's,* America would need to strike first, and from the air, or be prepared for every one of its major cities to be transformed into a "heap of dead and smoldering ashes," bridges shattered and citizens slain by the thousands.[49]

The picture of complete annihilation, of total war, visited upon civilians from the air, as painted by Baldwin and Mitchell, would not be fully realized until August 1945. The atomic bomb seared the international imagination and radically reconfigured dreams and nightmares of aerial warfare. In 1936, however, for most Americans, 1945 was far off. Still, the Spanish Civil War produced glimpses of mass destruction never seen before on such a scale—and certainly, in America, not heard before, even in a mimetic liveness. The terrified void in the minds of the post–World War I public over what aerial warfare would be in the next war was given form and content during the Spanish Civil War. Radio dramatists participated in the process. During the Spanish Civil War, the air-raid script became a kind of genre unto itself, as Michael Denning points out. In 1939, CBS reported that they had "been flooded with scripts about bombing planes."[50]

The technologies of aerial warfare and radio formed a powerful conjunction in relation to the Spanish Civil War. From northern Spain in 1936, Kaltenborn brought the sound of battle into American homes. This live sound track, mimicked in radio air-raid plays, combined with the proliferation of visual images of aerial and urban warfare that poured out of Spain: the ground was littered with the corpses of non-combatants, cities were reduced to rubble, and a battle might be fought across a city square or from the living rooms of half-smashed houses, their chandeliers glittering in the sunlight. As MacLeish's play shows and Welles's *War of the Worlds* used, in this seemingly new kind of war, cities, towns and homes—along with women, children, and refugees—were as likely to be targeted as munitions factories, military bases, and soldiers.

Both radio and aerial combat elided boundaries between what had been understood as civilian and military, private and public, home front and battlefront. This specific aural and visual iconography of the public imagination had been initiated in the final months of World War I, but it was not completely fathomable until the Spanish Civil War. The heightened awareness of the power of aerial warfare as proven in Ethiopia and Spain resonated domestically in the United States. It also brought with it far larger implications in terms of international responsibility. American radio listeners' identities were imaginatively transformed from civilian, protected bodies into a population of potential combatants and causalities. The Spanish Civil War opened up a liminal space in the American imagination: how the United States reacted to air raids in Spain would distinguish Americans' international responsibility for civilian populations, regardless of the political, cultural, or diplomatic status of their geography. Through air-raid drama, American ideas of the company they kept, and might keep, were radically expanded.

Although the Spanish Civil War was reduced to binary oppositions such as fascism versus democracy, Spain in civil war also actualized a fraught space in the American imagination, one in which ideas about legitimate military action were challenged. The Hague Conventions of 1899 and 1922–23 stated that strategic bombing—attacks on civilian populations and undefended towns or cities—was unlawful. In practice, however, up through the 1930s, these rules were consistently overlooked in colonial territories, as H. Bruce Franklin points out. "The bombing of non-white civilians," he writes, "was routine." France developed an aircraft specifically for the purpose of "subduing" Moroccans and Syrians. Britain regularly used aerial bombardment in India.[51] Spain presented a dilemma. As a nation, Spain "sat out" World War I. In fact, Spain had not been a major player on the international stage since its 1898 loss of the Spanish-Cuban-American War. In the 1930s, such a long-standing diplomatic and militaristic absence effectively negated Spain as European. Yet it was not a colonial geography either. Spain had not participated in World War I, and since the 1890s it had been exoticized by Europe and the United States as a kind of "internal other"—a mystical playland of Moors and Gypsies, or a backwards place of barbarians.[52]

Stories, as Certeau writes, transform places. Stories change the patterns of daily life by reconfiguring the landscape in one's imagination. Aerial warfare on civilian populations materially altered space. Favorite coffee shops were incinerated. City blocks and entire towns were obliterated. Child, female, and elderly bodies were the dead and injured. Mimetic representations of aerial warfare mapped damages wrought in Spain onto America, and, in the process, challenged American corporeal and ethical awarenesses. Not only were American radio listeners made into potential casualties, protected neither by oceans nor battlefronts; Americans were also asked to consider their relationship to air-raid victims in other parts of the world. Spain was and was not European. That it could be subjected to such devastation from the air brought the realities of air raids in Ethiopia closer to Americans and carried the potential to reconfigure the racialization of geopolitical prejudices.

At the Lenin Memorial, a meeting held at Madison Square Garden in January 1937, a spectacular dance piece was planned that would depict the siege of Madrid. At the end of the piece, "a bomb (created of sound effects) [would be] dropped into the center of the group of dancers." The dancers would scatter, as if felled by injuries, but, after a few moments, they would rise "again, fanning out into the audience."[53] The dance piece apparently never took place. Its sketch, however, indicates that *madrileños* were imagined as impervious to injury, innumerable and unconquerable, a heroic model, perhaps, for Americans to emulate. If the dancers had fanned out into the audience, the Spanish bodies they represented would have mingled with the American spectator bodies, linking both nationalities and rendering them interchangeable through physical proximity. Similarly, air-raid dramas, in conjunction with radio and aerial warfare, reconfigured the boundaries of American identity, forcibly positioning it within a global framework.

Notes

1. Archibald MacLeish, preface to *Air Raid,* in *Six Plays by Archibald MacLeish* (Boston: Houghton Mifflin, 1980), 98.
2. "City in Theoretical Ruins from Air Raid," *New York Herald,* July 30, 1921, 16.
3. "City 'Wiped Out' in Big War Game," *New York Times,* July 30, 1921, 5.
4. Michel de Certeau, "Spatial Stories," in *The Practice of Everyday Life,* trans. Stephen Randall (Berkeley: University of California Press, 1984), 117.
5. For an examination of both Charles Lindbergh and Henry Ford in relation to Germany, see Max Wallace, *The American Axis: Henry Ford, Charles Lindbergh and the Rise of the Third Reich* (New York: St. Martin's Press, 2003).
6. Lidell Hart, "Wings of Terror over Europe," *New York Times,* February 9, 1936, SM 1.
7. "Emperor Voices Bitter Protest to League after Italians Bomb Dessye," *Chicago Defender,* December 14, 1937, 1.
8. Spain democratically elected its second Republic in 1931. Although the king left without bloodshed, monarchists, landowners, the clergy, and the military immediately organized opposition to the largely leftist Republic. The Republic flipped from left- to right-

leaning over the next five years. Tensions reached a final breaking point in July 1936 when the Spanish military engineered a revolt against a semi-reinvigorated leftist coalition government. Wishing to contain the conflict, the Western democracies, including the United States, Britain, and France, along with Germany, Italy, and Russia, signed a nonintervention pact outlawing the sale of arms or grant of aid to Spain. Spain garnered more press, if not official international support, than Ethiopia. In terms of logistics, the Spanish Civil War lasted longer, larger numbers of internationals were residing in Spain at the time, and journalists quickly arrived. The signing and subsequent partial violation (by Germany, Italy, and Russia) of the nonintervention pact galvanized public demonstration for and against both sides of the Spanish Civil War. For a concise interpretation of the events, see Helen Graham, *The Spanish Civil War: A Very Short Introduction* (Oxford: Oxford University Press, 2005).

9. See Linda Robertson, *Dream of Civilized Warfare: World War Flying Aces and the American Imagination* (Minneapolis: University of Minnesota Press, 2003), and John Buckley, *Air Power in the Age of Total War* (Bloomington: Indiana University Press, 1999).
10. Although he was assigned by the *New York Times* to the Nationalist side, Carney lived in Madrid, a city that had managed to stave off Nationalist forces for months, despite infighting and street violence between political factions. See William P. Carney, "Madrid Situation Revealed: Uncensored Story of Siege," *New York Times*, December 7, 1936, 1+. For further discussion of the Spanish Civil War and urban damage as documented in European newspapers, see Caroline Brothers, *War and Photography: A Cultural History* (London: Routledge, 1997). For U.S. coverage see *A City in War: American Views on Barcelona and the Spanish Civil War, 1936–39*, ed. James W. Cortada (Wilmington, Del.: Scholarly Resources, 1985).
11. Robert Eichberg, *Radio Stars of Today: Or Behind the Scenes in Broadcasting* (Boston: LC Publishing, 1937), 86–88.
12. H. V. Kaltenborn, *Kaltenborn Edits the News* (New York: Modern Age Books, 1937), 14; George N. Gordon and Irving A. Falk, *On-the-Spot Reporting: Radio Records History* (New York: Julian Messner, 1967), 87–88.
13. Kaltenborn, *Kaltenborn Edits the News*, xiii.
14. Ibid., 25, 27, 28, 29.
15. Ibid., 24.
16. David Eldridge, *American Culture in the 1930s* (Edinburgh: Edinburgh University Press, 2008), 119.
17. Howard Blue, *Words at War: World War II Era Radio Drama and the Postwar Broadcasting Industry Blacklist* (Lanham, Md.: The Scarecrow Press, 2002), 4.
18. Bruce Lenthall, *Radio's America: The Great Depression and the Rise of Modern Mass Culture* (Chicago: University of Chicago Press, 2007), 68. See also Douglas B. Craig, *Fireside Politics: Radio and Political Culture in the United States, 1920–1940* (Baltimore: Johns Hopkins University Press, 2000), and Edward D. Miller, *Emergency Broadcasting and the 1930s American Radio* (Philadelphia: Temple University Press, 2003).
19. Blue, *Words at War*, 6.
20. Michael Denning, *The Cultural Front: The Laboring of American Culture in the Twentieth Century* (New York: Verso, 1997), 383.
21. Lenthall, *Radio's America*, 196.
22. For MacLeish and Robson's work with crowd scenes, for example, see Erik Barnouw, *The*

Golden Web: A History of Broadcasting in the United States, vol. 2, *1933–1953* (New York: Oxford University Press, 1968), 121–23.

23. Susan J. Douglas, *Listening In: Radio and the American Imagination* (Minneapolis: University of Minnesota Press, 2004), 178.
24. Anthologized in *Best Broadcasts of 1938–39,* ed. Max Wylie (New York: McGraw-Hill, 1939); Orrin E. Dunlap, "Exploring in Drama: MacLeish, Poet Dramatist, Talks about the Task of Writing a Broadcast Play," review of *Air Raid, New York Times,* October 30, 1938, X12; "Radio: *Air Raid,*" review of *Air Raid, Time,* October 31, 1938, http://www.time.com/time/magazine/article (accessed August 3, 2009); Scott Donaldson, *Archibald MacLeish: An American Life* (Boston: Houghton Mifflin, 1992), 262; Boris Todrin, review of *Air Raid, One Act Play Magazine,* December 1938, 606.
25. "Books and Authors," *New York Times,* April 30, 1939, 115.
26. Archibald MacLeish, *Air Raid* (New York: Harcourt, Brace, 1938), 3.
27. Ibid., 3–4.
28. Ibid., 4–5.
29. Ibid., 7.
30. Ibid., 28–29.
31. Ibid., 32.
32. Ibid., 34–35.
33. Archibald MacLeish, *Reflections,* ed. Bernard A. Drabeck and Helen E. Ellis (Amherst: University of Massachusetts Press, 1986), 119.
34. Ibid., 112.
35. Phillip Knightley, *The First Casualty: From the Crimea to Vietnam: The War Correspondent as Hero, Propagandist and Myth Maker* (New York and London: Harcourt, Brace and Jovanavich, 1975), 203. For more on the events, coverage, and responses surrounding Guernica, see Jordana Mendelson, *Documenting Spain: Artists: Exhibition Culture and the Modern Nation, 1929–1939* (University Park: Pennsylvania State University Press, 2005); Ian Patterson, *Guernica and Total War* (Cambridge: Harvard University Press, 2007); and Herbert Rutledge Southworth, *Guernica! Guernica! A Study in Journalism, Diplomacy, Propaganda and History* (Berkeley: University of California Press, 1977).
36. MacLeish, preface to *Air Raid,* 98.
37. MacLeish also worked on *The Spanish Earth* with Ernest Hemingway, John Dos Passos, and Joris Ivens.
38. Donaldson, *Archibald MacLeish,* 265.
39. Dunlap, "Exploring in Drama." Emphasis mine.
40. Blue, *Words at War,* 183.
41. See ibid., 83–84, for further discussion, including the following: "Although it escaped the notice of all but a few listeners, 'Air Raid' featured a technical mistake resulting more from the novel quality of aerial warfare than from the oversight of MacLeish. The script describes the bombers strafing the women on the ground below with machine gun fire. That, as even casual students of modern warfare know, is beyond the capability of bombers."
42. Dunlap, "Exploring in Drama."
43. "Radio: *Air Raid.*"
44. MacLeish, *Reflections,* 119.
45. MacLeish, *Air Raid,* 59.
46. Ibid., dedication.

47. Bernd Huppauf, "Experiences of Modern Warfare and Crises of Representation," special issue of *New German Critique* 59 (Spring–Summer 1993): 49.
48. Hanson W. Baldwin, "The Terror That Rides the Air," *New York Times,* May 24, 1936, SM4.
49. William Mitchell, "When the Air Raiders Come," *Collier's,* May 1, 1927, 9.
50. Denning, *The Cultural Front,* 383.
51. H. Bruce Franklin, *War Stars: The Superweapon and the American Imagination* (New York: Oxford University Press, 1988), 82–88.
52. See María de Guzmán, *Spain's Long Shadow: The Black Legend, Off-Whiteness and Anglo-American Empire* (Minneapolis: University of Minnesota Press, 2005).
53. Barbara Stratnyer, "'Significant Historical Events . . . Thrilling Dance Sequences': Communist Party Pageants in New York, 1937," *Studies in Dance History* 5, no. 1 (1994): 33.

A Failed Attempt at World Domination

"Advanced Vaudeville," Financial Panic, and the Dream of a World Trust

—MARLIS SCHWEITZER

In February 1907, the once-distinct worlds of vaudeville and the legitimate theatre collided when Marc Klaw and Abraham Erlanger, the two most vilified members of the Theatrical Syndicate, announced plans to enter the vaudeville arena.[1] Joining forces with their former rivals E. D. Stair and J. H. Havlin, who owned and controlled a national chain of lower-priced theatres, Klaw & Erlanger declared their goal of uplifting vaudeville from its lowbrow associations by presenting only the finest, "high class" acts.[2] "Advanced Vaudeville," they claimed, would bring to vaudeville the kind of cultural legitimacy that leading vaudeville impresario B. F. Keith had been struggling to achieve for years.[3]

Klaw & Erlanger's vaudeville declaration was big news on Broadway. As members of the Syndicate, an organization formed in 1896 by six prominent theatre owners and managers in an attempt to streamline booking processes, the duo dominated legitimate theatrical production in North America. By 1907 the Syndicate directly owned or leased well over eighty theatres and controlled the booking of five hundred theatres across the continent.[4] But it was Klaw & Erlanger's dual status as producers and booking agents that gave them the greatest competitive advantage over their rivals; through their centralized booking office, they secured the best routes for their own touring productions while reserving the worst for their rivals. Those who opted *not* to book with the Syndicate soon found themselves shut out of most first-class theatres in North

America with little option but to play in second-rate houses or other alternative venues.[5]

By 1907, however, the Syndicate was beginning to lose ground to the Shubert brothers from Syracuse, New York, who had begun an aggressive theatre-building campaign in most major cities throughout the United States. Like Klaw & Erlanger, the Shuberts also produced plays and musical comedies, but their approach to booking was markedly different. Rather than insist on an exclusive booking arrangement, the Shuberts adopted an "open door" policy, whereby they agreed to allow any and all other managers to use their theatres if they were available. This policy quickly won the Shuberts a number of influential friends, including the independent manager David Belasco, the publisher and manager Harrison Grey Fiske, and Fiske's actress wife, Minnie Maddern Fiske. Together, these allies launched a formal attack against the Syndicate, accusing them of trust-building and other criminal activities.

Ironically, it was the attempt on the part of vaudeville impresario B. F. Keith to establish his own Syndicate-like monopoly over vaudeville booking processes that presented the ideal opening for Klaw & Erlanger's vaudeville venture. In early February, Keith and fellow vaudeville entrepreneur F. F. Proctor finalized a merger with Willie Hammerstein and Percy Williams, two independent vaudeville managers who had formerly booked their acts through talent agent William Morris. Although initially hesitant to work with Keith, Williams and Hammerstein were enticed by the prospect of sharing profits with Keith's newly formed United Booking Office (UBO). At Keith's insistence they agreed to abandon Morris and book their acts exclusively through the UBO.[6] Blindsided by the merger, Morris turned to Klaw & Erlanger for help. In less than a week, plans for a new vaudeville combine were under way, prompting journalistic speculations of impending "vaudeville war."[7]

Theatre historians have offered numerous theories to explain why Klaw & Erlanger agreed to help Morris and enter the vaudeville playing field. Writing in 1909, Robert Grau argued that the duo had little actual interest in remaining in vaudeville but wanted to ensure that Keith and Albee stayed *out* of the legitimate theatre. By entering the vaudeville arena they effectively forced Keith and Albee to buy them out, which they eventually did in November 1907.[8] Grau's contemporary M. B. Leavitt offered a different interpretation, suggesting that Klaw & Erlanger gave little thought to their vaudeville venture, assuming that they would be able to challenge Keith for dominance with relative ease, thereby securing a monopoly over both vaudeville *and* legitimate theatre production.[9] Arthur Frank Wertheim echoes Leavitt in his 2006 book, *Vaudeville Wars*, noting the confidence with which Klaw & Erlanger declared their plan to offer the public "distinctive and unique" acts that would set apart "Advanced Vaudeville" from the competition.[10] Other historians have been more reticent in identifying Klaw & Erlanger's motives. In his landmark 1932 study *The Business of the Theatre,* Alfred L. Bernheim gives no definitive explanation for the duo's decision but observes that they had been "undoubtedly motivated largely by the necessity of filling the time of theatres in its circuit, a more difficult problem than ever owing to the growing power of the Shuberts."[11] In his 1991 essay on the Shubert/Syndicate rivalry, Peter A. Davis similarly concludes that small houses and the threat of shrinking profits were significant factors in Klaw & Erlanger's move into vaudeville.[12]

Yet despite offering an array of theories to explain why Klaw & Erlanger entered vaudeville (and almost as many to explain why they failed), few historians have examined the events leading up to their declaration, nor have they offered any extensive analysis of what happened during the ten-month-long vaudeville war that followed.[13] In fact, most historians treat Klaw & Erlanger's foray into vaudeville as little more than a bizarre blip in the history of commercial American theatre, assuming that it had very few, if any, long-term effects on legitimate and vaudeville theatre practices.[14]

Drawing from journalistic accounts and the Klaw & Erlanger papers housed in the Shubert Archive, I aim to complicate previous understandings of the duo's motives for entering (and eventually exiting) vaudeville by identifying the specific legal and financial challenges they faced circa 1907. By investigating the intense rivalry that developed between the talent scouts sent abroad by Klaw & Erlanger and the UBO, I also highlight the transnational aspect of the vaudeville wars. More than signing some of Europe's best acts, these globetrotting agents formed relationships with European managers that made the prospect of a world theatre circuit a distinct possibility. Finally, I show that despite its brevity, Klaw & Erlanger's advanced vaudeville had a lasting effect on commercial Broadway theatre by broadening the geographic scope of its business practices and encouraging (if only indirectly) the rise of labor activism among vaudeville performers.

A Strange Partnership: The Formation of the United States Amusement Company

On January 31, 1907, a New York State grand jury indicted all six members of the Syndicate on charges of criminal conspiracy and restraint of trade. Producing managers David Belasco and Lee Shubert had been among those who testified that their business interests had been negatively affected by the Syndicate's refusal to book a show into their theatres "unless the person who owned the attraction would consent to play only in theaters controlled by the syndicate."[15] Although the Syndicate soon moved for a dismissal of the charges, claiming that the indictment was improper and illegal,[16] Klaw & Erlanger's move into vaudeville less than three weeks after the indictment suggests that they were eager to diversify their operations and reposition themselves within the theatrical business landscape should the grand jury decision hold.[17]

One of their first challenges was securing appropriate theatres. Although in February 1907 Klaw & Erlanger already owned or controlled hundreds of first-class theatres throughout North America, they were understandably wary of turning too many these houses over to vaudeville, even advanced vaudeville. By collaborating with Stair & Havlin, who had maintained their monopoly on "popular priced" theatre through a tacit agreement with the Syndicate to stay out of the legitimate field, Klaw & Erlanger gained access to theatres more ideally suited to vaudeville entertainment.[18] These included the New York Theatre in Manhattan, the West End Theatre in Harlem, the Circle Theatre in Columbus Circle, and the Globe Theatre in Boston. Fellow Syndicate members Samuel F. Nixon and J. Frederick Zimmerman also agreed to give over one of their Philadelphia theatres, extending the geographic scope of advanced vaudeville. The unfolding vaudeville war quickly reached a national scale as Klaw & Erlanger hinted that they would soon control vaudeville theatres in New Orleans, Chicago, San Francisco, Denver, and other key western cities.[19]

Klaw & Erlanger's need for appropriate vaudeville theatres helps to explain one of the most surprising theatrical business deals of the pre–World War I period. In April, less than three months after the grand jury indictment, they announced the formation of the United States Amusement Company (USAC), a joint venture with their archrivals, the Shuberts. According to the terms of incorporation, both parties agreed to turn over a specified number of theatres located throughout the United States to the expanding advanced vaudeville circuit. Klaw & Erlanger retained a 51 percent controlling interest in the corporation, while the Shuberts had 42 percent and other participants took up the remaining 7 percent.[20] With an authorized capital of $50 million—$1 million of which was paid directly into the company, the USAC was poised to become one of the most influential corporations in the commercial theatre industry.[21]

In a public statement, Klaw & Erlanger expressed their belief that the new corporation would address a perceived glut in the number of theatres "devoted exclusively to high-class attractions." Whereas theatres dedicated to "popular-priced" and vaudeville attractions had little trouble attracting audiences, "higher class theatres [that] necessarily catered to a minority," especially those in smaller urban centers, were less successful. By re-designating some of these first-class theatres along more popular lines, Klaw & Erlanger anticipated that the "theatrical atmosphere" would be cleared and the imbalance corrected.[22]

Klaw & Erlanger's decision to collaborate with the Shuberts—the same men who had so recently accused them of criminal conspiracy—is undoubtedly curious. But closer examination of Shubert Archive records suggests that it was a strategic move. Through contract negotiations, Klaw & Erlanger not only (temporarily) neutralized the competition by re-designating their theatres as vaudeville houses but also, more importantly, set limits to the future expansion of the Shubert enterprise. In a January 28, 1909, letter to Lee Shubert, written after the collapse of "Advanced Vaudeville," Shubert lawyer Willie Klein describes a clause in the USAC contract that effectively prevented the Shuberts from acquiring or otherwise becoming interested "as owner, partner, officer, director, stockholder, trustee, lessee, manager, agent, employee or in any position or capacity whatsoever in any Theatre" in locations where the Syndicate already owned or operated a theatre.[23] Although Klein reassured his client that he had identified several loopholes that would allow the Shuberts to circumvent the contractual restriction, the clause's inclusion offers insight into Klaw & Erlanger's ulterior motives.

The USAC agreement benefited Klaw & Erlanger in other, more direct ways. Peter A. Davis argues that small houses in Syndicate-owned or -controlled theatres were major factors in the formation of the corporation, noting that "the prospect of a 51 percent share in the new company's $50 million capitalization must have seemed the perfect remedy for shrinking profits."[24] This statement is corroborated by financial data for the twenty-five theatres directly owned by Klaw & Erlanger, although the major decline seems to have come in the 1908–9 season. Yet while Klaw & Erlanger may have anticipated greater financial gains with the success of the USAC, their primary objective in April 1907 seems to have been challenging the UBO's monopoly. The formation of the USAC gave Klaw & Erlanger the theatres they needed to extend their advanced vaudeville circuit into Brooklyn, Buffalo, Chattanooga, Columbus, Denver, Kansas City, Louisville, Milwaukee, New Orleans, Pittsburgh, Rochester, Springfield, and Worchester.[25] Although this circuit was still relatively small compared to the 150 houses operated by the UBO, it nevertheless represented a growing challenge to Keith and his partners. "A forecast of the future seem[s] . . . to indicate a new line-up of theatrical hostilities founded on the vaudeville business," the *New York Times* concluded. B. F. Albee, general manager of the United Booking Agency, brushed off the challenge, claiming that the development was "nothing but what we have been expecting for months. . . . We see no cause to be in the least disturbed about it."[26] But as the ensuing competition for first-class acts suggests, the UBO viewed the USAC and advanced vaudeville as a major threat to their interests and were determined to do whatever they could to stop Klaw & Erlanger from taking over vaudeville.

The Great Talent Chase

Although Klaw & Erlanger represented advanced vaudeville to the press, William Morris remained a key architect in the development of the enterprise, especially where talent was concerned. Prior to the formation of the UBO and his subsequent break with F. F. Proctor, Willie Hammerstein, and Percy Williams, Morris had been responsible for booking a staggering five thousand vaudeville acts.[27] Keith, Albee, and the other members of the UBO recognized and were understandably threatened by Morris's considerable influence as an agent. When Morris insisted on remaining independent, rejecting several offers to enfold his operations into the UBO, Keith and Albee instituted blacklisting measures to prevent vaudeville performers from working with him. The terms of the UBO contract prohibited performers from appearing in any theatre not affiliated with the UBO; those who failed to comply with this demand would be released from their contract immediately. Similar terms applied to independent theatre owners who used the UBO's services; those who booked with agents not affiliated with the UBO faced the prospect of empty houses for an entire season or more.[28] Although he lost many of his clients, bookings on forty theatres, and an estimated $125,000 to $250,000 in annual income to the UBO, Morris remained optimistic. Within a few months of the formation of the USAC, he had signed hundreds of acts with the assistance of future film producer Jesse L. Lasky, who opened up a Chicago branch for the agency.[29]

Klaw & Erlanger were no strangers to such blacklisting tactics; in fact, Keith, Proctor, and other members of the UBO modeled their booking system and subsequent tactics on those used by the Syndicate.[30] Now finding themselves on the wrong side of the blacklist, Klaw & Erlanger decided with Morris that in addition to finding new or unsigned talent at home, their best prospect was signing foreign artists who had never performed in the United States. Morris had offices in London and Berlin and had already established a reputation for attracting top international acts.[31] And so it was that in late March and early April 1907, several weeks before the official establishment of the United States Amusement Company, Klaw & Erlanger dispatched agents to Europe and prepared to wage vaudeville war on foreign shores.

Klaw & Erlanger's two leading agents in Europe were Clifford C. Fischer, who would go on to become a successful agent and producer with Morris Gest, and Alfred E. Aarons, a manager and producer of musical comedies.[32] By the first week of April, Fischer claimed that he had already signed several leading artists of the British music-hall stage including Harry Lauder for $2,250 a week, Gus Elen for $1,500 a week, and Will Ewans for $1,250 a week.[33] Aarons left New York for Europe on April 2 to join Fischer in the hunt.

The UBO responded quickly to Klaw & Erlanger's challenge, enlisting the services of the H. B. Marinelli agency, one of the largest booking agencies in Europe, and those of vaudeville manager Percy Williams, who left for Europe in early May on board the *Kaiser Wilhelm der Grosse*.[34] "He is taking his large automobile and his chauffeur along," the *Dramatic Mirror* reported, "and in the machine, will visit the principal cities of Europe, and many of the smaller places, keeping his eyes open all the time for novelties to be secured for next season."[35] Without referring directly to the developing vaudeville war or to his former association with William Morris, the *Dramatic Mirror* said that Williams felt that "a personal scrutiny of the many acts that have been offered to him will be the most satisfactory method of determining what he does and does not want for his theatres and those of his associates in the United Booking Offices."[36] Playing up his own talents as a scout—the *Dramatic Mirror* noted that most of Williams's previous imports had been "gold mines"—he implied that the services of an intermediary like Morris were ineffective and therefore unnecessary.[37]

Williams's decision to travel through Europe in his own automobile suggests that he anticipated the need for speed, mobility, and flexibility in his quest for talent. Over the following three months, representatives for the warring vaudeville trusts "[fought] each other all over Europe," traveling through England, Scotland, Ireland, France, Germany, Italy, and Egypt in the hunt for big names and undiscovered talent.[38] In addition to scouring the major theatrical centers, Fischer, Aarons, and Williams toured the English provinces and visited small towns throughout the Continent where they attended music festivals, summer garden shows, and other forms of local entertainment. A May 7 letter from Aarons to Erlanger details his grueling itinerary and the further challenges brought about by hot summer weather:

> It has been so warm in Germany, Italy, and surrounding countries that all the Music Halls are closing up for the summer. So after I finish my present route, already made

> out, I shall return to Paris to see the opening of the summer gardens, then to London to see the new programmes which change weekly, also the provinces of England. In other words, I shall keep doubling from Paris to London [and] the English provinces every week. And I feel satisfied that by the end of July we will have all that is worth having over here, or at least our share of it. . . . I shall see the performance here to night then go to Achen. Essen—Elberfeld—Duren—Amsterdam—Hague—Rotterdam—etc.[39]

It is unclear from this letter whether Aarons was traveling by train or automobile, although given the intensity of his rivalry with Williams, the latter is most likely. By early June, Aarons revealed to the *New York Times* that he had signed between two hundred and three hundred acts, "the very cream of Europe."[40] Williams, who had zealously followed Aarons from location to location, claimed the same. "In the course of a little over two weeks," he boasted to the *Times* reporter, "I saw more than 200 turns."[41]

As Aarons and Williams chased one another all over Europe with little (apparent) regard for the costs involved, they signaled the dramatic expansion of the vaudeville playing field. American managers and agents had, of course, traveled to Europe for years in pursuit of talent, competing with one another as well as European-based agents to sign big-name acts. In the 1860s, producer Henry C. Jarrett and his business partner Henry Palmer had traveled to Paris, Berlin, and Milan in pursuit of the "most accomplished artistes and the prettiest women" from the ballet world. Enticed by promises of high salaries, these dancers traveled to New York and became the centerpiece of Jarrett and Palmer's landmark production, *The Black Crook.*[42] Other impresarios, from P. T. Barnum to Florenz Ziegfeld, had followed a similar path. But the great "vaudeville chase" of 1907 differed from these earlier talent quests in several respects: first, the scale and scope of the pursuit; second, the number and range of acts being signed; third, the amount of money being offered for them; and fourth, the extent of the agents' travels throughout Europe. English newspapers marveled at the "the magnitude of these American trusts," which made "the English music hall syndicate look small," further noting that music-hall proprietors were "greatly disturbed over the approaching exodus of talent."[43] Without the seemingly vast resources available to the UBO or Klaw & Erlanger, they could do little to stop their performers from abandoning their contracts and fleeing to America. Indeed, as the cartoon in figure 1 suggests, few agents could compete with the vast resources behind agents like Aarons and Fischer.

Aarons's letters provide detailed information about the wide range of acts he was seeing. On May 7 he sent Erlanger contracts for seven of the acts he had recently signed with salaries ranging from $165 to $800 a week for an average weekly salary of $383.57; these acts included the Tschin-Maa troupe of

STILL FISHING

Figure 1. Clifford C. Fischer "catches" another famous performer for Klaw & Erlanger. *Variety,* November 9, 1907, 17.

seven Chinese jugglers; the mimic dancer Mlle La Camargo; the Brothers Gautschmidts acts with two comedy dogs; La Esmeralda, an eighteen-year-old Spanish dancer from Madrid; and Little Pisch, a comedian and dancer.[44] The diversity of these acts, both in terms of the performers' nationalities and their particular talents, highlights Aarons's skills as an agent and complicates previous assumptions about Klaw & Erlanger's vaudeville motives. Although (inflated?) reports that he had signed between two hundred and three hundred acts in just over two months might indicate a reckless approach to scouting, Aarons's letters to Erlanger suggest (to the contrary) that he was signing only the most promising acts. In his May 7 letter he apologized for not sending more contracts, explaining that he had "visited four and five towns in succession without finding one act suitable. So you can realize what slow work it is over here."[45] In his early June return letter, Erlanger encouraged Aarons to maintain his high standards, going so far as to warn him not to book any more animal acts, as they did not "fit with our bills." "[T]he public looks for something different from us," Erlanger wrote. "We are doing an enormous business everywhere; in fact, the success that we have made has been wonderful, and instead of losing money, as everybody predicted we would with our expensive bills, we have made a handsome profit up to date, notwithstanding that we have given the public the biggest vaudeville programmes that have ever been seen anywhere."[46] Although squeezing the UBO to the point of a buyout may have been one of Klaw & Erlanger's objectives, their investment in talent and their attention to crafting high-class bills seem to indicate that they had long-term goals for advanced vaudeville.

For their part, foreign music-hall performers welcomed the invasion of American vaudeville agents. In January 1907, labor unrest among British variety artists had culminated in a three-week strike that had affected over twenty London music halls and thousands of performers. Although, as Lois Rutherford explains, the strike led by the newly formed Variety Artistes' Federation "petered out" in mid-February "with the establishment of a board of conciliation for all parties," the prospect of a full season of employment in North American vaudeville at a weekly salary much higher than what most music-hall performers could earn playing five or six houses in a single night was almost irresistible.[47] "The English performers seem to be in a state bordering upon hysteria in their expectations of gold galore," remarked the *Chicago Daily Tribune*, "and the London newspapers are promoting that condition by quoting figures which are amusing to those who know."[48] Percy Williams concurred: "People in England seem to think that money grows in the streets of New York like grass in the English lanes and that they can get whatever price they feel like asking." In an interview with the *New York Times* he told the story of a female performer who earned little more than $50 or $60 a week performing in multiple London music halls. When offered a $300 contract with the UBO she balked, insisting that she would only go for $500.[49]

Yet while less-established players entertained outlandish salary expectations, performers who consistently drew large audiences were in a much stronger negotiating position. In April, London newspapers reported that British music-hall stars Vesta Tilley, Marie Lloyd, Ethel Levey, Albert Chevalier, and Harry Lauder had all received offers of $1,500 a week or higher—double or in some cases triple their weekly earnings. So extreme were these salary increases that the *Chicago Daily Tribune* found it difficult to believe that the Scottish singer and comedian Harry Lauder, who was "entirely unknown on this side of the water," had received an offer for $2,500 a week, especially when previous visits by music-hall stars had been unsuccessful. Citing the failure of Dan Leno, "the pet of the London music halls," the *Tribune* found "the probability of an American manager taking the long chance of $2,500 per week on an unknown Scotch comedian . . . consequently amusing."[50] The *Tribune* would ultimately be proven wrong; Lauder would go on to become one of the most successful acts in vaudeville history.[51]

In July, Aarons returned to the United States with his "pockets filled" with contracts that reflected the extent of his travels and Klaw & Erlanger's interest in finding new and novel acts.[52] The press release announcing his return included a list of performers from eleven different countries: England, Scotland, Ireland, Switzerland, Belgium, Holland, Germany, Egypt, Japan, Russia, and China.[53] Many of these performers had never appeared in the United States and thus promised to bring new performance traditions and a fresh perspective to vaudeville.

But Aarons's and Williams's great chase also had broader implications for American vaudeville and variety entertainment worldwide. As the following section details, through their extensive travels these agents encouraged greater collaboration between European and American theatre owners and managers, giving rise to competing schemes for the establishment of a world theatre trust.

The $100 Million Merger: World Theatre Trust Fantasies

Judge Otto Rosalsky was largely responsible for reinvigorating Klaw & Erlanger's dreams of world domination. Presiding in the Court of General Sessions on June 18, the New York City judge dismissed the January indictment of the Syndicate for criminal conspiracy and restraint of trade.[54] Referring directly to the 1899 New York State law defining trust activities as "against public policy, illegal and void," Rosalsky determined that, "In the light of the lexicographer's definition of trade, commerce, play, entertainment, and theatres, it seems to me that plays and entertainments of the stage are not articles of or useful commodities of common use, and that the business of owning, leasing, and controlling theatres is not trade, and that, therefore, the defendants did not commit acts injurious to trade or commerce."[55]

By defining "plays and entertainments of the stage" as something *other* than "articles of or useful commodities of common use," Rosalsky did not exclude theatrical entertainment from the commodity category altogether but rather distinguished it from *common use* commodities (i.e., coal, ice, hairbrushes, toothpicks). Since the state did not consider a play to be a "commodity of common use," those who engaged in the business of producing plays, owning theatres, and setting up booking offices for the circulation thereof were not *technically* engaging in trade activities and were therefore exempt from antitrust legislation. In his lengthy decision, Rosalsky further noted that neither Belasco nor Shubert was unduly harmed by the Syndicate; "instead of being prevented from doing business," he chided, "[they] were actually able to and were owning and controlling many theatres" and even (in the case of the Shuberts) ran their own booking agency.[56] Rosalsky therefore dismissed the indictments against the Syndicate and "virtually sustain[ed]" the defending counsel's position that they had been the product of "spite work."[57]

Rosalsky's decision was a metaphorical green light for Klaw & Erlanger. With all charges of trust-building dismissed and any future charges forestalled by Rosalsky's exemption of theatrical commodities from the "common use" category, they were free to build upon the groundwork laid by Aarons during his exhaustive European tour. Klaw & Erlanger had long entertained dreams of establishing a transnational theatre circuit; in a fall 1906 interview, for example, Erlanger suggested that a "definite understanding" between booking agencies in North America, Europe, and Australia would be in the best interests of all involved.[58] Now, thanks to the vaudeville war with the UBO and Rosalsky's dismissal, they were in a position to actively pursue this objective.

On July 17, one week after Aarons had returned to New York declaring his victory in the vaudeville talent hunt,[59] Klaw & Erlanger announced plans "for an international theatrical merger." With a capital stock of $100 million, the proposed world syndicate would extend beyond North American borders to include England, Germany, France, and possibly Austria and Switzerland. The new trust's primary focus would be streamlining booking processes for vaudeville acts, but it would also provide services for the legitimate theatre.[60] In an interview with the *New York Times,* Erlanger explained that "the new corporation will be an institution entirely separate from the United States Amusement Company and the Syndicate. But it will work in harmony with and prove beneficial to both."[61] The *Times* observed that the "recent trip of an agent of the American firm," undoubtedly Aarons, had been instrumental in "bringing the final negotiations to a head."[62] Indeed, Klaw's presence in London and Paris in June 1907 suggests that negotiations had begun well before Rosalsky's decision.[63]

Within days of Aarons's return, Klaw & Erlanger secretly dispatched their lawyer, Levy Mayer, to Europe on board the *Kronpriz Wilhelm* to formalize arrangements with the European managers and theatre owners.[64] During his time abroad, Mayer reportedly attended a meeting with several managers in Berlin and secured options on two theatres in the city. As he explained to a reporter en route, Klaw & Erlanger aimed to purchase "theatrical realties [theatres] in various parts of Europe and the United States," which would allow them to expand their base. Many of these realties had already been offered to Klaw & Erlanger—or so Mayer claimed—and it was his job to discuss terms with the interested parties.[65]

The immediate reaction to Klaw & Erlanger's proposed world theatre trust was one of surprise and disbelief. American managers argued that such an agreement was both impossible and unnecessary, and they expressed serious doubts as to whether London's independent managers would ever agree to such a coalition.[66] Their British counterparts, most notably Charles Wyndham, Herbert Beerbohm Tree, and George Edwardes, similarly scoffed at Klaw & Erlanger's "preposterous" plans for world domination. "I presume that Baron Münchausen, that distinguished financier, is to be chairman," Tree joked.[67] While Tree accused Klaw & Erlanger of Münchausen-like fantasies, other observers were much less willing to dismiss the world theatre trust, noting that the two men possessed "brains and money and audacity" and were "flushed with their victory in the New York court," which had "made them supreme in the United States."[68] These writers expressed grave concerns about the Syndicate's expanding influence on theatrical production worldwide. "The new International Theatre Trust will control not only almost every high-class theatre in Europe and America," warned the *New York World,* "but the productions presented in them as well. It will be able to dictate the efforts of dramatists, composers and librettists, make its own terms and place dramatic art upon a strictly commercial basis if it so desires."[69] The *Cleveland Plain Dealer* echoed this sentiment: "There seems to be a possibility not far distant that all the theaters, plays, playwrights, operas, composers, actors, singers, musicians and managers in the world will be parts of one big trust, and dramatic and musical entertainments of all varieties will be handled with the mechanical precision and inflexibility of the steel trust, with every artistic ideal subordinated to the necessity for bigger dividends."[70] A cartoonist for the *New York World* captured these anxieties in a foreboding caricature in which a giant, mask-wearing octopus representing the Theatrical Trust seizes unsuspecting actors (fig. 2).[71]

Despite characterizing Klaw & Erlanger's plans as a clever bluff and "moonshine," Keith, Albee, and their colleagues were unwilling to simply sit by and watch. In fact, they may have even anticipated their rivals' move. On July 12, Martin Beck, the owner of the Orpheum Circuit, sailed for Europe on board the *Kaiser Wilhelm der Grosse* for a meeting with his business partner, Morris Meyerfeld Jr., and Percy G. Williams, fresh from his chase with Aarons. The *Dramatic Mirror* speculated that when the three vaudeville managers returned to the United States in early August they would have "some startling announcements to make."[72] As it happened, the announcement came much sooner, likely in response to Klaw & Erlanger's July 17 declaration.

After arriving at Bremmen, Beck traveled to Paris, where he met with Meyerfeld, Williams, and several other prominent American and European man-

Figure 2. *New York World* caricature depicting the Syndicate's global reach. *New York World*, July 18, 1907, 5.

agers at the Hotel Continental for a series of talks. On July 25, eight days after Klaw & Erlanger's announcement, the group declared the formation of a rival trust. According to the *Baltimore Sun*, the proposed International Booking Syndicate would include "practically all the vaudeville theatres in America, 38 of the best known theatres of the Continent and a large number in England." Although the names of participating English managers were "guarded from the public," other key members of the trust included "F. Steiner, of the Berlin Wintergarten; Percy G. Williams and Martin Beck; M. Ruez, H.B. Marinelli, who manages the booking of attractions for the Continental tour, and W. Passaret, European rep of Beck, and Mr. Meyerfeld, working on English combination."[73] Speaking to the *New York Times*, Meyerfeld admitted that "the organization [was] much further advanced in France and Germany than in England" but nevertheless suggested that the speed of the vaudeville field made the involvement of all managers immaterial. H. B. Marinelli, head of the Marinelli booking agency, revealed that part of his motive in joining the syndicate was to ensure that vaudeville salaries did not continue to escalate. "Vaudeville artists have been getting far too much lately," he explained, alluding to the ongoing vaudeville war, "and it occurred to us that a powerful combine, insuring long engagements on good terms, might be able to obtain artists at far cheaper rates."[74] Boasting that his agency could already guarantee artists two years playing the European circuit, Marinelli anticipated an easy victory over Klaw & Erlanger.

Financial Panic and the Collapse of Advanced Vaudeville

It is impossible to know what might have happened had both groups succeeded in establishing their proposed world theatre syndicates. Klaw & Erlanger may well have been bluffing to force the UBO's hand. Or perhaps they believed that they had sufficient resources to establish a monopoly in Europe just as they had established one in the United States. As it happened, fallout from the disastrous panic of 1907 brought an abrupt end to Klaw & Erlanger's grand vaudeville scheme both at home and abroad.

In mid-October, just as many of Aarons's prized European performers began arriving in New York, Wall Street erupted in chaos when an attempt to corner the copper market failed, prompting a series of bank runs.[75] Within days of the reckless attempt, some of the nation's largest financial institutions were teetering on the verge of collapse and the stock market had plummeted. Although financier J. P. Morgan managed to bring an end to the weeklong chaos by organizing a series of meetings with the city's most influential bankers, the effects of the panic were felt throughout the country for months afterward. Many banks outside New York responded to news of the panic by suspending the withdrawal of deposits, a decisive action that, as historians Robert F. Bruner and Sean D. Carr explain, "immediately cut off liquidity for individuals and companies, causing hardship and spreading fear."[76] In late November, the *New York World* reported that while some areas of the country had been unaffected by the panic, the Pacific states and the Midwest were "almost paralyzed." Still recovering from the San Francisco earthquake of 1906, California "suffer[ed] practical suspension of all payments in specie and currency," while in Chicago, St. Louis, and Cincinnati, local businessmen had introduced "extreme measures to carry on business and scrip and certificates of many kinds have been issued."[77] Within such an environment, commodity prices fell and industrial production dropped, while the number of bankruptcies grew. Unemployment rates also increased rapidly from 2.8 to 8 percent, leading to the mass exodus of recently arrived immigrants.[78] By early December a reported 75,000 foreign laborers had returned to Europe because they were unable to find work. On November 30 alone, eight transatlantic ocean liners transported upwards of 12,000 "home-rushing aliens," a record for emigration from the United States, with another twenty-one liners scheduled to leave later in the week.[79]

The financial panic hit Broadway hard. By mid-November an estimated three thousand actors were unemployed, significantly more than in previous panic years, with similar results for production personnel ranging from stage carpenters and "wardrobe women" to business managers and advance agents.[80] Many of the unemployed *had* in fact held jobs in early fall, but a record number of failed productions—the *New York Times* reported that 80 percent of the "new serious plays were pathetic fiascos"—had resulted in early dismissals.[81] Other factors, including "overcompetition" between managers, "a scarcity of good plays," careless booking of road attractions, and the perceived construction of "too many" theatres on Broadway and throughout North America had contributed to a disastrous season even before the mid-October panic.[82] Anxieties about economic depression further impinged upon managerial decisions. Whereas managers had previously responded to failed productions by reorganizing, trying new plays, or sending the production out on the road to recoup costs, managers faced with the prospect of committing more resources to untried plays now opted to take the losses rather than risk more failure.[83]

In an interview given days before the panic, Broadway manager William A. Brady predicted that the current financial depression would have a debilitating effect on theatrical production throughout the country, especially on the road. "It will be felt first on the road and later in New York," he explained in an interview. "One of the reasons for this is that the man in the small town reads the papers which discuss the state of financial depression in New York, becomes frightened, really before there is anything to become frightened about, loses his nerve and decides to save his money."[84] Brady's words were prophetic. On December 1, 1907, the *New York World* reported that over fifty road companies had "gone to smash within the last ten days" with "more than a thousand" unemployed actors stranded in Chicago alone. Conditions were just as bad, if not worse, in small towns: "Every incoming organization tells of meeting stranded troupes along the whole line of one-night stands, the members of which are penniless and forlorn."[85]

Bad business on Broadway was one thing, but for Klaw & Erlanger, as well as the other members of the Syndicate, bad business on the road was potentially devastating. Since so much of their revenue came from booking receipts for the five hundred theatres they owned or operated—anywhere between 5 and 10 percent of total gross receipts—they stood to lose much more than the Shuberts, who relied on venture capitalists and other third-party investors to finance their new theatres and related projects and were therefore much less vulnerable to market fluctuations.[86] But in the fall of 1907, even venture capitalists were shying away from theatrical investments, making it difficult for other managers to secure the capital to build theatres and mount shows. Indeed, while William A. Brady asserted that "reputable managers do not depend upon [outside capital] for making productions" because they had "money enough . . . to brave a few storms," these resources seemed to be dwindling, leaving many managers dependent upon box-office receipts.[87]

As word of road conditions reached New York, Klaw & Erlanger had little choice but to call a truce in their vaudeville war with Keith and the UBO. On November 6, 1907, three weeks after the panic had overtaken Wall Street and only days after the markets had begun to stabilize, the members of the USAC signed an agreement with the UBO promising to withdraw from the vaudeville field by February 1908 and remain out of it for at least ten years. In exchange, the UBO agreed to pay the USAC a total of $250,000 in two installments—$100,000 upon signing of the agreement and an additional $150,000 on February 3, 1908, the official end of advanced vaudeville. The UBO also agreed to take responsibility for all contracts made with vaudeville performers prior to October 28, 1907.[88]

Writing in 1909, Robert Grau interpreted this aspect of the deal as a major coup for Klaw & Erlanger. By passing on an estimated $1,750,000 in contracts, they not only relieved themselves of all obligation to pay the substantial salaries their agents had promised performers but also protected their own legitimate enterprise by ensuring that the UBO remained tied up in vaudeville.[89] In late October, Keith and his partners had announced plans to establish a chain of thirty "legit" houses that would stand in opposition to both the Syndicate and the Shuberts, but these plans quickly dissipated once the USAC agreed to abandon advanced vaudeville.[90]

Curiously, if not surprisingly, William Morris was absent from the negotiations that led to the USAC's withdrawal from vaudeville, an absence that Joe Laurie interprets as further evidence that Klaw & Erlanger and the Shuberts "were only in the vaude business to get a big price from Keith to quit."[91] Although, as I have argued above, Klaw & Erlanger appear to have had more complicated motives for entering vaudeville than Laurie and subsequent historians have allowed, their failure to involve Morris in the negotiations suggests they were motivated by self-preservation and perhaps by fear that Morris would have refused any settlement with the UBO.

The Legacy of Advanced Vaudeville

While Klaw & Erlanger's advanced vaudeville ultimately failed, the ten-month-long war between the United States Amusement Company and the United Booking Office had several significant long-term effects on vaudeville. First, Alfred E. Aarons's and Percy Williams's extensive travels throughout Europe brought hundreds of foreign performers to North America, many of whom had never before played in the United States. The diversity of these acts, which ranged from Chinese jugglers and Japanese singers to Spanish dancers and German acrobats, not only introduced vaudeville audiences to new styles of performance but also offered a much richer reflection of the racial and ethnic diversity of America itself. At a time when mass immigration was radically transforming the sights and sounds of the urban environment, vaudeville's cosmopolitan bills gave voice to immigrant communities working to make new homes for themselves.[92]

Second, in extending the geographic reach of advanced vaudeville beyond North America to Europe, Klaw & Erlanger, Keith, Beck, Procter, Williams, and their colleagues (temporarily) strengthened their ties with foreign booking agents, managers, and performers. In fact, while Klaw & Erlanger were obligated to stay out of vaudeville following the UBO "buyout," they continued to court foreign vaudeville and variety performers for their musical comedies and revues, often competing directly with vaudeville agents for top acts.[93] For its part, the UBO continued to pursue plans for an International Vaudeville Trust long after the collapse of Klaw & Erlanger's proposed World Theatre Trust. In August 1909, Martin Beck reported from Berlin that he was in the process of finalizing a deal with foreign music-hall managers that would guarantee "practical control of the foreign vaudeville market." With the assistance of Morris Meyerfeld, Beck met with "Director Steiner of the Wintergarten, Ben Tieber of the Vienna Apollo, Charles Aumont of Paris, E. K. Tichy of Prague, H. B. Marinelli for Paris, and Director Thurin of the Apollo, in St. Petersburg, representing the leading music halls of the Continent" to formalize arrangements.[94] Despite Beck's efforts, however, the International Vaudeville Trust never materialized.

Ironically, one of the most significant barriers to the formal establishment of a transnational vaudeville agency appears to have been the number of agencies vying to do business with the UBO following the collapse of advanced vaudeville. In August 1913 the UBO published notices in theatrical newspapers in New York and Berlin declaring that they were no longer using the booking services of H. B. Marinelli, Ltd. In November, Marinelli responded by suing the UBO for $3 million, alleging that the trust had "blacklisted artists and theatres with the result that they [had] entirely destroyed the business of Marinelli in [North

America]."[95] Perhaps fearing the outcome of an antitrust hearing, the UBO reconciled with Marinelli and cut off its relations with other booking offices, including those of Clifford C. Fischer and those of Charles F. Bornhaupt. In April 1915, Fischer and Bornhaupt filed their own suit against the UBO, demanding $600,000 in damages.[96]

Third, as previously noted, the competition for first-rate foreign stars led to a dramatic increase in performers' salaries. This in turn contributed to greater economic stratification among vaudeville players, which fueled the rise of labor activism. Prior to the transatlantic chase between Aarons and Williams, the most a vaudeville performer could expect to make was $1,000 a week (not counting headliners appearing at major vaudeville halls such as Koster and Bial's or the Olympia). By 1909, Robert Grau observed that $3,000 a week was "by no means uncommon" for such stars as Lillian Russell, Lily Langtry, and Harry Lauder.[97] The following year, *Variety* published a list of nine headliners who earned more than $2,000 a week. The rapid rise in star salaries did not trickle down to established or emerging performers, however, who continued to earn between $100 and $500 a week depending on experience and popularity.[98] Unsatisfied with the increasing economic disparity, many performers began agitating for reform. As early as January 1908, the *New York Times* reported that vaudeville artists "[had] already begun to make preparations to meet the new conditions in their field, caused by the recent amalgamation of all the leading vaudeville managerial firms, with only the opposition of William Morris in sight."[99]

English vaudeville artists, many of whom traveled to the United States in 1907 hoping to capitalize on the rivalry between the UBO and the USAC, played a key role in the rise of labor activism among vaudeville performers. In December 1907 the *New York World* observed that "among the hardest hit of the players are the great numbers of English actors who crossed the ocean this season, expecting to sell their services at their own figures." When their dreams of doubling or tripling their weekly salaries ended in unemployment, many of these performers found themselves stranded in the United States, without sufficient funds to return home.[100] Many of these stranded actors brought their labor politics with them. While established stars, such as Cecilia (Cissie) Loftus, proposed the formation of a club "confined to English actors, actresses, and vaudeville artists,"[101] others, most notably Harry Mountford, looked to unite all performers—regardless of nationality or income—in fighting the injustices they experienced at the hands of vaudeville management. Prior to his arrival in the United States, Mountford had played a key role in the organization of the Variety Artistes' Federation in 1906 and the subsequent strike against London theatre managers in January 1907. When the federation forced him out for his refusal to negotiate with management, he traveled to the United States, where he soon became a leader within the American vaudeville union, the White Rats.[102] In much the same way that immigrant laborers from eastern and southern Europe fueled the rise of labor activism in factories and sweatshops, Mountford transformed the White Rats into a much more powerful organization by encouraging a more militant approach. By July 1908, thanks in large part to Mountford's charismatic leadership, membership in the White Rats had increased to twenty-five hundred, with new chapters opening across the United States.[103]

Finally, Klaw & Erlanger's decision to abandon advanced vaudeville effectively freed William Morris to remain in vaudeville. For as much as Klaw & Erlanger's backdoor deal outraged Morris—Joe Laurie claims that he tore up his contract in front of Erlanger—his exclusion from the agreement meant that he was not only free to continue working as an independent agent but also free to set up his own rival circuit, which is exactly what he did. The story of Morris's continued struggle against the UBO has been well documented by historians such as Arthur Wertheim. I nevertheless want to note that one of Morris's key tactics in his continued war with the UBO involved extensive travel to Europe, where he enlisted the support of foreign artists like Harry Lauder and continued to build his relationship with foreign music-hall managers and agents. In this respect, Morris followed the lead of Alfred E. Aarons and Percy Williams, extending vaudeville's geographic reach far beyond American borders.

In *The Economics of the British Stage, 1800–1914*, Tracy C. Davis writes, "Not everyone in business acts rationally, and it is certainly more than competitiveness that explains market success."[104] To this I would add that it is more than competitiveness that explains market *failure*. As this essay has detailed, it was a complex interplay of legal decisions, business rivalries, economic conditions, and individual aspirations that led Klaw & Erlanger into the vaudeville arena and eventually forced them out of it. While advanced vaudeville may have been one of the duo's greatest professional failures, it also had a lasting effect on the structure, content, and scope of vaudeville as well as the lives of the men and women who enlivened its stages.

Timeline

January 31, 1907	New York Grand Jury indicts all six members of the Syndicate on charges of criminal conspiracy and restraint of trade
January 1907	Labor unrest among British variety artists leads to a

	three-week strike; many of these performers later sign with American vaudeville agents
February 1907	Percy Williams and Willie Hammerstein join B. F. Keith's United Booking Office, abandoning William Morris in the process
mid-February 1907	Klaw & Erlanger announce plans for advanced vaudeville, supported by William Morris
March–April 1907	Klaw & Erlanger, with William Morris's assistance, send agents to Europe to scout for talent
April 2, 1907	Alfred E. Aarons leaves for Europe to scout for Klaw & Erlanger
April 26, 1907	Klaw & Erlanger join with the Shuberts to form the United States Amusement Company
early May 1907	Percy Williams travels to Europe on board the *Kaiser Wilhelm der Grosse*
May–June 1907	Williams and Aarons chase each other over Europe searching for talent
early June 1907	Marc Klaw leaves for Europe, begins preparations for "World Theatre Trust"
early June 1907	Aarons returns from Europe with contracts for advanced vaudeville
June 18, 1907	Judge Otto Rosalsky dismisses January indictment of the Syndicate
July 12, 1907	Martin Beck leaves for Europe on board the *Kaiser Wilhelm der Grosse*
July 17, 1907	Klaw & Erlanger announce their plans for a "World Theatre Trust"
July 25, 1907	Percy G. Williams, Martin Beck, Meyerfeld, Marinelli Ltd. announce formation of the "International Booking Syndicate"
mid-October 1907	European performers begin arriving in the United States to begin their vaudeville tours
October 17, 1907	Panic overtakes Wall Street
November 6, 1907	Klaw & Erlanger and the Shuberts sign an agreement with B. F. Keith and the other members of the UBO to remain out of vaudeville for ten years in exchange for $250,000
December 1, 1907	*New York World* reports that at least fifty road companies have "gone to smash"
February 3, 1908	Official end of Advanced Vaudeville

Notes

The research for this article was made possible by financial support from the Social Sciences and Humanities Research Council of Canada and the John W. Kluge Center at the Library of Congress. I am extremely grateful to both institutions. Thanks as well to Daniel Guadagnolo, Catherine Mayhew, and Rhona Justice-Malloy.

1. "Vaudeville War Expected," *Baltimore Sun,* February 18, 1907, 12; "Vaudeville War May Start Anew," *New York Times,* February 14, 1907, 9.
2. My use of the ampersand for "Klaw & Erlanger" is consistent with the pair's official producing name.
3. On B. F. Keith's vaudeville aspirations see M. Alison Kibler, *Rank Ladies: Gender and Cultural Hierarchy in American Vaudeville* (Chapel Hill: University of North Carolina Press, 1999); Arthur Frank Wertheim, *Vaudeville Wars: How Keith-Albee and Orpheum Circuits Controlled the Big-Time and Its Performers* (New York: Palgrave Macmillan, 2008); and Robert Snyder, *Voice of the City: Vaudeville and Popular Culture in New York* (New York: Oxford University Press, 1989).
4. Alfred E. Bernheim, *The Business of the Theatre: An Economic History of the American Theatre, 1750–1932* (New York: Benjamin Blom, 1932), 51–52. "Controls 500 Theaters," *Washington Post,* January 25, 1907, 5.
5. Bernheim's and Jack Poggi's studies offer a thorough analysis of the Syndicate's activities. See Bernheim, *The Business of the Theatre,* and Jack Poggi, *Theater in America: The Impact of Economic Forces, 1870–1967* (1966; Ithaca: Cornell University Press, 1968). See also John Frick, "A Changing Theatre: New York and Beyond," *The Cambridge History of American Theatre,* vol. 2, ed. Don B. Wilmeth and Christopher Bigsby (London: Cambridge University Press, 2000), 196–232.
6. For a detailed description of Keith's establishment of the UBO and his success in convincing Hammerstein and Williams to join him, see Wertheim, *Vaudeville Wars,* esp. 117–33.
7. "Vaudeville War Expected."
8. Robert Grau, *Forty Years Observation of Music and Drama* (New York: Broadway Publishing Company, 1909), 12.
9. M. B. Leavitt, *Fifty Years in Theatrical Management* (New York: Broadway Publishing Company, 1912), 190.
10. Quoted in Bernheim, *The Business of the Theatre,* 139.
11. Ibid., 68.
12. Peter A. Davis, "The Syndicate/Shubert War," in *Inventing Times Square: Commerce and Culture at the Crossroads of the World,* ed. William R. Taylor (New York: Russell Sage Foundation, 1991), 147–57.
13. Peter A. Davis is one important exception. In "The Syndicate/Shubert War" he associates the Syndicate's decline with fallout from the panic of 1907, which included the collapse of Advanced Vaudeville.
14. There are numerous reasons why this perspective has held for so long. Vaudeville's frequent designation by critics and historians as lowbrow (occasionally middlebrow) entertainment has led to a division within American theatre historiography, whereby the history of vaudeville is often treated as something quite distinct from the history of legitimate theatre. Lingering academic anxieties about commercial theatre and a general

antipathy toward examining the business practices of commercial theatre managers, especially those characterized by their contemporaries as artless villains, has likewise led many historians to overlook or disavow Klaw & Erlanger's contributions to American theatre. On this tendency see Mark Hodin, "The Disavowal of Ethnicity: Legitimate Theatre and the Social Construction of Literary Value in Turn-of-the-Century America," *Theatre Journal* 52 (2000): 211–26; and Vincent Landro, "Media Mania: The Demonizing of the Theatrical Syndicate," *Journal of American Drama and Theatre* 13 (Spring 2001): 23–50. Until recently, historians of early-twentieth-century commercial theatre in North America have largely focused on the development of national theatre culture and practices, without taking into full account the transnational networks to which many of Broadway's leading theatre impresarios, agents, playwrights, and performers belonged. Of course, scholarly analysis of the formation of national theatre cultures has been very productive. Recent work by theatre scholars has interrogated the idea of "the nation" as performed and constructed onstage. Some of the best work includes S. E. Wilmer, *Theatre, Society and the Nation: Staging American Identities* (Cambridge: Cambridge University Press, 2002); Loren Kruger, *The National Stage: Theatre and Cultural Legitimation in England, France and America* (Chicago: University of Chicago Press, 1992); Jeffrey D. Mason and Ellen Gainor, *Performing America: Cultural Nationalism in American Theatre* (Ann Arbor: University of Michigan Press, 1999); Alan Filewod, *Performing Canada: The Nation Enacted in the Imagined Theatre,* Textual Studies in Canada 15 (Kamloops, B.C.: University College of the Cariboo, 2002); and Jen Harvie, *Staging the UK* (Manchester: Manchester University Press, 2005).

15. "Play Trust Men Indicted: Six Accused of Conspiracy to Control Theatrical Business," *Chicago Daily Tribune,* February 1, 1907, 1; "Stage Combine Feels the Law," *Atlanta Constitution,* February 1, 1907, 5; "Theatre Trust Indicted," *Baltimore Sun,* February 1, 1907, 11.
16. "Theatre Trust Defiant," *New York Times,* March 21, 1907, 9.
17. Bernheim suggests that they may also have been motivated by the need to ensure that they had enough acts to fill their theatres as the rivalry with the Shuberts intensified. Bernheim, *The Business of the Theatre,* 68.
18. "C. E. Blaney Leases the Lincoln Square," *New York Times,* May 7, 1907, 7.
19. "Vaudeville War Now On," *New York Times,* February 17, 1907, 9.
20. Bernheim, *The Business of the Theatre,* 68.
21. Ibid.
22. "New Combine Born in Theatre Land," *New York Times,* April 28, 1907, 9.
23. Klein to Shubert, January 28, 1909, Klaw & Erlanger Papers, Shubert Archive, New York City.
24. Davis, "The Syndicate/Shubert War," 155.
25. "New Combine Born in Theatre Land," 9.
26. Ibid.
27. Frank Rose, *The Agency: William Morris and the Hidden History of Show Business* (New York: HarperBusiness, 1995), 25.
28. Wertheim, *Vaudeville Wars,* 132.
29. Ibid., 134, 138–39.
30. Ibid., 97.
31. Ibid., 136.
32. Grau, *Forty Years Observation of Music and Drama,* 32. Grau credits Aarons with con-

tributing to a rise in performer salaries: "When Klaw and Erlanger entered the vaudeville field as opposed to the coterie of vaudeville managers then in control, Aarons was selected to go abroad, which he did, and it would be far easier to state whom he did not engage than those whom he did; but it can be truthfully stated that as a result of Aarons' activity abroad, the price which the vaudeville managers had to pay to end the famous 'war' of 1907 was not lessened."

33. Fischer's claims may have been premature. It was a common practice for managers and agents to announce that they had signed stars before any contracts had been finalized.
34. "Profit by Music Hall War: Noted English Arts Engaged for Long Tours in This Country," *New York Times,* April 5, 1907, 9. "Theatre Season Ending: Rival American Vaudeville Combination Active in London," *New York Times,* June 30, 1907, C2.
35. "Percy G. Williams Going to Europe," *New York Dramatic Mirror,* May 5, 1907, 17. See also "May Move to Montauk," *New York Times,* May 8, 1907.
36. "Percy G. Williams Going to Europe," 17.
37. Ibid.
38. "Vaudeville Chase All Over Europe," *New York Times,* June 9, 1908, C2.
39. Aarons to Erlanger, May 7, 1907, Box 1 (Alberg, J. A. to Abarbanell, Lina), Klaw & Erlanger Collection, Shubert Archive.
40. "Vaudeville Chase All Over Europe."
41. "Hammerstein Union with Paris Opera," *New York Times,* June 9, 1907, C1. Speaking with the same reporter while on a brief stopover in Paris, Marc Klaw explained that he was "not looking for anything in Paris, for we have, through our agent, already booked all we want in this gay city." See also "Williams Secures Vesta Tilley," *New York Dramatic Mirror,* July 6, 1907.
42. Robert Lewis, ed., *From Traveling Show to Vaudeville: Theatrical Spectacle in America, 1830–1910* (Baltimore: Johns Hopkins University Press, 2003), 198–99. Quote is from Joseph Whitton, "*The Naked Truth*": *An Inside History of the Block Crook* (Philadelphia: H. W. Shaw, 1897), [5]–6, 10, 32.
43. "Throw Figures in Vaudeville War," *Chicago Daily Tribune,* April 28, 1907, 14.
44. Aarons to Erlanger, May 7, 1907, Box 1 (Alberg, J. A. to Abarbanell, Lina), Klaw & Erlanger Collection, Shubert Archive.
45. Ibid.
46. Erlanger to Aarons, June 3, 1907, Box 1 (Alberg, J. A. to Abarbanell, Lina), Klaw & Erlanger Collection, Shubert Archive.
47. Lois Rutherford, "'Managers in a Small Way': The Professionalization of Variety Artistes, 1860–1914," in *Music Hall: The Business of Pleasure* (Milton Keynes, U.K.: Open University Press, 1986), 107–8.
48. "Throw Figures in Vaudeville War," 14.
49. "Hammerstein Union with Paris Opera," C1. Williams repeated this story to the *New York Dramatic Mirror.* "Percy G. Williams in Paris," *New York Dramatic Mirror,* June 22, 1907, 17. See also short notes in *Variety* from November 2, 1907, for a similar story of a female baritone singer refusing a $75 a week offer, explaining that she had received an offer for $500 a week and would only settle for $1,000 (3).
50. "Throw Figures in Vaudeville War."
51. "5,000 a Week for Lauder," *New York Times,* September 1, 1908, 1.
52. "Percy G. Williams Going to Europe," 17.

53. "Imported Vaudeville," *Baltimore Sun*, July 11, 1907, 2.
54. Appointed in April 1906, Rosalsky was reportedly the youngest judge ever to sit in the Court of General Sessions. "Rosalsky Is a Judge," *New York Times*, April 26, 1906, 1.
55. "Theatrical Trust a Legal Combine," *New York Times*, June 20, 1907, 7. The 1899 law reads: "Every contract, agreement, arrangement, or combination whereby a monopoly in the manufacture, production, and sale in this State of any article or commodity of common use is or may be created, established, or maintained, or whereby competition in this State in the supply or price of any such article or commodity is or may be restrained or prevented . . . is hereby declared to be against public policy, illegal, and void." "The Law and the Ice Trust," *New York Times*, May 10, 1900, 6.
56. "Theatrical Trust a Legal Combine," 7.
57. Ibid.
58. "World Merger in Theatricals," *New York Times*, July 7, 1907, 1.
59. "Theatrical News," *New York Tribune*, July 11, 1907, 7.
60. "World Merger in Theatricals," 1.
61. Erlanger quoted in "A Theatrical Trust for the World," *Current Literature* 43, no. 3 (1907): 319.
62. "World Merger in Theatricals," 1.
63. "Hammerstein Union with Paris Opera," C1. In a July 18 interview with the *New York Herald*, Erlanger stated that Klaw had been working on the merger for months. "Mr. Erlanger Talks on New Syndicate," *New York Herald*, July 18, 1907, 16. On July 19, Klaw returned to New York after nine weeks abroad. "Mr. Klaw Talks of Big Syndicate," *New York Herald*, July 20, 1907, 10.
64. "World Merger in Theatricals," 1.
65. "Meyer [*sic*] in Berlin," *New York Dramatic Mirror*, August 10, 1907, 15. Erlanger had previously explained that their primary goal was in acquiring major vaudeville/variety houses in Europe. "Mr. Erlanger Talks on New Syndicate," 16.
66. "Organize World Theatre Trust at $100,000,000," *New York World*, July 18, 1907, 1. See also "Mr. Erlanger Talks on New Syndicate," 16.
67. "A Theatrical Trust for the World," 319. Tree may have had other motives for challenging Klaw & Erlanger's claims. In May, during his annual trip to Germany, he had reportedly met with German managers to discuss the possibility of a triangular exchange system between German and English and American companies. "The business part would be arranged upon a reciprocal relation," explained the *Dramatic Mirror*, "so that while the English and American companies were playing in the principal theatres of Berlin, Leipzig, etc., London and New York would be seeing Schiller and Goethe played in the mother tongue and also the modern productions of Germany." Tree undoubtedly knew that a world theatre trust overseen by Klaw & Erlanger would jeopardize this kind of exchange relationship. "An English-German Exchange," *New York Dramatic Mirror* June 1, 1907, 13. On French reactions to the news see "Agents in Paris Doubt Trust Story," *New York Herald*, July 19, 1907, 16.
68. *Cleveland Plain Dealer* qtd. in "A Theatrical Trust for the World," 319.
69. "Organize World Theatre Trust," 1.
70. *Cleveland Plain Dealer* qtd. in "A Theatrical Trust for the World," 319.
71. "In the Spot Light," *New York World*, July 17, 1907, 5.
72. "Martin Beck Sails," *New York Dramatic Mirror*, July 13, 1907, 14.

73. "World's Theatre Trust Real," *Baltimore Sun*, July 25, 1907, 9; "Vaudeville Trust Formed in Paris," *New York Times*, July 25, 1907, 1.
74. "Vaudeville Trust Formed in Paris," 1. See also "Meyer in Berlin," *New York Dramatic Mirror*, August 10, 1907, 15.
75. "War Begins in Chicago," *New York Dramatic Mirror*, October 19, 1907, 16; "Advanced Rumours," *New York Dramatic Mirror*, November 11, 1907, 14.
76. Robert F. Bruner and Sean D. Carr, *The Panic of 1907: Lessons Learned from the Market's Perfect Storm* (Hoboken, N.J.: Wiley, 2007), 135.
77. "Effect on the Money Panic Varies in Different Parts of the Country," *New York World*, November 25, 1907, 2.
78. Bruner and Carr, *The Panic of 1907*, 141–42.
79. "12,000 Aliens Sail from New York," *New York World*, December 1, 1907, 1. Bruner and Carr report that between 1907 and 1909 immigration dropped from 1.2 million to 750,000. It was not until 1910 that immigration rose to 1 million again. *The Panic of 1907*, 142.
80. "Actors Out of Work," *Baltimore Sun*, November 18, 1907, 11. The rapid growth of the acting profession in the early twentieth century offers some explanation for the increase in unemployment numbers. According to census records, there were 6,734 actresses in 1900; by 1910 that number had almost doubled, to 11,992. Benjamin McArthur, *Actors and American Culture, 1880–1920* (Iowa City: University of Iowa Press, 2000), 30–31.
81. "Actors Out of Work," 11.
82. "The Theatrical Situation," *New York Times*, November 17, 1907, 8; "Thousands of Actors Left Out of Work," November 11, 1907, 4.
83. "Thousands of Actors Left Out of Work."
84. "Wall Street and the Drama: Opinions of the Managers on the Effects of Financial Depression," *New York Times*, October 6, 1907, X1.
85. "Winter of Actor's Discontent to Bring About Stage Reforms," *New York World*, December 1, 1907, 6M.
86. Bernheim, *The Business of the Theatre*, 56; Davis, "The Syndicate/Shubert War," 155–56.
87. "Wall Street and the Drama," X1.
88. Agreement between the UBO and the United States Amusement Company, Corporation Series: Klaw & Erlanger, Box 34, Folder 10, Shubert Archive.
89. Grau, *Forty Years Observation of Music and Drama*, 12.
90. Bernheim, *The Business of Theatre*, 68.
91. Joe Laurie Jr., *Vaudeville: From the Honky Tonks to the Palace* (New York: Henry Holt, 1953), 372.
92. Robert Snyder makes this general observation about vaudeville's appeal in *Voice of the City*.
93. For example, in 1908, dancer Maud Allan was pursued by B. Keith, Marc Klaw, and Florenz Ziegfeld. "Allan Wants to Capture America," *Chicago Daily Tribune*, July 5, 1908: G2; "Maude Allan's Dance Here," *New York Times*, July 8, 1908, 7.
94. "Control Foreign Vaudeville: Orpheum Circuit Arranges to Interchange Acts for Long Engagements," *New York Times*, August 19, 1909, 7.
95. "Vaudeville Trust Sued for $3,000,000," *New York Times*, November 12, 1913, 7; "$3,000,000 Vaudeville Suit: H. Marinelli Asks Damages under Sherman Antitrust Law," *Washington Post*, November 12, 1913, 10.
96. "Big Vaudeville Agencies Sued," *Chicago Daily Tribune*, April 28, 1915, 15. For a discus-

sion of booking abuses, see Robert Grau, "Fortunes Made on Actors' Salaries," *Overland Monthly and Our West Magazine* February 1959, 131–34.

97. Grau, *Forty Years Observation of Music and Drama*, 10.
98. Wertheim, *Vaudeville Wars*, 171.
99. "Vaudeville Men Getting Together," *New York Times*, January 23, 1908, 9.
100. "Winter of Actor's Discontent to Bring About Stage Reforms," 6M.
101. "Club for English Actors," *New York Dramatic Mirror*, July 6, 1907, 15.
102. Wertheim, *Vaudeville Wars*, 186.
103. Ibid. Not surprisingly, Klaw & Erlanger showed their support for the White Rats organization by publishing a full-page ad in George Fuller Golden's 1909 book, *My Lady Vaudeville and her White Rats*, in which they declared their "sincere regards and appreciation." A full-page ad for William Morris, Inc., appeared on the following page.
104. Tracy C. Davis, *The Economics of the British Stage, 1800–1914* (Cambridge: Cambridge University Press, 2007), 1.

The Company She Kept

The Radical Activism of Actress Kitty Marion from Piccadilly Circus to Times Square

—CHRISTINE WOODWORTH

At the end of the nineteenth century in a small provincial music hall, while the lead performers were singing a popular ballad, from the back of the house came the clarion voice of actress and radical activist Kitty Marion. In her unpublished autobiography, Marion writes: "The song 'Bluebelles' was very popular that season and our Principal Boy and Girl sang it as a duet, but never got a hand. It was also the vogue to have someone sing from a box or any other part of the house, so our musical director picked a voice—mine—to repeat the chorus in front of the house, after which the P.B. and G. on the stage 'took calls' while the applauding audience cheered into the dark whence came the voice."[1] Kitty Marion's voice was her greatest asset as a music-hall and pantomime performer throughout the English provinces and in London during the last decades of the nineteenth century and the early years of the twentieth. As Viv Gardner notes, Marion garnered a mere "modicum of success" as an actor, yet she achieved iconic status in both England and the United States through her work in various social justice movements.[2] Her strong, clear, and resonant voice became a principal tool in advocating for political change. Fueled by the injustices toward women that she perceived and experienced in the world of professional theatre and musical entertainment, Marion found herself gravitating toward a variety of campaigns. Her work in the labor, suffrage, and birth-control movements was inspired by the unfair and often dangerous working conditions for women in the theatre. Her training as a performer made her a strong voice within these movements yet her activism in many ways harmed her career. Her protest work often placed her in perilous situations that at times caused her physical harm. Additionally, her involvement in and affiliation with various organizations garnered her the notorious reputation as a radical and, therefore, ultimately an unsavory addition to any theatrical company. In reference to Marion's unpublished autobiography, Gardner notes that "the calling *that frames the memoir,* is the fight against the sexual, economic and legal abuse of women."[3]

While the fight began in her brief music-hall career, she soon found a home in a number of activist campaigns. In turn, the company she kept within these campaigns at once afforded her entry into new social justice opportunities while alienating her from others. Not all of her political affiliations, it turned out, were considered to be good company. Several scholars have examined Marion's work within activist campaigns in England and the United States. This essay will explore the interrelationship of these movements and the ways in which Marion's clarion voice and physical sacrifice can be situated as the connecting (and at times unraveling) thread. In spite of the literal and metaphorical gulf between her activist involvement on two separate continents, the inscription of her experiences with labor, suffrage, and birth-control reform serve as palimpsests whose imprints and tracings shade all of her work on the activist stage.[4]

Kitty Marion was born in Germany in 1871 as Katherina Maria Schafer. Although her relationship with her disciplinarian, abusive father was fraught, her memoir recounts some happy moments from her childhood, including her early aspirations for the theatre. While in school, she notes,

> [A]t singing and reciting I excelled simply because it came easily to me and I loved it. . . . I developed quite a voice by learning and singing . . . songs which I harmonized. Singing "seconds" came quite natural to me. . . . We used to ramble through the nearby forest, singing with might and main, with heart and soul, awakening the echoes with songs, extolling war, victory, heroism, liberty, "Deutchland über Alles" as well as volk songs of gentler German sentiments. I indulged in visions and dreams of the day when I would go on the stage and dress and sing like my step-mother's friends at the theatre in Dartmund, for talk of the Bühne was always discreetly discouraged.[5]

Marion moved to England in 1886 to live with an aunt and learn English. By 1889 she appeared on the pantomime stage.[6] Her career on the stage was largely unremarkable; she often appeared in large choruses and small featured roles. In the early years of her theatrical career she was not even listed as a member of the cast. Eventually, however, she was able to take on more prominent roles and serve as understudy for the leads in pieces such as *The Lady Slavey,* which toured to Glasgow, Newcastle upon Tyne, Dublin, and Belfast, and in *Kitty Grey,* which she performed in for two years.[7]

During the period in which Marion was touring throughout the provinces, music-hall performances had long since attained a semblance of respectability. Peter Bailey, in his book *Music Hall: The Business of Pleasure,* goes so far as to suggest that as early as the 1870s "performers became a more or less professionalized labour force, appearing in London at several different halls each night under the intensive turns system, and working the provincial halls in frequent tours that made the medium a prime agent in the construction of a national taste in entertainment."[8] This was not without cost, however. Bailey discusses the ways in which music-hall performers felt their labor was exploited, equating the evolution of the music-hall industry to the "shift from domestic to factory production" and likening the performers to an "alienated labour in rebellion."[9] For Marion, as with many other young women performing at this time, that alienation and exploitation was decidedly gendered.

In her autobiography, Marion describes an encounter with an agent whom she calls Mr. Dreck. Upon Marion's signing a contract for appearances in a series of small music halls, Dreck attempted to kiss her. She struggled, fell, hit her head on his desk, and lost consciousness. When she awoke, Dreck warned her that she would not be able to secure future employment if she continued to reject sexual advances.[10] This was a matter of much public debate at the end of the nineteenth century. Marion notes, "About this time there was much excitement, consternation and indignation in 'the profession' and the press over a statement made by Clement Scott, theatrical critic of the *Daily Telegraph,* to the effect that it was impossible for an actress to rise to success except through the manager's bedroom."[11] In an interview for a publication titled *Great Thoughts,* Scott stated, "What is infinitely more to be deplored is that a woman who endeavors to keep her purity is almost of a necessity foredoomed to failure in her career." Scott ultimately resigned in 1898 as a result of the uproar that his comments generated.[12] While the *Daily Telegraph* initially gave him a raise following his remarks, theatre professionals called for his dismissal.

In 1906, however, the topic was once again in the public spotlight as Marion wrote a letter to the London *Era* newspaper in response to an article written by a theatrical agent bemoaning successful actors' lack of loyalty to the agents who gave them their start. Marion asserted, "I have, with others almost given up hope for a woman who wants to earn her own living, and at the same time rise in the profession on her merits only, without influence of any sort."[13] Christine Anderson notes, "Over the next six weeks, many female performers replied to Kitty's letter in the newspaper, supporting her argument with similar experiences of their own."[14]

That same year, Marion ultimately joined the Actors' Association and the Variety Artists Federation (VAF). At one VAF meeting held to discuss financial woes and the corruption of agents, Marion noted that there was no mention of the particular difficulties of women: "Someone gave a short speech ending with, 'that's why they wont [*sic*] give me work.' Instantly I blurted out, 'and they won't give me work because I won't kiss them!' The meeting exploded with laughter, applause, shouts of bravo and support of my statement. 'Kiss your agent!' was the daily catch phrase, full of meaning as to how to get work. It was 'meat' or 'poison' according to the individual's reaction to it. Many thanked me for speaking up."[15] As a result of this exclamation at the VAF gathering, Marion was invited to a London County Council meeting to share concerns regarding women in theatre; however, she had to submit her concerns in writing because she was out of town.

In the midst of her involvement in the labor campaigns within the theatre, Marion was drawn into the militant suffrage campaign in England. She had a natural affinity for this, since "as a member of the Actor's Association and the Variety Artists' Federation, I 'voted' for the executives so why should not women vote for members of Parliament? So I joined the 'Militants,' wore the colors, 'purple, white and green' and gradually absorbed the gospel of 'Votes for Women' as it had developed up to its reaching my ears."[16] Marion joined the Women's Social and Political Union (WSPU) in 1908[17] and the Actresses Franchise League (AFL) in 1909.[18] The WSPU's motto was "Deeds not Words."[19] Marion's militancy within the suffrage campaign reached legendary status as she participated in public demonstrations, window smashing, and arson. She was arrested many times for her militant activities, waged hunger strikes in prison, and was forcibly fed a staggering 232 times.[20] Yet Marion's involvement within the campaign began in a much less dramatic manner. One of the first tasks she was charged with by the WSPU was selling their publication *Votes for Women.* She described the experience in her autobiography: "What a great lesson in self-denial, self abnegation, self-discipline. The first time, I took my place on the 'island' in Picadilly Circus, near the flower sellers. I felt as if every eye that looked at me was a dagger piercing me through, and I wished the ground would open and swallow me. However, that feeling wore off and I developed into quite a champion paperseller."[21] Barbara Green notes that Marion "wrote of the sensationalism attached to the activist woman in the street, the sexualization of the female body on display, and the aggressive quality of a masculinized gaze in ways that seemed to predict some of the insights of late-twentieth-century film theory."[22] Little did Marion know that in a few short years she would find herself in Times Square in New York City, engaged in a similar task and on display for a very different social movement. She had, of course, been on display in a theatrical context, but the stakes of suffrage performances were much higher.

Marion embraced the "Deeds not Words" of the WSPU, writing that "'Suffragettes' was an intended insult to the Militants by the *Daily Mail,* but became a title of honour which I was proud to share and live up to."[23] She avidly participated in processions and marches, often returning home bruised and sore from the rough handling she received from suffrage opponents and policemen. Her more violent deeds, including smashing the windows of a post office, professional association, and grocery store and setting fire to the grandstand at the Hurst Park Racecourse, landed her in prison. When Marion was arrested the night after setting the fire with another suffragette, she found her theatrical and suffrage worlds colliding:

> When Inspector Pride brought Betty [Giveen] in he fairly "barked" at me "what's your name?" Mocking his tone, I barked back, "Kitty Marion!" "Oh," he said. Then in a quite pleasant, friendly manner, "Do you know Mr. Finden?" Trying to place "Mr. Finden" in the Suffrage movement, I hesitated a moment, then "Mr. and Mrs. Harold Finden in the Music Halls? I've played on the same bill with them." "That's it," he said. "What a strange coincidence, I met Mr. Finden at a club last night and in the course of conversation, we touched on Women's Suffrage, he said he knew a Suffragette and mentioned your name. I little dreamed I would arrest you this morning."[24]

Of course, Marion's involvement with the WSPU and their radical tactics harmed her theatrical career in a number of ways. Her reputation was forever damaged: "A girl with whom I had played the leading part in a dramatic sketch told me how in course of conversation with her agent, he asked who had played the other part and when she mentioned my name, he said, 'Oh, that bloody Suffragette, she'd better not come here for anything.'" Indeed, agents expressed similar statements directly to Marion: "'If you'll take off those colors, I'll see that you get booked up for life,' he said. And I said 'No, you should have booked me before I put them on, it's too late to take them off now.'"[25]

Marion's theatrical career and, indeed, physical well-being were often in jeopardy due to her numerous jail terms. As Jane Purvis notes, "[E]ven one night in a cell, resulting in one missed performance, 'was sufficient to damage the chances of future employment.'"[26] Marion and her fellow crusaders continued their protests within the jails. She broke windows, took doors off hinges, ripped pillows and mattresses, broke gas lines, and even set fire to her cell. Additionally, she embarked upon numerous hunger strikes, which were met with exceptionally violent forcible feedings. Marion describes being held down by teams of wardresses and doctors as feeding tubes were forced into her nostrils or mouth and pushed down her throat, as liquefied food was poured in. Sometimes the tubes were administered so forcefully and incorrectly that the resultant stabbing pain caused her to lose consciousness. On some occasions these forcible feedings were conducted up to three times a day. Fearful of the effects of these forcible feedings on her throat and vocal chords, Marion repeatedly asked the prison officials to spare her this treatment so that her livelihood would not be jeopardized. Even though Marion recounts some of these feedings in explicit detail, she notes that "there are no words to describe the horrible revolting sensations."[27]

Marion received support from the WSPU leadership and also from her fellow AFL members, many of whom shied away from militant activities because of their fear of the impact they would have on their theatrical careers. One prominent AFL member, actress and playwright Elizabeth Robins, launched a letter-writing campaign on behalf of suffrage political prisoners and appealed directly to actresses to support Marion during her incarceration.[28]

Following her release from prison after a month's sentence in 1909, Marion told the WSPU newspaper *Votes for Women,* "I am more than ever convinced of the necessity for militant action."[29] Marion was outspoken in her opposition to forced feeding and recounts an incident in which she interrupted Minister Lloyd George, who was speaking at the annual Welsh cultural festival: "I jumped up and shouted, 'How dare you have political prisoners fed by force!'"[30] She was then thrown out of the hall, and her clothing was ripped and her hair pulled by an angry mob. Amazingly, in spite of her militancy and jail time, and the physical toll they took on her body, Marion was able to sustain something of a theatrical career in London. Elizabeth Crawford notes that following her arrests in 1909, Marion received a hunger strike medal from the WSPU in early December and went on to appear in holiday pantomimes.[31] In 1910 she fit stage performances in between political protests. Sometimes she was even able to combine performance and political activism, as she did at an appearance at the Colchester Liberal Unionist Association meeting where she was billed as "Music Hall Artiste and Militant Suffragette."[32]

At the onset of World War I, Marion was forced to leave England due to her German birth and her militant activities. Initially, she was supposed to be deported to Germany, but several colleagues worked on her behalf and she was able to move to the United States. Her reputation preceded her, however. Friends "had been certain I would easily find something in the Suffrage Movement or on the Stage. Considering how 'Notorious Characters' have been welcomed by theatrical and vaudeville enterprise, they thought my militant suffrage notoriety would help me, whereas it went against me."[33] She notes that much like in England, "My connection with suffrage prejudiced some managers, who were most facetiously afraid I might smash their windows or burn the theatre."[34] Additionally, she was alienated from U.S. suffragists, whose more conservative campaigns were disdainful of British militancy. She was reunited with Elizabeth Freeman, a former militant colleague who "reminded me of how we became acquainted at a meeting at the Queen's hall, London, when she and her mother, sitting next to me, had remarked on my fine voice, joining [me in] militant songs, and I answered, 'Oh yes, I earn my living with it, I am on the stage.'"[35] Yet it took some time for her "fine voice" to discover a new cause. Eventually, Marion began following the court case of Margaret Sanger and her colleagues following their operation of the Brownsville birth-control clinic.[36]

When Marion called to make a reservation to attend a meeting at Carnegie Hall where Sanger was speaking, the voice on the phone allegedly said, "Kitty Marion? We've heard of you, won't you come and help us, we've so much work to do."[37] Marion soon found herself in the role she would occupy for the next thirteen years, selling Sanger's *Birth Control Review* (*BCR*) publication. Fittingly, the *BCR* made its debut in Carnegie Hall, and as Marion notes, "Elizabeth Freeman and I help[ed] to sell it in true British Suffragette style, among the audience."[38] In her autobiography, Sanger notes that "selling *The Suffragette* on the streets of London had been part of the initiation which duchesses and countesses and other noble auxiliaries to the Pankhurst cause had had to undergo. Kitty had stood side by side with them. Since we had so experienced a veteran ready for service we began to offer the *Review* on the sidewalks of New York."[39] Esther Katz, in her editorial commentary in *The Selected Papers of Margaret Sanger*, goes so far as to describe Marion as a "militant street hawker," once more linking her to the militancy of her suffrage campaigning.[40] Marion quickly moved the sale of the *BCR* out into the streets, and for thirteen years she could be found in Times Square, in front of Grand Central Station, in Harold Square along Broadway, and occasionally on Coney Island. Bundled up with a satchel of *BCR*s over her shoulder and one in her hand raised above her head, Marion became a New York icon.[41] In fact, an anecdote regarding a small child who mistook Marion for the Statue of Liberty was parodied by at least two different cartoons.[42]

Unlike in London, Marion was not able to sustain a theatrical career in the midst of her political activism in the United States. Eventually, her commission from selling the *BCR* became her sole source of income. She did find herself in close proximity to theatres, after discovering a great deal of success selling papers outside of them.[43] Marion used her voice to call out to passersby, many of whom engaged in heated debate with her, some going so far as to physically assault her or call the police. Not surprisingly, Marion was arrested several times for her work within the birth-control campaign. In comparison with her work in British suffrage, however, her deeds were much less militant. Most of her arrests stemmed from perceived violations of Comstock Laws, and in one instance she was entrapped by a member of the Society for the Suppression of Vice.[44] A 1927 *New Yorker* article noted that Marion "has sold 86,478 copies, as of the first of August, we are informed, and all told has had much success and little trouble. Once an Irish lady engaged her in a one-sided fencing match with an umbrella, once some of Billy Sunday's followers denounced her publicly as immoral and upon one occasion the Vice Society had her arrested. She has come through each experience unscathed, however, and last month she even sold a copy of her magazine to a policeman."[45] Marion did spend some time in American jails for her work selling the *BCR,* however. In November 1918 she spent thirty days in prison after her entrapment by the member of the "Vice Society." While there, she met political dissident Agnes Smedley.[46] Smedley noted Marion's strong voice: "Kitty came clattering down the stone corridors every morning with her scrub pail in her hand. 'Three cheers for birth control,' she greeted the prisoners and the matrons. . . . When visitors or keepers came into the prison Kitty was always heard cheering for birth control."[47]

As in England, many political prisoners utilized the tactic of hunger striking to protest arrests. Margaret Sanger, her sister, and others involved in birth-control reform were among those who engaged in hunger strikes and were subsequently forcibly fed. A year and a half prior to her own arrest, Marion used her booming voice to interrupt a town meeting held in Carnegie Hall with the commissioner of corrections. As the *New York Tribune* noted, Commissioner Lewis had begun talking about "'so-called political offenders,' when Miss Marion arose and in a high-pitched voice shouted: 'Why do you use force to feed political prisoners?'"[48] In her autobiography, Marion notes that a friend "showered birth control leaflets from the gallery" as she was forcibly escorted out the door by a "chucker-out."[49]

Many of the tactics employed by the birth-control reform campaign bore similarities to those used by the British suffrage organizations, albeit on a much less violent scale. For Marion, the links between suffrage and birth control were clear. Her work with the WSPU and the AFL directly shaped her work selling the *BCR.* Yet for many older suffragettes, birth control had no place in the suffrage campaign. In one particularly poignant demonstration of this alienation,

Emmeline Pankhurst, one of the iconic leaders of the WSPU, visited New York, and Marion eagerly looked forward to a reunion: "I pictured a joyous meeting, should she come along and see me sell the *Birth Control Review.* I felt sure that with her knowledge of the unspeakable poverty-stricken, overcrowded slum conditions in England she would be delighted with my present activities." Unfortunately, as Marion continued,

> One afternoon at Macy's corner she did appear with Miss Pine, dear old "Piney" who, in her Nursing Home had been such a good, Ministering Angel to me and other hungerstrikers. I saw them crossing Broadway and my heart beat high in anticipation of our mutual pleasure of a reunion. I stood ready to "pounce on them," like a cat on two mice, at the moment of recognition. But oh, what a crashing of castles upon my unwary head when they did see me. Their faces hardened, their heads went up and they passed me, staring stonily in front of them. I felt stunned, hurt to the quick.[50]

Although Marion was deeply upset by this slight, she did return to England a few years later to witness the unveiling of a statue of Mrs. Pankhurst.[51] Shortly before she departed on this trip, she was let go from her position selling the *Birth Control Review.* As a writer for *The World* noted, "Kitty Marion whose voice was always so deceptively gentle when she inquired if you'd care to buy a copy of the *Birth Control Review,* is abandoning her stands in front of Grand Central and Macy's and the Astor to go back to England."[52] Prior to her departure, Marion told the *Brooklyn Daily Eagle* that she was not sure what her new cause would be but that "I'll probably be in mischief soon."[53] In honor of her thirteen years of service, the American Birth Control League gave Marion a luncheon and five hundred dollars.[54] When Marion did return to New York, she was at loose ends for some time until she found a new use for her strong voice. She eventually took a job with the Speech Improvement Project of the WPA, helping children learn proper English. In a roundabout way, she returned to her own roots as a young woman struggling to master a language that would ultimately become her medium.

Throughout the early decades of the twentieth century, actress Kitty Marion raised her clarion voice within and outside the theatre, advocating for social justice. The connections between her work in labor, suffrage, and birth-control reform were natural, with each movement inspiring the others. The injustices she observed led her to a life dedicated to agitating for political change. The tactics she learned in one movement shaped the ways in which she worked within the others. The company she kept within these movements simultaneously led her to greater involvement and increased her alienation. In spite of the severing of certain ties, however, Marion's experiences with each cause left its tracings, upon which she wrote the next phase of her radical activism.

Notes

1. Kitty Marion Papers, Manuscripts and Archives Division, The New York Public Library, Astor, Lenox, and Tilden Foundations, 71. It should be noted that the page numbering of the Marion Papers is in a shambles. Page numbers are skipped, page numbers are duplicated, and certain sections restart the pagination. I have listed the page numbers as marked on each page; however, there are multiple pages with the same number in vastly different segments of the autobiography.
2. Viv Gardner, "The Three Nobodies: Autobiographical Strategies in the Work of Alma Ellerslie, Kitty Marion and Ina Rozant," in *Auto/biography and Identity: Women, Theatre and Performance,* ed. Maggie B. Gale and Viv Gardner (Manchester: Manchester University Press, 2004), 12.
3. Ibid., 23.
4. Thomas Postlewait, "Theatre Autobiographies: Some Preliminary Concerns for the Theatre Historian," *Assaph C.* no. 16 (2000): 157–72. It should be noted that Marion's papers, primarily her unpublished autobiography, comprise a major source for this work. Postlewait has articulated four primary concerns for any historian utilizing autobiographies as evidence: quantity, reliability, quality, and narrative traits and types. Borrowing from Postlewait, Maggie B. Gale and Viv Gardner note in *Auto/biography and Identity* that "Actresses, as one of the first groups of professional women, have used, and use, autobiography and performance as both a means of expression and 'control' of their public selves, of both the 'face and the mask'" (3). Additionally, as Gardner cautions, "Unpicking the 'inner-life'—or even the 'real life'—from the complex matrix that informs and defines the performer's autobiography is no simple task" ("The Three Nobodies," 11). Wherever possible, I have attempted to verify Marion's claims with additional sources.
5. Marion, 8–9.
6. Christine A. Anderson, "(Per)forming Female Politics: The Making of the 'Modern Woman' in London, 1890–1914" (Ph.D. diss., University of Kansas, 2008), 36, http://kuscholarworks.ku.edu/dspace/bitstream/1808/4535/1/Anderson_ku_0099D_10060_DATA_1.pdf.
7. Gardner, "The Three Nobodies," 25. George Dance was the "author and 'director'" of both productions. Joseph Macleod notes that "George Dance, a reporter, owned a number of Drury Lane dramas, together with twenty-four touring companies. He was also the 'Westby and Co.' who made a fortune from the theatre bars. Macqueen Pope says he has the poorest opinion of the theatrical art; his object was to make money." Macleod, *The Actor's Right to Act* (London: Lawrence and Wishart, 1981), 83.
8. Peter Bailey, ed., *Music Hall: The Business of Pleasure* (Milton Keynes, U.K.: Open University Press, 1986), x.
9. Ibid., xv.
10. Gardner explicates this encounter as well as other run-ins with nefarious agents as a means of explaining the ways in which Marion may have been "using anecdote in the

development of her 'campaign' against abuses in the theatre" ("The Three Nobodies," 27). She also notes that Marion relates positive examples of her relationships with agents and managers who did not assault or threaten her. Anderson (not unproblematically) attributes Dreck's treatment of Marion to her perceived social class ("(Per)forming Female Politics," 45–46).

11. Marion, 69.
12. "Clement Scott Resigns," *New York Times,* December 11, 1898, 1. The *Times* article notes that the public debates extended to New York on their own pages and to Paris in the pages of *Le Figaro.* When Scott resigned, the *Daily Telegraph* published his letter of apology, and Sir Henry Irving accepted Scott's apology on behalf of the theatre profession.
13. Anderson, "(Per)forming Female Politics," 38.
14. Ibid., 48.
15. Marion, 9. In 1909 Marion once again joined the public debate regarding women's sexuality and professional theatre. The Longon *Sunday Chronicle* published an article and a series of letters to the editor, including one by Marion herself.
16. Ibid., 2–3.
17. Katherine Roberts, *Pages from the Diary of a Militant Suffragette* (London: Garden City Press Limited, 1910), 143. In this book, Roberts describes her involvement with the WSPU. In the final pages she has grown tired of discussions with anti-suffrage challengers while selling *Votes for Women* on the street. She writes, "I am getting tired of quoting Australia, so I pointed out that the stage is the only place where women have equal rights with men in their profession. 'Yet is there any place,' I asked, 'where women retain their womanliness more than on the stage?'"
18. Antonia Raeburn, *The Militant Suffragettes* (London: Michael Joseph, 1973). Raeburn notes that "the majority of members of the Franchise League were classical actresses, but the society was open to anyone connected with the theatrical professions, including singers and musicians; Kitty Marion was a red-headed variety artiste" (86). Although there are no records of Marion appearing in any of the suffrage propaganda plays produced by the AFL, Elizabeth Crawford notes that "on 13 April 1909 [Marion] helped carry the AFL banner in a procession from Marble Arch to Aldwych to celebrate Mrs. Pethic-Lawrence's [a WSPU leader] release from Holloway [prison]." Crawford, *The Women's Suffrage Movement: A Reference Guide, 1866–1928* (London: Routledge, 2001), 376.
19. Lisa Ticknor, *The Spectacle of Women: Imagery of the Suffrage Campaign 1907–1914* (Chicago: University of Chicago Press, 1988), 8.
20. Rebecca Lenkiewicz, *Her Naked Skin* (London: Faber and Faber, 2008). In this play about the British suffrage campaign, Lenkiewicz chronicles some of these tactics. While Marion is not a character in the play, she is referenced. During a Hyde Park speech, Florence states, "Over a thousand women have been to prison during the course of this agitation. Last summer there were one hundred and two suffragettes incarcerated at one time. Of these ninety were forcibly fed. Some of them twice a day. Our comrade Kitty Marion has been force-fed up to two hundred times to date" (26). Lenkiewicz's use of Marion is evidence of Marion's enduring iconic status within the suffrage campaign.
21. Marion, 6.
22. Barbara Green, *Spectacular Confessions: Autobiography, Performative Activism, and the Sites of Suffrage 1905–1938* (New York: St. Martin's Press, 1997), 11. Green also asserts that Marion's foray into selling *Votes for Women* was a "perilous encounter with a condemn-

ing masculine gaze" (39). Yet Marion does not specify that "every eye" was male, making Green's assertion somewhat problematic.

23. Marion, 4.
24. Ibid., 63.
25. Ibid., 7.
26. Jane Purvis, "Doing Feminist Women's History: Researching the Lives of Women in the Suffragette Movement in Edwardian England," in *Researching Women's Lives from a Feminist Perspective,* ed. Mary Maynard and June Purvis (London: Routledge, 1994), 174.
27. Marion, 22.
28. Angela V. John, *Elizabeth Robins: Staging a Life, 1862–1952* (London: Routledge, 1995), 160.
29. "Miss Kitty Marion Released," *Votes for Women,* November 19, 1909, 106. Throughout the campaign, hunger-striking suffragettes were released temporarily from prison to recover under what became known as the Cat and Mouse Act. Marion protested the act upon her 1913 conviction for the arson at the racetrack, asserting, "I shall hunger strike and I shall refuse to leave prison under the Cat and Mouse Act. I shall insist upon staying here until dead or released a free woman." "Says She'll Refuse to Leave Prison," *New York Times,* July 4, 1913, 2.
30. Marion, 53.
31. Crawford, *Women's Suffrage Movement,* 376.
32. Ibid., 376. Crawford writes that "the resulting report notes that 'the awe experienced by the audience was quickly succeeded by delight, for the lady proved a charming vocalist'" (376–77).
33. Marion, 1.
34. Ibid., 3.
35. Ibid., 3–4.
36. Marion notes in a eugenic manner, which was common among birth-control reformers of this time, "As I followed the case in the Press, I realized more and more that here was the most fundamental plank, even more important than Woman's Suffrage, in the abolition and prevention of future poverty, over-crowding, un-employment, war, and all the unspeakable misery they bring in their wake. This was the 'Ark' by which the fit and useful members of society could save themselves from the 'Deluge' of the unfit, the unwanted, the useless and unnecessary" (ibid., 1).
37. Ibid., 2.
38. Ibid., 3.
39. Margaret Sanger, *Margaret Sanger: An Autobiography* (New York: Norton, 1938), 256.
40. Esther Katz, ed., *The Selected Papers of Margaret Sanger,* vol. 1, *The Woman Rebel, 1900–1928* (Urbana: University of Illinois Press, 2003), 196.
41. "Lost Lady," *New Yorker,* February 22, 1930, 18. Published upon her retirement from selling the *BCR,* the article noted that "through her years of selling the *Birth Control Review* in Times Square, Grand Central Station, in front of Macy's, and other places crowded enough for her she became one of the best known figures in town."
42. Clippings of these cartoons are contained in the Marion Papers. Their sources are not identified.
43. One evening, Sanger's documentary film on birth control was scheduled to be shown but was barred by the police. Marion decided to see another picture instead. "*The Hand That Rocks the Cradle* appeared at [a] Broadway Theatre, just below 41st St. 'Some sloppy sen-

timentality,' I thought, feeling sore at the fate of Mrs. Sanger's picture, and just to wallow in disgust I went in to see it when lo and behold, I found a perfectly fine Birth Control story, similar to Mrs. Sanger's. I rushed home, snatched all the *Reviews* I had, nearly 100, and got back to the Theatre just in time to catch the audience coming out. The psychological moment—'*the Birth Control Review,* 15 cents a copy' I called out, holding it aloft for people to see, and they bought it like hot cakes. The picture ran three weeks, the management having had the foresight to procure an injunction restraining the police from interfering, though they did prevent it from being shown in the future in New York. Every night I sold outside the theatre, doing exceedingly good business, to the delight of Dr. Blossom and the rest of 'the office'" (6).

44. Margaret Sanger, "Trapped!" *Birth Control Review,* October 1918, 3.
45. "Malthus on Broadway," *New Yorker,* August 27, 1927, 12–13.
46. Ellen Chessler, *Woman of Valor: Margaret Sanger and the Birth Control Movement in America* (New York: Simon and Schuster, 1992), 170.
47. Agnes Smedley, "Cell Mates," ed. Jan MacKinnon and Steve MacKinnon, *Signs: Journal of Women in Culture and Society* 3, no. 2 (1977): 538.
48. "Woman Put Out of Carnegie Hall for Baiting Lewis," *New York Tribune,* March 8, 1917, 6.
49. Marion 5–6.
50. Ibid., 38.
51. Jared L. Manley, "Crusader," *New Yorker,* July 4, 1936, 23.
52. "Kitty Marion, Birth Control Worker, Quits Her Post Here," *The World,* February 10, 1930, 1.
53. Isabelle Keating, "Kitty Marion, Fighter, Looks for New Cause," *Brooklyn Daily Eagle,* February 11, 1930, 3.
54. "Birth Control Leaders Honor Kitty Marion," *New York Herald Tribune,* February 12, 1930, 10.

"The Picture Postcard is a sign of the times"

Theatre Postcards and Modernism

—PENNY FARFAN

The invention of the postcard in 1869 and the introduction of picture postcards not long after resulted in an international postcard craze that lasted until the onset of World War I. As theatre historian Veronica Kelly has noted in a study of the theatrical dimensions of this popular phenomenon, actresses, particularly those specializing in musical comedy, were a favorite subject within the postcard industry, extending the actresses' images beyond their theatrical origins to a much broader range of contexts and making those images available for a variety of consumer usages.[1] It is worth noting, however, that the postcard vogue coincided with the rise of modernism and that, in addition to popular musical-comedy actresses, some of the more elite stage performers and controversial theatre artists of the period were represented on postcards. This essay considers the use of the postcard to circulate images of turn-of-the-twentieth-century star performers not typically considered in relation to modernism and of seemingly high-art modernists not typically considered as popular entertainment. In doing so, I raise questions about the relation of popular entertainment and modernism and suggest how postcards might be seen to problematize the perceived boundaries between high art and popular culture that have traditionally effected the segregation of popular entertainment studies and modernist cultural studies. At the same time, I consider how theatre postcards complicate the conventional geographic and temporal boundaries by which modernism has most often been understood. In these ways, the essay suggests how late-nineteenth- and early-twentieth-century theatre postcards provide evidence to support recent reconceptualizations of the field of modernist studies and of the centrality of theatre and performance within modernist cultural production.

Plain postcards, with the postal address and postage on one side and space for a message on the other, were initially proposed by a German postmaster in 1865 and came into use in Austria in 1869 with such success that sales are estimated at a million cards per month in the first year alone.[2] Picture postcards followed soon after and were especially popular with tourists at European resorts in the 1880s and 1890s. Plain postcards were adopted in Britain in 1870, with picture postcards following in 1894, and the United States began issuing plain postcards in 1873 and picture postcards in 1893. During the peak of their popularity, postcards functioned as a form of popular entertainment as individuals around the world engaged in correspondence, collection, and exchange.

A few examples will give some sense of the range and focus of theatre- and performance-related postcards during the period in question. For representations of actresses, Ellen Terry provides a useful example, with a large number of postcards featuring her in costume for various roles, as well as out of character (figs. 1-4).[3]

Postcards featured scenes from plays as well, as shown in the examples of productions of *The Second Mrs. Tanqueray, The Lower Depths,* and *Hedda Gabler* (figs. 5–7).[4] Dance artists were also popular subjects for postcards and were represented in genres ranging from ballet to modern dance to cabaret (figs. 8–11). Theatre- and performance-related postcards were not limited to performers but also included such key modernist playwrights as Henrik Ibsen, August Strindberg, Anton Chekhov, Maxim Gorky, and George Bernard Shaw, as well as less widely recognized figures such as writer Cicely Hamilton and producer/manager Lilian Baylis (figs. 12–16).[5] Such postcards were most often formal studio portraits, but there were also occasional snapshots and cartoons (figs. 17 and 18).

In "The Work of Art in the Age of Mechanical Reproduction," Walter Benjamin notes that the "uniqueness of a work of art is inseparable from its being imbedded in the fabric of tradition."[6] Detaching a work of art from its "aura" of authenticity—its original "presence in time and space, its unique existence at the place where it happens to be"—thus inevitably detaches "the reproduced object from the domain of tradition" and from the "ritual function" associated with "the location of its original use value." In the case of theatre-related postcards, they were detached from the rituals of theatre-going and perhaps even play-reading.[7] Indeed, as theatre scholar Viv Gardner has observed, postcards contributed to a "fissure between performance and the sale of the image. You could live in Barrow-in-Furness, never go to the theatre, and yet still collect pic-

Figure 1. Ellen Terry as Portia, *The Merchant of Venice,* Lyceum Theatre, London, 1879–1880. J. Beagles & Co. postcard. All postcards reproduced in this essay are courtesy of the author's collection.

Figure 2. Ellen Terry as Beatrice, *Much Ado about Nothing,* Lyceum Theatre, London, 1882–1883. Raphael Tuck & Sons postcard; postmarked U.K., 1905.

Figure 3. Ellen Terry. C. W. Faulkner & Co. postcard; postmarked Macclesfield, U.K., 1904.

Figure 4. Ellen Terry with her dog. Rotary Photo postcard; postmarked London, 1906.

Figure 5. Mrs. Patrick Campbell as Paula Tanqueray and George Alexander as Aubrey Tanqueray, act 1, *The Second Mrs. Tanqueray,* St. James Theatre, London, 1893. J. Beagles & Co. postcard.

Figure 6. *The Lower Depths,* Moscow Art Theatre, 1902. Phototype Scherer, Nabholz & Co. (Moscow) postcard; postmarked Sophia, Bulgaria, 1904.

Figure 7. Lydia Yavorska as Hedda and Franklin Dyall as Judge Brack, *Hedda Gabler,* Kingsway Theatre, London, 1911. Photo by Daily Mirror Studios; postmarked U.K., 1914.

tures of Gertie Millar."[8] As Benjamin says, "by making many reproductions," the mechanical reproduction of the work of art "substitutes a plurality of copies for a unique existence. And in permitting the reproduction to meet the beholder or listener in his own particular situation, it reactivates the object reproduced. These two processes lead to a tremendous shattering of tradition. . . . [and] are intimately connected with . . . contemporary mass movements."[9]

The rise of the postcard industry was linked to advances in photographic development and reproduction; and theatre- and performance-related postcards were often photographic in nature. For Roland Barthes, the essence (*noeme*) of photography—its fundamental quality of "That-has-been"—derives from its chemical processes. As he notes,

> a scientific circumstance (the discovery that silver halogens were sensitive to light) made it possible to recover and print directly the luminous rays emitted by a variously lighted object. The photograph is literally an emanation of the referent. From a real body, which was there, proceed radiations which ultimately touch me, who am here . . . the photograph of the missing being . . . will touch me like the delayed rays of a star. A sort of umbilical cord links the body of the photographed thing to my gaze: light, though impalpable, is here a carnal medium, a skin I share with anyone who has been photographed. . . . [T]he thing of the past, by its immediate radiations (its luminances), has really touched the surface which in its turn my gaze will touch. . . . [T]he photographed body touches me with its own rays and not with a superadded light.[10]

The owner of a photographic postcard of a "star" was thus, in a sense, in physical contact with the star's being, and so in a relationship of distanced possession.[11]

While unsent postcards were sometimes preserved as collectors' items, many cards were sent through the mail; indeed, as C. W. Hill has noted, in addition to developments in photography that enabled the mass circulation and private ownership of images of art and artists, the postcard craze was linked to modernizing developments in national and international postal services that set uniform inland postal costs, established regular home delivery, and devised "methods of co-ordinating the transport of mail between countries and of simplifying the calculation of postage."[12] The General Postal Union, later the International Postal Union, was established in 1875 "with the task of organizing and regulating the exchange of 'letters, postcards, books, newspapers and printed matter, samples and commercial paper'" among its member nations.[13] Historians of the international post have linked such innovations to global expansions in trade and commerce, as well as to developments in transportation associated with the Industrial Revolution; they have also noted the role of postal innovations, particularly those relating to reduced mailing rates for newspapers and periodicals,

Figure 8. Adolf Bolm, *Polovtsian Dances,* Ballets Russes, Théâtre du Châtelet, Paris, 1909. Photo: W. Willinger, Berlin.

Figure 9. Tamara Karsavina, *Firebird,* Ballets Russes, Théâtre du Châtelet, 1910. Postcard sold on behalf of the Society of Saint Evgenia, Dressler Phototype and Printing, St. Petersburg.

Figure 10. Maud Allan, *The Vision of Salome* (1906). Postcard advertising a performance by Allan, with Leo, Jan, and Mischel Cherniavsky, at Warwick Town Hall (Australia, 1914); Swift Print, Sydney, Australia.

Figure 11. Josephine Baker. Photo: Cliché Walery, Paris; Cinémagazine—Edition postcard, Paris.

Figure 12. August Strindberg.

Figure 13. Anton Chekhov.

Figure 14. Maxim Gorky. Sent from Stara Zagora to Kazanlak, Bulgaria, 1904.

Figure 15. George Bernard Shaw.

Figure 16. Cicely Hamilton and Lilian Baylis. P. & A. Photo, K. Ltd. postcard.

in "the international exchange of ideas."[14] Similar claims have been made about national postal systems. In a study of the U.S. post, for example, Richard John identifies postal innovations as one aspect of a larger "communications revolution" that has "figured conspicuously in the making of the modern world." For John, "the postal system [was] a powerful agent of change."[15]

Veronica Kelly has noted that postcards' "small scale as written documents provided an informal medium for fast communication which risked little loss of cultural face whether for the youthful or the adult poorly-schooled."[16] Similarly, historian David Henkin has written that "since postcards supplied a built-in excuse for being brief, they . . . lowered the threshold for mail exchange" and "accentuated the ease with which letters could be produced as well as transmitted"; in these ways, along with "lowered participation costs"—that is, reduced postage rates—postcards "democratized the exchange of interpersonal greetings."[17]

Postcards were, moreover, regarded by some who used them as a particularly modern form of communication. As one enthusiast wrote in 1900,

> The Picture Postcard is a sign of the times. It belongs to a period peopled by a hurried generation which has not many minutes to spare for writing to friends. What with the express trains going at the rate of a mile a minute, with telegrams and telephones, the world has become a small place. We go all over it, we have acquaintances in all parts of it. When we rush from Rome to Paris, do the galleries of Italy in one week and those of

Figure 17. Henrik Ibsen. J. F. Eftf. [Norway]; inscribed "1908."

Figure 18. Henrik Ibsen. Cartoon by G. S. Shepheard, Raphael Tuck & Sons postcard.

Holland the next, fly . . . off to the Holy Land, take Mount Olympus on our way, how can we pause to do more than send a signal of safe arrival and a sign of remembrance to our numberless acquaintances? The Picture Postcard is with us. It suits us. It meets our needs.[18]

At a time when distances were traversed with greater ease and the pace of life seemed to be accelerating, postcards were an apt, and trendy, mode of communication.

The short messages people wrote on theatre postcards sometimes related to the subject of the card and sometimes did not. Postcards of Ellen Terry, for example, included such messages as the following:

—"Hope you like this of E. Terry. With Love, AB"
—"This is another for your collection."
—"I like this one very much, don't you?"
—"Dear Doris, Thought you would like this better than a view. we are very busy Auntie & Uncle Harry coming Mary Best love [Over.] have you gone back to the same school."
—"She has too much lace on for me but she is rather nice looking. I think she is Mrs. [Tuck?]. She looks like a [Binyer?]. With love from your father alm [?]."
—"Dear Mrs D many thank for P.C. glad to hear you are enjoying yourself & the nice weather. did you get the letter alright hoping you are well Bertha"
—"Darling—Little Mother Dada and I wish you a very happy Birthday—and hope you will like this pretty P. P. Card. With every loving wish—and praying God to bless and take care of you—darling Mother—always—.Loving Dada—and Isoline."
—"from Yours ever to be respected Maurice"
—"Will see you Wednesday. Always yours. E. L." [This last addressed to a Miss Wasdell in Winnipeg, Canada.]
—"Dear Ada. How are you progressing with your sums. Are they not fearful? Don't worry. Think of ————————. M."
—"To Dear [Louie?]. With love & all good Wishes for Xmas & the coming New Year. From yours lovingly Fannie."

Terry's image was also used on postcards advertising goods such as needles and soup (figs. 19 and 20). These postcards and their messages democratized not only written communication by post but also access to an elite stage actress celebrated for her artful performances, particularly of Shakespeare.

Figure 19. Ellen Terry, advertisement for Milward's Needles. Photo: Window and Grove; postmarked Wellington, New Zealand, 1907.

Figure 20. Ellen Terry, advertisement for Symington's Soups. Postmarked U.K., 1911.

Figure 21. Henrik Ibsen. RPH [Rhotophot] postcard; postmarked Tromso, Norway and Darmstadt, Germany, 1906. "Tromso—July 10–06.—Dear E. You must [have/save?] this card for it is of a deep thinker—am well etc. [. . .] Love." Sent to Miss Edith A. Gundebach, c/o Frau Louisa Wagner in Darmstadt, Germany.

If such widespread and casual circulation of images of a well-known actress who toured extensively and internationally is not surprising,[19] postcards of artists more closely associated with modernist ideas and aesthetic innovations may be; and the latter, like the actress postcards described above, included messages that occasionally referred to the subject of the card but as often did not. A postcard of Ibsen written in English and sent from Tromsø to Darmstadt in 1906 (fig. 21) included a message relating to the playwright's high art status: "Dear E. You must [have? save?] this card for it is of a deep thinker—am well etc. [Illegible: initials?] Love." More tersely, an Ibsen card sent from Montevideo, Uruguay, in 1905 included only a handwritten notation identifying the subject of the card as a Norwegian dramatist, the name "Oscar" (presumably that of the sender), and the name and address of the recipient, a Señora Nilsen. Still another Ibsen card (fig. 22), posted in 1903, again from Montevideo, included a lengthy message written on the picture side that made no mention of the playwright at all but instead chatted about the winter weather and boredom due to a cold that prevented the sender from being able to go out. Perhaps more meaningful was an exceptionally handsome double-portrait postcard (fig. 23) of Maxim Gorky

Figure 22. Henrik Ibsen, drawing by L. Reig. Postmarked Montevideo, Uruguay, 1903. "Dear Fela [Señorita Fela Dorr Hillner (?)]: I received your brief letter the other day, which made me very happy. I will respond to it one of these days. I won't do so today because my hands are so cold that I can't even hold a pen. All I can say is if this is what winter is going to be like we should get ready because it is very cold at the moment. I have a cold so I can't go out which has me bored because I love to go out. Lot of kisses to your mom and Lalito and for you. A warm hug. [Unreadable signature.] PS. This week I also received a postcard." (Trans. Lourdes Arciniega.)

and Feodor Schaliapin that was sent without comment from Vienna in 1904 to a female schoolteacher in the Bulgarian village of Ferdinandovo. The sender of an Isadora Duncan postcard (fig. 24) postmarked in Stockholm in 1906 thanked the recipient for a postcard and mentioned the preceding day's local news—a fire and an accident—with no reference to the great dancer. A postcard of Chekhov written in Bulgarian and dated 1921 sent a schoolboy best wishes on the occasion of his name day and hoped for his "happiness and progress in school."[20] As Veronica Kelly has argued and as these postcards make clear, the remediated images of the theatrical personages who figured on postcards were put to new uses in the process of recontextualization within "a complexity of early twentieth-century everyday practices."[21]

As the variety of examples illustrating my analysis may suggest, theatre and performance postcards from the early twentieth century present challenges to the conventional periodization of modernism. For example, internationally circulated cards of a leading but primarily late-nineteenth-century performer

Figure 23. Maxim Gorky and Feodor Schaliapin. Posted from Vienna to Ferdinadovo, Bulgaria, 1904. "For Miss Rada Obshtinska, teacher in the village of Ferdinandovo."

such as Ellen Terry remediated her stage presence through modern technologies (photography, the postal system, the postcard form, advertising)[22] to contribute to her ongoing currency in the early twentieth century.[23]

But the "modern" itself was also curiously temporalized by the vivid quality of some "real photo" postcards. Remarking that "the portrait was the focal point of early photography," Benjamin notes that although "mechanical reproduction emancipates the work of art from its parasitical dependence on ritual" and the auratic, "for the last time the aura emanates from the early photographs in the fleeting expression of a human face. This is what constitutes their melancholy, incomparable beauty."[24] In "A Short History of Photography" he further observes, "However skillful the photographer, however carefully he poses his model, the spectator feels an irresistible compulsion to look for the tiny spark of chance, of the here and now, with which reality has, as it were, seared the character in the picture; to find that imperceptible point at which, in the immediacy of that long-past moment, the future so persuasively inserts itself that, looking back, we may rediscover it."[25]

For Barthes, that "tiny spark" is the *punctum* —the unintentional detail that punctures the photograph to wound the viewer with the unique reality of

Figure 24. Isadora Duncan. Postmarked Stockholm, Sweden, 1906. "Dear Miss! Dearest thanks for the postcard I received a couple of days ago. Yes, now the Miss does not have more than 2 whole days left to be in peace and quiet. Here in the city it is an unfortunate time. The 13th fire started yesterday and that is in 9 out of 10 days. There was also an accident by Stadgården yesterday. I was nearby but did not want to go over and see. The Miss will probably get to read about it in time. [?] are all well. Dearest greetings from Hilda. Welcome soon to Gerda." (Trans. Hanne Wiseth.)

the photographic referent. Most theatre and performance postcards fall under the category of what Barthes calls the *studium*, by which he means those photographs that "provoke only a general and, so to speak, *polite* interest: they have no *punctum* in them: they please or displease me without pricking me: they are invested with no more than *studium*. The *studium* is that very wide field of unconcerned desire, of various interest, of inconsequential taste: *like/don't like*. The *studium* is of the order of *liking*, not of *loving*."[26]

Occasionally, however, a postcard pierces the *studium* of conventional theatrical postcard imagery with an unexpectedly wounding *punctum*. In a Rotary Photo postcard (fig. 25), for example, the strikingly vivid texture of the fabric of Ellen Terry's garment suggests the feeling on and of the body that wears it and thus connects the spectator sensually with the mortal flesh of the immortal actress.

Figure 25. Ellen Terry. Rotary Photo postcard.

As Benjamin indicates in his reference to that "imperceptible point at which, in the immediacy of that long-past moment, the future so persuasively inserts itself," and as Barthes so movingly argues in *Camera Lucida,* the *punctum* that wounds is not only the unintentional yet piercing detail but also time itself.[27] In the most literal sense, to pose is to experience one's transformation from subject into object.[28] More fundamentally, though, the photograph might be said to capture the experience of the living becoming dead, and thus it is in essence the return of the living/dead, an uncanny doubling of the living past of the dead and the now-dead/then-living's then-future death: in Barthes's words, "This *punctum,* more or less blurred beneath the abundance and the disparity of contemporary photographs, is vividly legible in historical photographs: there is always a defeat of Time in them: *that* is dead and *that* is going to die."[29] Two images may serve here to exemplify this notion of time as *punctum.* The first (fig. 26), a Rotary Photo postcard of a seemingly resigned and strikingly melancholy Ellen Terry, out of her live-theatre element and pinned by the camera (or pinioned—note the gloved hands); the second (fig. 27), a 1905 stereo-card (close relative of the postcard) of the stroke-afflicted Ibsen at home in his apartment in the last year of his life. Barthes notes that while photographs are "'modern,' mingled with our noisiest everyday life," they also have "a strange stasis, the stasis of an *arrest.*"[30] The postcard image of the melancholy, gloved Terry modernizes the non-modern, while the stereo-card of Ibsen historicizes the modern. In doing so, these oddly wounding images suggest a paradox at the heart of modernism that corresponds with August Strindberg's claim that modern characters are "torn and divided, a mixture of the old and the new"[31] and Georg Lukácz's observation that the modern stage is "the point of intersection for pairs of worlds distinct in time; . . . where 'past' and 'future,' 'no longer' and 'not yet,' come together in a single moment."[32]

Beyond problematizing the temporality of the "modern" and the periodization of modernism, early-twentieth-century theatre and performance postcards extend modernism's geographic range and make clear that it was not simply an urban, western European, and American phenomenon. The specific postcards that I have referred to in this essay circulated in places as diverse and far-flung as rural and urban England and Scotland, eastern and western Europe, Russia, the United States, Canada, South America, New Zealand, Australia, and, to add one more example, Turkey, where Josephine Baker's image appeared on a postcard advertising chocolate (fig. 28).

Finally, theatre postcards—the form and also the similarities in circulation and usage of images of popular performers, controversial playwrights, and modern dance artists alike—bridge, equalize, or collapse the categories of "high

Figure 26. Ellen Terry. Rotary Photo postcard.

Figure 27. "Henrik Ibsen, the dramatic poet to whom all the world pays homage, in his home at Christiania, Norway." Stereocard, Underwood & Underwood, U.S.A., 1905.

Figure 28. Josephine Baker, advertisement for Besler Çikolatasi (Turkey).

art" and "popular entertainment," making clear the falseness of this conventional dichotomy. Through postcards and the popular practices of postcard collection and exchange, not only the musical comedy starlets that Veronica Kelly has studied but also elite actresses, controversial modern dancers, and now-canonical pioneers of modern drama were implicated in an emergent celebrity culture dependent on new technologies and modern mass media.

Douglas Mao and Rebecca Walkowitz have described "the new modernist studies" as challenging the "temporal, spatial, and vertical" dimensions that have traditionally defined modernism as an early-twentieth-century movement centered in western Europe and the United States and favoring "high art" and aesthetic experimentation over more popular cultural forms.[33] Scholars of modernist performance studies have further complicated such critical challenges by demonstrating the centrality of theatre and performance within modernism.[34] Through the complexities of their "temporal, spatial, and vertical" dimensions, the theatre and performance postcards I have considered in this essay—the artists they represented, the messages that were written on them, the uses to which they were put, and the postal routes they traveled—validate challenges to conventional understandings of modernism, including the role of theatre, drama, and performance in modernism's emergence, development, and circulation.

Notes

All illustrations and citations of postcard correspondence are from items in the collection of the author. Thanks to Matthew Farfan for sharing his postcard expertise.

1. Veronica Kelly, "Beauty and the Market: Actress Postcards and their Senders in Early Twentieth-Century Australia," *New Theatre Quarterly* 20, no. 2 (2004): 99–116. For another account of the intersection of the popular entertainment and postcard industries that gives particular attention to the "glamour card" of musical comedy actresses, see Viv Gardner, "Gertie Millar and the 'Rules for Actresses and Vicars' Wives,'" *Extraordinary Actors: Essays on Popular Performers*, ed. Jane Milling and Martin Banham (Exeter, U.K.: University of Exeter, 2004), 83–96. David Mayer's "'Quote the Words to Prompt the Attitudes': The Victorian Performer, the Photographer, and the Photograph," *Theatre Survey* 43, no. 2 (2002), includes a discussion of theatre postcards (245–47). Richard Bonynge's *A Collector's Guide to Theatrical Postcards* (London: B. T. Batsford, 1988) reproduces a selection of theatre- and performance-related postcards with accompanying biographical information on the subjects of the cards.
2. C. W. Hill, *Discovering Picture Postcards* (Tring, U.K.: Shire Publications, 1970), 9.
3. As David Mayer has pointed out, Victorian and Edwardian photographs of actors in costume were usually taken in photographers' studios rather than onstage and should therefore not be understood as images of stage performances per se. Rather, while a photograph "may show an actor in a role, or a variety artist wearing the costume or showing the apparatus of his or her act, or a dancer posed as if in midstep, the photograph is made, distributed, acquired, and collected because it is, first and foremost, a *portrait* —a likeness—of the performer" ("'Quote the Words to Prompt the Attitudes,'" 227).

   The dates of the photographs used on postcards do not always correspond with the dates of the production of the postcards themselves; instead, the postcard images are often reproductions of earlier photographs. The stage production dates provided in these captions suggest approximate dates of the photographs, whereas franking dates on postally used postcards suggest approximate dates of the postcards.
4. Laurence Senelick has noted that "[i]nsufficient lighting and bulky equipment prevented on-stage photos from being taken before 1872" ("Melodramatic Gesture in Carte-de-Visite Photographs" *Theatre* 18, no. 2 [1987]: 5). Whereas the photographs reproduced in the postcards of *The Lower Depths* and *Hedda Gabler* included in this essay appear to

have been taken on actual stage sets, the photograph of *The Second Mrs. Tanqueray* may have been taken in a photographic studio.

5. Hamilton and Baylis were close friends and coauthored a history of the Old Vic that was published in 1926.
6. Walter Benjamin, "The Work of Art in the Age of Mechanical Reproduction," *Illuminations*, trans. Harry Zorn (London: Pimlico, 1999), 217.
7. Ibid., 214, 215, 217.
8. Gardner, "Gertie Millar," 104.
9. Benjamin, "The Work of Art," 215.
10. Roland Barthes, *Camera Lucida: Reflections on Photography*, trans. Richard Howard (New York: Hill and Wang, 1981), 80–81. As Barthes notes, he is here following Susan Sontag, who states in *On Photography*: "While a painting, even one that meets photographic standards of resemblance, is never more than the stating of an interpretation, a photograph is never less than the registering of an emanation (light waves reflected by objects)—a material vestige of its subject in a way that no painting can be" ([New York: Picador, 1973], 154). Elizabeth Barrett Browning wrote in 1843 of the early photographic form of the daguerrotype, "several of these wonderful portraits, like engravings—only exquisite and delicate beyond the work of graver—have I seen lately—longing to have such a memorial of every Being dear to me in the world. It is not merely the likeness which is precious in such cases—but the association, and the sense of nearness involved in the thing, the fact of the very shadow of the person lying there fixed for ever!" (quoted in Peter Hamilton, "The Beautiful and the Damned," *The Beautiful and the Damned: The Creation of Identity in Nineteenth Century Photography*, by Peter Hamilton and Roger Hargreaves [Aldershot, U.K.: Lund Humphries in association with the National Portrait Gallery, London, 2001], 11; see also Sontag, *On Photography*, 183).
11. As Sontag notes, "a photograph is not only like its subject. . . . It is part of, an extension of that subject; and a potent means of acquiring it, of gaining control over it" (*On Photography*, 155). In a somewhat different sense, Laurence Senelick has written of collectors of erotic cartes de visite that, "to some small degree, to own the image was to possess its subject" ("Eroticism in Early Theatrical Photography," *Theatre History Studies* 11 [1991]: 8); see also Laurence Senelick, "Early Photographic Attempts to Record Performance Sequence," in which he states, "A sense of property rights in the actress was provided by the reduced format [of cartes de visite], for these photographs were rather smaller than a playing card" (*Theatre Research International* 22, no. 3 [1997]: 258).
12. Hill, *Discovering Picture Postcards*, 7.
13. Ibid., 8.
14. Gottfried North, Arthur Wyss, Pierre Le Saux, Howard Daniel, and André Savoie, *The Post: A Universal Link among Men* (Lausanne: Vie Art Cité, 1974), 135–36, 142.
15. Richard R. John, *Spreading the News: The American Postal System from Franklin to Morse* (Cambridge: Harvard University Press, 1995), 3, 7.
16. Kelly, "Beauty and the Market," 105.
17. David M. Henkin, *The Postal Age: The Emergence of Modern Communications in Nineteenth-Century America* (Chicago: University of Chicago Press, 2006), 173–74.
18. Quoted in Tonie and Valmai Holt, *Picture Postcards of the Golden Age: A Collector's Guide* (London: MacGibbon & Kee, 1971), 20.
19. In a discussion of Gaiety Theatre performer Gertie Millar, Gardner has argued that the

picture postcard was central to the "star industry" in the days before the emergence of "the film star and the mass production of film fanzines, posters and all the other commercial paraphernalia of 'fandom'" ("Gertie Millar," 98). Historians of photography more generally have noted the integral relationship between photography and celebrity; see, for example, Abigail Solomon-Godeau, "The Legs of the Countess," *October* 39 (Winter 1986): 92-94; Hamilton, "The Beautiful and the Damned," 1–15; and Roger Hargreaves, "Putting Faces to the Names: Social and Celebrity Portrait Photography," in Hamilton and Hargreaves, *The Beautiful and the Damned*, 17–55.

20. Translated by Cody Olson.
21. Kelly, "Beauty and the Market," 101. Kelly is particularly interested in the hegemonic "codings of femininity" on "glamour" postcards of actresses in popular entertainment forms such as musical comedy (99).
22. See Julian Murphet for a discussion of how the older media of painting and literature "became remediated and so *modern* within the complex photomechanical medium of halftone photography, photogravure and machine-set print." *Multimedia Modernism: Literature and the Anglo-American Avant-garde* (Cambridge: Cambridge University Press, 2009), 41.
23. In another context, I have argued elsewhere that while Terry has been traditionally regarded as a Victorian actress who was out of step with modernist aesthetic and political innovations, she remained a central figure for such key modernists as George Bernard Shaw, Isadora Duncan, and Virginia Woolf, and that her views on drama—and particularly on Shakespeare and Ibsen—need therefore to be considered in relation to feminist stances within modernist culture. See Penny Farfan, *Women, Modernism, and Performance* (Cambridge: Cambridge University Press, 2004), 34–48.
24. Benjamin, "The Work of Art," 218–19.
25. Walter Benjamin, "A Short History of Photography," trans. Stanley Mitchell, *Screen* 13, no. 1 (1972): 7.
26. Barthes, *Camera Lucida*, 27.
27. Benjamin, "Short History of Photography," 7.
28. Barthes, *Camera Lucida*, 14.
29. Ibid., 96.
30. Ibid., 91.
31. August Strindberg, "Preface to *Miss Julie*," in *Dramatic Theory and Criticism: Greeks to Grotowski*, ed. Bernard F. Dukore, trans. E. M. Sprinchorn (Fort Worth, Tex.: Harcourt Brace Jovanovich, 1974), 567.
32. George Lukácz, "The Sociology of Modern Drama," trans. Lee Baxandall, in Dukore, *Dramatic Theory and Criticism*, 934.
33. Douglas Mao and Rebecca L. Walkowitz, "The New Modernist Studies," *PMLA* 123 (2008): 737.
34. See, for example, Penny Farfan and Katherine E. Kelly, "Staging Modernism: Introduction," *Staging Modernism*, spec. issue of *South Central Review* 25, no. 1 (2008): 1–11; and Olga Taxidou, *Modernism and Performance: Jarry to Brecht* (Houndsmills, U.K.: Palgrave MacMillan, 2007).

A More Aggressive Plantation Play

Henrietta Vinton Davis and John Edward Bruce Collaborate on *Our Old Kentucky Home*

—THOMAS ROBSON

When discussing the earliest African-American woman playwrights, conversation in theatre history classes tends to focus on the 1920s and 1930s. The Harlem Renaissance brought writers like Angelina Weld Grimke, Zora Neale Hurston, and Georgia Douglas Johnson to the stage, and any history of the black woman playwright naturally must mention them. Contrary to this prevailing narrative, however, black woman playwrights existed in the United States prior to the Harlem Renaissance. In 1898 the celebrated African-American actress and public elocutionist Henrietta Vinton Davis added "author" to her list of titles with her plantation play *Our Old Kentucky Home*. Davis did this through one of the most lauded—if not always practiced—traditions of theatre: collaboration. Davis composed *Our Old Kentucky Home* with the noted black journalist John Edward Bruce, aka "Bruce Grit."[1] In the period prior to the explosion of African-American literary and cultural output in the 1920s, black woman writers faced significantly more challenging working conditions. Without the benefit of belonging to a larger movement—and without the benefit of white-dominated organizations like the National Association for the Advancement of Colored People—woman writers of the preceding generation needed to find alternate paths in order to bring their voices to the public.[2]

A black woman playwright faced two particular obstacles en route to the stage: her gender and her race. As Sandra M. Gilbert and Susan Gubar explain in *The Madwoman in the Attic: The Woman Writer and the Nineteenth-Century Literary Imagination*, nineteenth-century culture viewed woman writers as an oddity. Writing was considered the purview of men—the ability to compose words and sentences a uniquely male attribute—thus discouraging women from attempting the craft. Gilbert and Gubar pose the question, "What does it mean to be a woman writer in a culture whose fundamental definitions of literary authority are, as we have seen, both overtly and covertly patriarchal?"[3] The racial obstacle stood as an even greater societal hindrance. In *Staging Whiteness*, Mary F. Brewer writes, "To be White is to be culturally denominated as possessing and instantiating a set of moral and 'civilized' traits and habits."[4] Conversely, blackness connoted the antitheses of these "civilized" traits and values. "White" represented more than a mere skin color; it represented a way of behaving—of existing—thought to be desirable, while "Black" stood for everything that "White" was not.

The culture of the late nineteenth and early twentieth centuries thus defined "Black" as immoral and uncivilized, and "Woman" as silent. How, then, was a woman writer of color to express herself? Collaboration proved the key for Davis to break through this racist, patriarchal logjam. By forming a creative partnership with her friend Bruce, Davis overcame the cultural quieting of woman writers. This partnership then allowed her to speak her opposition to the second obstacle. Through the writing and production of *Our Old Kentucky Home*, Davis skillfully addressed racial issues in America. In her hands the play served as a vehicle to deliver skillfully crafted commentary on both racial and gender issues in the United States. Davis and Bruce used the form of the plantation play, familiar to American theatre audiences from such popular works as *Uncle Tom's Cabin* and *The Octoroon*, and twisted it to new, more aggressive ends.

Henrietta Vinton Davis

Between 1883, when Frederick Douglass first introduced her to Washington, D.C., as a public elocutionist, and 1919, when she began a long association with the radical black leader Marcus Garvey and his Universal Negro Improvement Association, Henrietta Vinton Davis was considered the foremost dramatic actress of her race.[5] Davis eschewed the popular minstrel-show stereotypes of her time, never "blacking up" in performance, and focused her energy instead on recitations from and performances of the plays of Shakespeare as well as numerous popular literary melodramas of the late nineteenth century. Audiences and critics lavished praise on the talented performer. Shortly after her 1883 debut, one audience member exclaimed, "Our race never before reached so high a point in histrionic art. This is indeed a revelation; it seems a delightful dream!"[6] Almost a de-

Figure 1. Henrietta Vinton Davis. Image courtesy of the Library of Congress's *Chronicling America* Web site, http://chroniclingamerica.loc.gov/lccn/sn83027091/1903–02–14/ed-1/seq-6/.

cade later a reporter declared her simply "the greatest living genius of the race."[7] Among her most famous roles in the first decade of her career were some of Shakespeare's greatest characters: Lady Macbeth, Portia, Juliet, Lady Anne, Desdemona, and Cleopatra—the only woman of color in all of Shakespeare's canon.

Errol Hill's outstanding book *Shakespeare in Sable: A History of Black Shakespearean Actors* effectively documents Davis's career performing the plays of the English bard, but it pays scant attention to her significant contributions in other areas. The entry on Davis in *Women in American Theatre* entirely avoids any mention of Davis performing material *not* written by Shakespeare, a stunning oversimplification of a complex career. A closer examination of Davis's life and résumé reveals that after devoting much of the first stage of her career to Shakespearean performance, she began a transition during the 1890s that would lead to her eventual departure from the stage and her embrace of radical black political philosophy. Davis increasingly sought out material by black writers, reciting poems by Paul Laurence Dunbar and performing in plays about imperial Haiti by William Edgar Easton.[8] During this same period she began her work on *Our Old Kentucky Home,* the single work of hers most directly addressing the condition of African-American life.

As a performer Davis was known for her commanding stage presence and her "resonant"[9] and "deep, sonorous voice"[10] that was reminiscent of Charlotte Cushman. Judging from articles and reviews in the period press, she possessed a tremendous ability to shift from character to character during the course of the performance; she frequently needed to use multiple dialects over the course of one evening's performance. She possessed a particular gift for impersonating men onstage. Indeed, she frequently played characters with cause to cross-dress, most notably Portia in *Merchant of Venice* and Valerie/Père L'Avenge in *Christophe.*[11] All of these skills proved useful in the performance of *Our Old Kentucky Home,* and an analysis of that play's text shows that Davis and Bruce clearly designed the character around her skill set.

Davis twice produced *Our Old Kentucky Home,* first after its composition in 1898 and again in 1903. In 1898 she performed the play in several cities in the eastern United States, reportedly with "marked success."[12] In 1903 she revived the play for a production in Denver, and it does not appear to have played in any additional cities. With *Our Old Kentucky Home,* Davis took a large step toward greater control of her own image onstage, serving not only as the leading actress but also as the de facto director of the play for both productions, and she was its producer in Denver. The resulting play presents the most realistic depiction of African-American life found in Davis's repertoire. While no one would ever confuse the play's style with that of Ibsen or other major European realists, when compared with the verse tragedies and other melodramas of the early portion of her career its representation of midcentury black life paints a far more recognizable picture of the African-American experience than any of her other material. The play comfortably fits into the stage image Davis cultivated for herself during her career, but it also raises additional questions about the conditions of the turn-of-the-century African-American stage.

The Authorship of the Play

Authorship of *Our Old Kentucky Home* is primarily attributed to journalist and newspaper editor John Edward Bruce. The play was never published and exists only in manuscript form in the John Edward Bruce Collection in the Schomberg Center for Research in Black Culture. In *Shakespeare in Sable,* Hill says that Davis wrote the play "in conjunction with the black journalist John E. Bruce."[13]

Hill's assertion is supported by an 1898 *Colored American* article written by Bruce (under his "Bruce Grit" pseudonym) that says, "J. E. Bruce (Bruce Grit) and Miss Henrietta Vinton Davis, the accomplished and talented elocutionist and tragedienne have written a five act drama, which they have copyrighted, entitled, 'Our Old Kentucky Home.'"[14] A 1903 article in the same publication, however, indicates that Bruce "wrote [the play] for Miss Davis some years ago."[15] This wording suggests that Bruce alone wrote the play, and the title page of the unpublished manuscript lists only Bruce as an author. Despite the title page's omission of her name, however, enough evidence exists to view Davis as a coauthor of the piece. Both period and secondary sources agree that the play was at the very least written as a vehicle for Davis, and an examination of its text shows its close alignment with many of the star's other roles.[16] Because Davis lived in a time and place that viewed women's contributions to the literary world with scorn—especially within the highly patriarchal African-American community—her opportunities to pen a full-length play for production without collaboration would have been few. These conditions call for a broader definition of authorship.

If the culture defines literary authority as male, the woman writer must find alternative routes to authorship. The scholar must keep this cultural limitation in mind when exploring the notion of authorship in the nineteenth century. Given a society where, in Gilbert and Gubar's words, "male sexuality . . . is not just analogically but actually the essence of literary power," critics and scholars have pointed to the need to consider less traditional forms of literary writing, like diaries and letters.[17] To this necessary expansion I would add the consideration of the uncredited coauthor, the influential woman who aids in the ideas and characters of the work, contributing to the story without necessarily putting pen to paper herself. Failing to use this expanded view of the notion of authorship when examining the nineteenth century suggests a historical acquiescence to the patriarchal silencing of women. A twenty-first-century perspective aids in the liberation of the oppressed woman's voice. With this in mind, I contend that the world and words of *Our Old Kentucky Home* represent an authorial collaboration between the hand of John Edward Bruce and the voice of Henrietta Vinton Davis.

The Play: Synopsis and Context

Davis and Bruce's play consists of five acts, each taking place in a different time and location, and the play stretches from 1859 to 1865.[18] The play begins in the

French Market in New Orleans, with two old women discussing the impending slave auction and marveling at the fact that Monsieur Sevier intends to sell his prized slave, "the beautiful Creole slave 'Clothilde,'" with whom he is in love.[19] The scene then shifts to the slave auction, where Clothilde, played by Davis, and numerous other slaves are sold to the highest bidder. Act 2 moves to the Kentucky plantation of Colonel Knott, Clothilde's new home. In this act Colonel Knott's son Courtney makes sexual advances toward Clothilde, who refuses to yield to him. Act 3 takes place three years later; Union soldiers have converted the Knott plantation into a military headquarters. Knott's former slaves, including the lead male character, Basil, become Union soldiers and aid in the fight.[20] The Confederate army captures Basil, but Clothilde, disguising herself as a boy, infiltrates their camp to free him. Act 4 sees the celebration of the return of Basil before the play jumps to Washington, D.C., for the celebration of the end of the war. The play closes with the wedding of Basil and Clothilde in New York and the return of the newly married couple to "the Old Kentucky Home," which Basil has now purchased.

On the surface, many elements of the play resemble other plantation dramas of the nineteenth century, most notably George Aiken's *Uncle Tom's Cabin,* William Wells Brown's *The Escape, or a Leap to Freedom,* and Dion Boucicault's *The Octoroon,* although it also borrows from elements of other plays of the abolition era. The first two acts of the play recycle scenes common to plays focused on the conditions of slavery: the auction block and the sexual abuse of slaves by the master. In both of these cases, however, Davis and Bruce extend the recognizable scenes beyond the bounds of those who preceded them. They present both scenarios in a far more horrific manner than did Aiken, Wells, and Boucicault, resulting in a more powerful and politically provocative play. The final three acts of the play take the plantation story in a new, more aggressive direction. In previous slavery plays, oppressed African Americans either accepted their lot and died as martyrs (Uncle Tom) or fled captivity to seek freedom in the North (numerous characters). In *Our Old Kentucky Home,* Davis and Bruce dramatize slaves fighting for their own freedom; Basil and Clothilde join with the Union army. They take an active, combative role in addressing racial inequality and seek change rather than mere escape. This delivers the message that true equality can only be achieved through confrontation, a perspective that presages the radical political sentiments of Marcus Garvey that would attract both Davis and Bruce in later years.

A review of the 1903 Denver production of *Our Old Kentucky Home* refers to the slave auction scene at the end of act 1 as "one of the strongest and most realistic in the play."[21] Only roughly one-quarter of this scene actually furthers the narrative of the play; Clothilde does not enter until extremely late. The first three and a half pages of this four-and-a-half-page scene feature an auctioneer selling several slaves who never return to the stage during the play. This seems an especially odd choice for a play that is formally a melodrama; devoting such a significant stretch of stage time to a scene that does not contribute to the progression of the plot defies that genre's emphasis on action. This protracted slave auction scene realistically and horrifically depicts the cruelty and dehumanization of the sale of human beings, and in so doing it establishes the emotional background against which the rest of the play will function. While not contributing directly to the play's narrative, the scene establishes tone early and prepares the audience for the vivid confrontations to come.[22]

Within the first few seconds of the scene the auctioneer calls a slave named Mose to the block. According to the stage directions, he "ascends the stand, the prospective purchasers crowd around the stand, some of them examine his arms, open his mouth, put their fingers in his mouth and examine his teeth, and so on."[23] This demonstrates the obvious lack of dignity afforded to these slaves, as a band of white men examines their bodies as if they were nothing more than cattle. In fact, a few lines later the auctioneer cries, "Why gentlemen, look at that darky, did you ever see a more perfectly formed critter?"[24] These prospective buyers even violate the slave's body by penetrating his mouth with their fingers, an especially degrading and emasculating act. The slave has no choice but to passively accept this de facto rape if he wishes to avoid harsh reprisal. This scene mirrors both *Uncle Tom's Cabin* and *The Escape*. The former features a slave auction scene in act 5, in which Simon Legree inspects Uncle Tom's teeth and forces him to "Strip up your sleeve and show your muscle."[25] In the latter, a prospective buyer performs the same dental examination on the slave Sam.[26]

The auctioneer of *Our Old Kentucky Home* next presents for sale the combination of an unnamed slave woman and her three-month-old child, saying, "I want to sell 'em both together if I can, as her master would not like to separate her from her cub." Again, note the animalization of one of the slaves; the reference to the child as a cub frames both the infant and mother as far less than human. The auctioneer continues, "Still, if we can't sell 'em to suit ourselves, we will sell 'em to suit you gentlemen, of course."[27] He further commodifies the slave woman by issuing a money-back guarantee that she will satisfy her new owner, as if this mother were nothing more than a common household item. After her acquisition at the hands of one owner, she begs him to also purchase her daughter. The auctioneer snarls at her, "Here you impudent hussy, stop your noise. Thar! the gentleman doesn't want your little Nigger. He wants you! Shet up your snuffling, d'ye hear me! Now gentlemen I am going to sell this little Nigger; it's a gal. Something that you can raise to your hand. You remember what the Bible says about bringing up a child the way it should go. But I ain't preaching this morning, gents, I am selling Niggers. How much am I bid for this little Pickaninny?"[28] Naturally, a different bidder purchases the child, leading the mother to scream and collapse to the ground in sobs, while the bidders mock her and tell crude jokes at her expense. This "concern" for keeping slave families together appears in numerous slavery dramas. In *The Escape* the same situation occurs: Mr. Pinchen says of Mr. Haskins, "He won't sell a man from his wife, if he can get any one to buy both of them together."[29] This statement, however, immediately precedes Dr. Gaines selling Sam separately from his wife, Hannah. In the anonymous abolitionist play *The Kidnapped Clergyman* (1839), the Kidnapper says, "Dont [*sic*] separate the mother from the children. That would be cruel, I have sold them all together."[30] This concern for the welfare of the slave family—ironic coming from a character solely named "Kidnapper"—recurs in *The Octoroon.* In that play's slave auction a prospective buyer, on hearing that his bid would separate a family, retracts his bid.[31] While the theme of family fracture appears in these other slavery plays, none so prominently features the perspective of the slave herself as does *Our Old Kentucky Home.* Davis and Bruce extend the idea beyond the point of previous writers, presenting a more complete picture of the impact of such family separations on the slaves.

The auctioneer next calls up "lot number 2071," a collection of six or seven young black men he intends to sell together. The sale of this group escalates the onstage depiction of degradation to a physical level, as the auctioneer strikes one of the slaves. On seeing one of the slaves droop his head, the auctioneer "strikes him on the back with a bull whip."[32] Where previous examples in this scene have shown the subjugation of blacks through intimidation, animalization, and mockery, this demonstrates the power of the slave owner to corporeally discipline the body, a reminder of the constant threat of violence and even death that hangs over the life of the slave. Any refusal to acquiesce to the demands of the master can be met with swift and brutal retribution. This moment of physicality also distinguishes *Our Old Kentucky Home* from the rest of the slave play corpus, as none of the other plays features such overt slave-auction violence.

The auctioneer and bidders further reduce this group of men to objects as the bidding begins. The bidding for the lot reaches the highest monetary value of the scene and also contains the most aggressive back-and-forth exchanges between multiple bidders. As the price quickly escalates from $1,600 to $1,800 to $1,850 to $1,900 to $2,000 to $2,100 and finally to $2,200 the bidders clearly compete with each other. The sale of humans takes on the form of a game, two men challenging each other for dominance and using the bodies of the slaves as their playing field. The pace of the bidding suggests an emotional investment in this particular purchase—more so than has been previously shown in this scene. This can be attributed to the need of these bidders to demonstrate their masculine dominance over not just the black slaves they intend to purchase but also over their white competition. These bidders treat the slave bodies as pieces of property to assert their ascendant position in the society of the South.

Finally, Clothilde climbs the auction block; she is the final slave to be sold in this scene. Bruce and Davis describe her as "a handsome Creole, with little black hair braided and hanging to her waist, blue linsey dress and little red plaid shawl, coarse shoes."[33] Possibly because of her strong reputation as established in the play's first scene, or more likely because of the lightness of her skin, Clothilde receives a different sort of reaction than the previous female slave. The stage directions read, "The white men leer at her and the Auctioneer with mock tenderness calls her by name and gallantly assists her to the platform, where she meets the gaze of the speculators with defiance."[34] This single sentence of stage directions requires division into three parts, each with its own significance. First consider the auctioneer's treatment of Clothilde. His mockingly gentle treatment of her serves a dual purpose: it elevates her from the rest of the slaves for sale while simultaneously disparaging the very idea of treating a black woman with kindness. He makes her special, and then uses her specialness to demean her. This treatment suggests that the auctioneer and bidders view her as an "uppity" black woman who considers herself to have a higher stature than the rest; the scorn with which he greets her enables the dominant white man to disparage her dignity.

In a fortunate coincidence, Bruce and Davis employ the extremely loaded word "gaze" to describe the spectators' relationship to Clothilde's body. Examining the scene, it becomes clear that the bidders view Clothilde's body, in Laura Mulvey's terms, "as erotic object for the spectator within the auditorium."[35] The display of Clothilde's body in front of a collection of men invites their gaze—invites them to leer. In a world governed by the white male visual perspective, the black woman inhabits the role of bearer of the look. Only the powerful dominant possesses the authority to gaze, and Clothilde's insistence on meeting the gaze of the spectators defies the accepted structure of white-black interaction in the slavery-era South, especially interactions between white males and black females. As bell hooks writes in *Black Looks: Race and Representation,* "The politics of slavery, of racialized power relations, were such that the slaves were denied their right to gaze."[36] By refusing to submit to this system of "racialized power relations," Clothilde gives an indication of the resistance leader she will become later in the play. This first and seemingly small instance of challenging the gaze develops into her later eagerness to challenge the Confederate military. No earlier work's slave-auction scene features such a moment of defiance, again demonstrating Davis and Bruce's concern for placing a more confrontational presentation of slavery and its effects onstage.

Perhaps most significantly, the authors use the word "leer" to describe the manner in which the white spectators view Clothilde. The word carries tremendous sexual overtones, suggesting the sexual domination and colonization of the black female body by white men. A few lines later the auctioneer specifically addresses the single men in the crowd: "Perhaps some of you old bachelors may need a housekeeper,—somebody to sew on your buttons and make themselves otherwise useful."[37] He need not explain the meaning of the phrase "make themselves otherwise useful"; the subtext is clear. The auctioneer offers up Clothilde as a surrogate wife for the single men in the crowd, with all the duties that position entails. He clearly implies that the winning bidder should consider Clothilde's body his to use as he wishes, including sexually.

This sexual abuse of slave women on the plantation features prominently but less explicitly in previous plays. In the anonymous *The Fugitives* (1841) the slave owner, Bandaloz, threatens to take Iola, a young female slave, away from her family and into his home. Iola's brother, Ghestler, makes Bandaloz's sexual desire for Iola clear when he recounts the master's "cursed hand smoothing her flowing hair."[38] In Lydia Maria Child's *The Stars and Stripes* (1858), Ellen, the slave, is the illegitimate daughter of her master, and of course Zoe in *The Octoroon* has the blood of both slave and master in her veins. Most similar to *Our Old Kentucky Home*, in *The Escape* Dr. Gaines makes strong advances toward his slave, Melinda:

DR. GAINES: I will set you free, let you live in this cottage, and be your own mistress, and I'll dress you like a lady. Come, now, be reasonable!

MELINDA: Sir, I am your slave; you can do as you please with the avails of my labor, but you shall never tempt me to swerve from the path of virtue.

DR. GAINES: Now, Melinda, that black scoundrel Glen has been putting these notions into your head. I'll let you know that you are my property, and I'll do as I please with you. I'll teach you that there is no limit to my power.[39]

Despite Gaines's harsh words, however, he makes no attempt to force himself on Melinda during this scene. He threatens her, but he does not elevate the situation to the level of violence.

In her essay "Reflections on the Black Woman's Role in the Community of Slaves," Angela Davis describes the sexual nature of the white man's conquest of the black woman: "Much has been said about the sexual abuses to which the black woman was forced to submit. They are generally explained as an outgrowth of the male supremacy of Southern culture: the purity of white womanhood could not be violated by the aggressive sexual activity desired by the white male. His instinctual urges would find expression in his relationships with his property—the black slave woman."[40] *Our Old Kentucky Home* reflects this sexual aggression through the figure of Courtney Proctor Knott, Colonel Knott's son. In contrast to Gaines's verbal assault in *The Escape*, Courtney forcefully and physically attempts to take Clothilde as his latest conquest. Where previous depictions of the same thought relied on words and offstage action, Davis and Bruce show the white man attempting to rape the black woman. The slave evades his advance, proclaiming, "Aldo I am a slav, M'sieur, I am a leddy." Courtney responds, "Ha! Ha! Ha! Ha! that is good, that is rich—a leddy, eh? Well, I will show you my leddy what we do to leddies of your kind in Kentucky. I'll make you bend, stiff as you are. If I don't, you'll be the first that ever got by me."[41] This furthers the ironic diminishment of Clothilde's ladylike status established during the slave auction scene, and also shows that Courtney habitually raped the black women on his father's plantation. Davis writes, "The slave master . . . knew that as female, this slave woman could be particularly vulnerable in her sexual existence."[42] Doubly diminished by her status as black and female, the typical slave woman had little choice but to submit to the sexual advances of the white slave owner. Clothilde's ability to evade Courtney and successfully resist his assault reinforces her strength and prepares the audience for her eventual heroism.

Disguise

To achieve her heroic act, Clothilde adopts a strategy utilized by numerous characters portrayed by Davis over her career: she cross-dresses.[43] In act 3, scene 4, she enters the Confederate camp at Fort Robert E. Lee, infiltrating the general's tent. Clothilde takes the clothes of a man who was a servant to a recently deceased colonel. She fools the guards and provides Basil the means to escape: a bottle of liquor (to drug the guard) and a pistol. Basil owes his freedom entirely to Clothilde's cleverness and courage; without her daring to infiltrate the Confederate camp, he would have remained a prisoner.[44] Once safely back at the camp of the United States Colored Troops—a division of the Union army—and after a general cry of "Three cheers and a Tiger for Clothilde," Basil praises his savior to a gathering of his fellow soldiers: "Boys, that gal has done something to-day dat any sojer would be proud of. I am proud of her because she are one of us, an' warn't afeard to take desperate chances. The blowin' up of Fort Lee will put an end to dis war sho' as you bawn, an' de credit of it will belong to a black 'oman."[45] Similar to so many of Davis's other characters, Clothilde refuses to be constrained by the societally imposed limitations of her sex. Crucially, Clothilde does not appear onstage for this scene, so no argument can be made for Basil saying these things publicly simply to please her. When Basil lauds her to a collection of other black men in the privacy of an all-male gathering, it is a chance for Davis and Bruce to put words praising black women into the mouth of a black man, an effort to respond to the significantly patriarchal culture of the nineteenth-century African-American community.

Chief among the elements of Clothilde's disguise is her cunning use of dialect, one of the most interesting aspects of this text. Both she and Basil undergo a substantial evolution in their speech over the course of the play, with Clothilde possessing the ability to alter it at will. Her first words in the play feature her heaviest accent: "Me name Clothilde; das ees all de name I haf."[46] Contrasting her language to Basil's reveals a clear difference: while she employs the phonetically spelled "ees," he speaks the same word as simply "is." Similarly, when discussing the fact that neither of them ever knew his or her parents, Clothilde says, "Me nevair haf no mudder nor fadder where I come from" in contrast to Basil's, "Well I ain't got no mammy and no fadder neither. I ain't nebber had none as I knows on."[47] Clothilde's "nevair" and "mudder" as contrasted with Basil's "nebber" and "mammy" assign them distinct regional dialects. Clothilde's possesses a vaguely French air, appropriate to a woman raised in New Orleans, while Basil's accent is more rooted in Kentucky. The French element of Clothilde's speech is evident when she calls Basil "Messieur Basil"[48] and uses terms like "ma chere."[49] This French inflection also contributes to Clothilde's somewhat elevated position over the other slave characters in the play, as the European connotation of the accent suggests a level of refinement and gentility that separates her from the others.

When Clothilde disguises herself to enter the Confederate camp and rescue Basil, however, she clearly adopts a different vocal pattern. Her first words to the guard display this shift: "Boss, I's Kunnel Fairfax's body servant. I wuz wid him at Petersburg whar he got wounded. I heerd he war heah an' I followed him. Does you knew Kunnel Fairfax, Boss?"[50] Clothilde has shaken all traces of the Louisiana accent—the French vowels and idioms replaced by a more stereotypical "Plantation Negro" dialect. Only two pages later, however, Clothilde reveals her true voice. After finding Basil, she speaks to him: "Basil, I am a Yankee spy. I followed you from the battlefield to rescue you from death. Young master has sworn to hang you. Here is a revolver, and Basil if you love me you will use it to make your escape this night. At midnight I will deliver you. Be ready. Good bye till then."[51] With these lines we see that Clothilde has lost all traces of any accent. She speaks perfect English with no regional dialect visible in the text. This demonstrates Clothilde's command of her voice; she possesses the ability to assume a vocal disguise just as easily as a physical one. Within the first thirty pages of the script Clothilde speaks in three distinct dialects, a challenge for an actress. When considering that Davis was one of the authors of this play, however, this challenge becomes an opportunity. Trained as she was in the elocutionary arts, she frequently assumed multiple character voices. Due to her participation in the writing of *Our Old Kentucky Home,* the play logically presents opportunities for Davis to showcase her particular skills.

The Play in Production

As mentioned, Davis produced the play on two occasions: the East Coast tour in 1898 and the Denver production in 1903. Beyond a few general statements that the tour was ongoing, no newspaper seems to have extensively reviewed the original staging.[52] The Denver production, however, prompted a somewhat lengthy article in the *Colored American,* which looked favorably on both the text and production.[53] An examination of the company listing for the Denver staging reveals that only Davis performed in both productions.[54] Looking at these few newspaper articles and cast lists raises one very significant question for the historian of the turn-of-the-century African-American theatre, a question with implications beyond the context of this single play. Of the twenty-eight speaking roles in the play, fifteen are white. While the play clearly focuses on Clothilde and Basil, whites comprise the most significant supporting characters, from the members of the Knott family to the Union general. Structurally the play proves interesting, as a number of the African-American speaking roles do not appear until the last two acts; the play thus mirrors the emergence of blacks from the shadow of southern whites. As blacks gain in power and southern whites lose it, black characters assume far greater prominence in the play and the white characters fade away. An audience could not help but notice the striking visual change, from a stage littered with white bodies at the outset to one populated with black ones at the close. The first scene of *Our Old Kentucky Home* includes no African-American characters, the final scene no white ones.

This analysis reveals one problem, however. How would these white characters have been cast in productions written, produced, and directed by African Americans? The *Colored American* article, the only extant review of the play in production, provides no concrete answers to this question, although it offers one compelling clue. While the review does provide a complete cast listing, it says nothing about the race of the individual performers. A play that hinges so significantly on issues of racial conflict would require some sort of physical differentiation between black characters and white. Without the epidemiological distinction between dominant and dominated portrayed in the play, many of its most powerful scenes lose their impact. Without such visual differences the potency of the slave auction scene radically diminishes, yet could they achieve this effect? Only two possible solutions spring to mind: either the production featured a mixed-race cast or the production utilized makeup to lighten the skin of black actors. Of the two options, the incorporation of white actors into a black cast seems more theatrically effective but also more unlikely. The existence of black and white actors side by side onstage would almost surely have provoked comment. African-American periodicals discussed *Our Old Kentucky Home* at least briefly on six occasions between 1898 and 1903, with no mention of the presence of a white actor in the company. With integration of commercial companies still many years away, it seems extremely improbable that Davis would have presented a multiracial cast in 1898 and 1903. Whiteface makeup, however, had existed on American stages since the mid-nineteenth century and was especially used by Anglo-Americans to burlesque newly arrived Irish immigrants.[55] With an accepted stage convention among the possibilities, I strongly suspect that Davis's company would have utilized this method of presenting white characters onstage. The cast list of the Denver production supports this theory. Albert Young's name appears twice in the cast list: first he is credited as Basil, but buried deep in the listing the name "Albert Young" also is credited as playing the auctioneer of the first act. Discounting the possibility that the company featured two actors named Albert Young, one white and one black, this confirms that African-American actors portrayed white characters.

The prospect of black actors in whiteface at the turn of the century provokes interesting questions about tone. To what extent does this black portrayal of whites represent a resistive act? Set against a backdrop of white appropriation of the black image in minstrelsy, the cast of *Our Old Kentucky Home* inverts this power relationship. Not only does the play permit black actors to seize control of their own image onstage, but it also allows them to impose the same parodic elements onto whites that whites had grafted onto them. Unlike previous slavery plays, *Our Old Kentucky Home* was always intended for full theatrical production by a company of black actors. Rather than expecting performance by a white company utilizing blackface, as in *Uncle Tom's Cabin* and *The Octoroon*, or a dramatic reading without staging, as in *The Escape*, Davis and Bruce expected to see their words embodied by actors of their own color. By controlling all means of production, from composition to presentation, African-American artists asserted their power to define not only their own image but also that of their historical oppressor. By controlling the means of representation, Davis and Bruce controlled the system of definition. With white characters in the play reduced to stereotypes, the authors cleverly transform the white man from figure of fear to figure of fun; the play shows their strength and menace but also shows how blacks need not cower to them. After all, these purportedly powerful whites are little more than minstrel buffoons themselves.

Despite this potential nod to parody, the play primarily dwells in the realm of the serious, and the gravity of the work appealed to at least the one critic whose thoughts survive. According to the *Colored American* reviewer, the play "is a great contrast to previous efforts at plays in Denver, being serious and having a plot dealing with the sterner side of life."[56] Based on the word of this single source, the production can be judged a success for Davis. A large crowd attended the play, and the reception given to it "was entirely complimentary and much applause [was] given." The reviewer goes on to remark that the play "is deserving of a place in the history of Denver's entertainment because of its being the most successful melodrama given here thus far."[57] As for the performers, the reviewer singled out Davis and Young as "all that could be expected" while indicating that the talents of the supporting cast varied: "in some cases of a high order, in others amateurish."[58]

Musical Resistance and Reappropriation

The play's title obviously references the popular Stephen Foster song most commonly known as "My Old Kentucky Home." The script calls for the singing of Foster's song on three separate occasions: at the beginning of act 2, when Clothilde arrives at the plantation, and at the beginning and end of the final scene of the play, when Clothilde and Basil return to the plantation. While Foster's song currently enjoys state pride—consider the enthusiastic singing of the song each year prior to the Kentucky Derby—when it is examined historically "My Old Kentucky Home" occupies a far more complex position. Foster did not even title the song "My Old Kentucky Home," but rather issued it the title "Poor Uncle Tom, Goodnight." Foster scholar Thomas L. Riis uses this information to assert that the composer originally envisioned the song for inclusion in a production of *Uncle Tom's Cabin*.[59] Foster's original version of the song contains several key differences from the more familiar current version. When Foster published the song in 1853, the first two lines read, "The sun shines bright in the old Kentucky Home, / 'Tis summer, the darkies are gay." It took House Resolution 159 in 1986 to alter the lyrics to their present form: "The sun shines bright in *My* Old Kentucky Home, / 'Tis summer, the *people* are gay."[60] The substitution of these two words significantly changes the tone of the song. Clearly, replacing the racist word "darkies" with the neutral "people" removes much of the plantation context of the song, but the shift from "the" to "My" accomplishes the same task. "My" suggests a personal connection between the singer and the state, and it references a specific memory for the singer. In this construction the singer lauds a personal dwelling and the bond he has with the larger notion of state pride. The word "the," on the other hand, brings with it the image of slavery; "the old Kentucky home" suggests the more generalized stately southern plantation.

Foster's song harnesses the powerful force of nostalgia to reinforce conservative notions of the American South. Despite his own pro-Union sympathies, and professed concern for the lives and social conditions of enslaved African Americans, he still utilized an idealized picture of the plantation South to help sell his songs.[61] Susan Key describes the nostalgia found in many of Foster's songs as an effective means for southerners "to express feelings of loss and alienation" during a time of great economic and political uncertainty.[62] These rose-colored images of serene plantation life in which the slaves—the symbol of conflict between North and South—"are gay" allowed white southern audiences to avoid the harsh realities of impending war and any possible feelings of guilt over their own treatment of blacks. As Key writes, "The world for which the slave waxed nostalgic was in fact another plantation full of pastoral bliss, such as that portrayed in the first stanza of "My Old Kentucky Home," where "the sun shines bright" and "the darkies are gay." By extension the slave's nostalgia acquired the same self-indulgent quality as the white listener's, humanizing along with the slave the harsh reality of slavery."[63] A native of Pittsburgh, Foster proved so successful in his exploitation of these southern tropes that many considered him a southern composer.[64]

By incorporating this song, loaded with plantation and minstrel baggage, into a play written, performed, and produced by African Americans, Bruce and Davis reappropriate it. A song replete with connotations of slavery transforms into a song of defiance. Its first appearance in the show serves a dual purpose: it provides the exposition that the scene has moved from New Orleans to Kentucky, but the song also provides an intensely ironic counterpoint to the content of the play. The stage directions for act 2, scene 1, read, "On the lawn below the verandah (R) are gathered a jolly quartette of slaves singing plantation melodies, ending with 'The Old Kentucky Home.'"[65] As this quartet of "jolly" slaves begins to sing Foster's song, Colonel Knott enters with the newly purchased Clothilde, who had last been seen in tableau weeping on the auction block. In this context the line "the darkies are gay" assumes a tone of bitter irony. Upon entering, Knott smiles at the singers and tosses them some coins, "for which they scramble."[66] This further shows the dehumanized situation of the black slave on the Kentucky plantation—outwardly "gay" to please the master, inwardly desperate for any scrap of money with which to control their own bodies. The song's chorus, "Weep no more my lady / Oh! weep no more today! / We will sing one song for the old Kentucky home / For the Old Kentucky Home far away," directly recalls Clothilde's sobs upon being sold.

When the song recurs at the end of the play, it appears in a radically different context. The Old Kentucky Home now belongs to Basil and Clothilde, the very slaves forced to work the land for no money. Bitter irony transforms into joyous celebration under these circumstances. With the white masters gone, the sun truly shines bright on the Old Kentucky Home. The "darkies" exhibit gaiety stemming from honest jubilation, not a need to please the oppressor. The song—and by extension the play—concludes with the exhortation to "weep no more," now a triumphant cry celebrating the end of slavery and the promise of burgeoning economic and political agency for African Americans. The final words, "For the Old Kentucky Home far away," now suggest not nostalgia but rather the historical distance from the cruelty of plantation life. The Old Kentucky Home Foster originally embraced with his song has vanished; it has gone far away, never to return. Through their use of title and song, Bruce and Davis attempt to banish the nostalgic aspect of Foster's famous tune, turning it from one in a series of Uncle Tom/minstrel songs into a song that black Americans could view with pride. This reappropriation of text functions as a transgressive act, resisting white oppression in an effort to assert black agency.

Conclusion

On its surface *Our Old Kentucky Home* seems like just another plantation play, but a close reading of its text and analysis of its production conditions reveals its progressive nature. Rather than simply re-treading the ground walked by William Wells Brown, George Aiken, Dion Boucicault, and others, Davis and Bruce use the familiar form of the plantation melodrama to deliver aggressive messages about gender and racial equality. The auction-block scene thrusts the horrors of slavery into the audience's face with more brutal detail than any preceding play. The writers explore the sexual exploitation and violence of white-black relations in a more physical manner than their predecessors. Perhaps most significantly, rather than showing African Americans running away from their lives of enslavement, Davis and Bruce show freed slaves taking up arms against their oppressors. By making a woman the protagonist of the play, Davis and Bruce deliver a powerful message about the resourcefulness, strength, and intelligence of women, ground that the previous race plays had largely avoided. Its production presented an opportunity for a transgressive reversal of the racial stereotyping of the minstrel stage, and its use of Stephen Foster's iconic song reappropriates a negative image and spins it into a positive one. All of these elements stem from Henrietta Vinton Davis's own personal beliefs and performance persona.

Examination of a spring 1916 letter from Davis to Bruce reveals a close and long-standing friendship between the coauthors of *Our Old Kentucky Home.* Davis alternately refers to Bruce as "My dear friend Brucey" and "'Grit,'" suggesting a certain level of closeness and informality to their relationship.[67] They shared a love of Shakespeare, and in later years both would become heavily involved in Garvey's Universal Negro Improvement Association. Their collaboration on *Our Old Kentucky Home* created a play that served as a formidable vehicle for Davis and her talents. It fit neatly into her previously established stage persona but also pushed her to more directly address the circumstances of the African American at the end of the nineteenth century. In her position as a black woman, the most disenfranchised of the disenfranchised at the turn of the twentieth century, Davis used her friendship with Bruce to amplify her voice. Bruce, who had no previous theatre experience but shared a kindred spirit with Davis, provided the pen, the vehicle to deliver Davis's perspective. Together they created a play that, although relegated to the sidelines of history, promoted an agenda for American racial and gender relations that was far more progressive than any previous writers had been on the same subject.

Notes

1. Bruce seems to have used the "Bruce Grit" moniker in most of his journalistic work and his proper name in other situations. He did not attempt to disguise the fact that "Bruce Grit" was a pen name. As he wrote *Our Old Kentucky Home* under the John Edward Bruce name, this article will refer to him as such.
2. While the NAACP was most prominently associated with the African American leader W. E. B. DuBois, when it was founded in 1909 DuBois was the only black member of its otherwise all-white board.
3. Sandra M. Gilbert and Susan Gubar, *The Madwoman in the Attic: The Woman Writer and the Nineteenth-Century Literary Imagination* (New Haven: Yale University Press, 1979), 46.

4. Mary F. Brewer, *Staging Whiteness* (Middletown, Conn.: Wesleyan University Press, 2005), 1.
5. For nearly two decades after her retirement from the stage in 1919, Davis was one of Garvey's most trusted allies and skilled advocates, even running the organization in Jamaica for a time while Garvey waited in jail to be deported from America. She frequently represented Garvey on international expeditions, first to the Caribbean and later to Africa, and held the title of Honorable International Organizer. She held a number of other leadership positions and was clearly the most powerful and influential woman in the organization. Davis's connection to politics preceded Garvey, however, as she wrote a letter to Populist Party founder Ignatius Donnelly in the 1890s offering to campaign on his behalf. For a more complete discussion of Davis's activities within the Universal Negro Improvement Association, see William Seraile, "Henrietta Vinton Davis and the Garvey Movement," *Afro-Americans in New York Life and History*, July 1983, 7–24.
6. *Christian Reporter*, September 6, 1883.
7. *Goldsboro Argus*, quoted in the *Savannah Tribune*, February 27, 1892.
8. Davis performed the first of these two plays, *Dessalines*, in 1893, and the second, *Christophe*, in 1912. Taken together the two plays present an almost entirely inaccurate portrayal of Haitian history, but they serve to effectively glamorize the first successful rebellion of African slaves over their European masters.
9. *Pittsburgh Courier*, August 12, 1911.
10. *New York Globe*, August 4, 1893.
11. In *Christophe*, Davis's character, Valerie, disguises herself as the male priest Père L'Avenge in order to seek vengeance on the title character who killed her lover.
12. "People Who Entertain," *Colored American*, December 24, 1898.
13. Errol Hill, *Shakespeare in Sable: A History of Black Shakespearean Actors* (Amherst: University of Massachusetts Press, 1984), 72.
14. Bruce Grit [John Edward Bruce], "'Tis Only a Fairy Tale," *Colored American*, June 18, 1898.
15. *Colored American*, February 14, 1903.
16. The play features a strong woman existing in a largely male world, staring down male authority. She cross-dresses, assumes multiple accents, and is noted for her beauty, as were numerous other roles in Davis's repertoire.
17. Gilbert and Gubar, *The Madwoman in the Attic*, 4.
18. The version of the play found in the Bruce Papers appears to be a working copy of the script, as there are occasional notes scribbled in the margins in a hand I suspect to be Bruce's—the handwriting clearly does not match Davis's. On the play's title page appears the phrase "A Drama in Five Acts," but the word "Five" is crossed out and replaced with "three." Renumbering of the scenes appears throughout the play, but not consistently, and there is no indication of any scene intended to be cut. For simplicity's sake I will refer to the act and scene numbers as typed in the manuscript and not the potential revision into a three-act version.
19. John Edward Bruce and Henrietta Vinton Davis, *Our Old Kentucky Home*, John Edward Bruce Collection, Schomberg Center for Research in Black Culture, New York Public Library, 2.
20. According to Bruce's 1898 *Colored American* article, Basil is also Courtney Knott's illegitimate half brother, which indicates that Courtney has inherited from his father his proclivity for sexual violence toward female slaves. This blood relationship between Basil

and Courtney, however, does not appear in the version of the play manuscript found in the Schomberg Center.

21. *Colored American*, February 14, 1903.
22. It is also worth noting that Davis and Bruce place their slave auction scene far earlier in their play than it was placed in the other plantation melodramas.
23. Bruce and Davis, *Our Old Kentucky Home*, 7.
24. Ibid.
25. George Aiken, *Uncle Tom's Cabin*, in *Major Voices: The Drama of Slavery*, ed. Eric Gardner (London: The Toby Press, 2005), 229.
26. William Wells Brown, *The Escape*, in Gardner, *Major Voices*, 396.
27. Bruce and Davis, *Our Old Kentucky Home*, 8.
28. Ibid.
29. Brown, *The Escape*, 393.
30. *The Kidnapped Clergyman*, in Gardner, *Major Voices*, 85.
31. Dion Boucicault, *The Octoroon*, in Gardner, *Major Voices*, 528.
32. *Our Old Kentucky Home*, 9.
33. Ibid., 10.
34. Ibid.
35. Laura Mulvey, "Visual Pleasure and Narrative Cinema," in *Film Theory and Criticism: Introductory Readings*, ed. Leo Braudy and Marshall Cohen (New York: Oxford University Press, 1999), 838.
36. bell hooks, *Black Looks: Race and Representation* (Boston: South End Press, 1992), 115.
37. Bruce and Davis, *Our Old Kentucky Home*, 11.
38. *The Fugitives*, in Gardner, *Major Voices*, 117.
39. Brown, *The Escape*, 409.
40. Angela Davis, "Reflections on the Black Woman's Role in the Community of Slaves," *Black Scholar* 3, no. 4 (1971): 12.
41. Bruce and Davis, *Our Old Kentucky Home*, 16.
42. Davis, "Reflections," 12.
43. It should be noted that Clothilde's donning of masculine apparel is true cross-dressing, and not a breeches role. The serious tone of the play does not lend itself to the winking sexuality often associated with the breeches role, and while *beauty* was often a part of Davis's stage persona, *allure* was not. In the only extant picture of Davis cross-dressing, from a production of Easton's *Christophe*, her masculine attire is actually quite billowy, designed to hide her physical form, not accentuate it.
44. As with other nineteenth-century melodramas like Daly's *Under the Gaslight*, the brave woman comes to the rescue of the imperiled man.
45. Bruce and Davis, *Our Old Kentucky Home*, 34.
46. Ibid., 13.
47. Ibid.
48. Ibid., 14.
49. Ibid., 15. Translated "My dear."
50. Ibid., 28.
51. Ibid., 30.
52. The November 12, 1898, *Indianapolis Freeman* did, however, provide additional names involved with the production. It names D. W. McCabe as the manager of the tour and

lists sixteen additional actors for the company: "Leo Relake, Eloise D. St. Clair, Bertha Young, Mercy Madden, Leona Bruce, Jennie Jennings, Mattie Wilson, Martha Hass, Nathan Spragne, Geo. Everette, Geo. Morris, St. Elmo Hart, John L. Conlin, Howard Bates, Johnson Stewart, and W. M. Will."

53. Two months after this initial review appeared, however, the *Colored American* included a brief mention that Davis and her company "are reported in Western Exchanges to have come to grief in Denver, Colorada [*sic*]. Praise is accorded to the Madam but her support is said to have been execrable. The company has disbanded." *Colored American*, April 25, 1903.

54. In addition to Davis, the Denver cast included Albert Young, Emmett Webster, H. B. Moore, E. S. Andrews, Frank King, David Gray, J. Berni Barbour, Robert Beatty, H. Reed, A. E. Pullam, Mrs. M. Clementine Travick, Mrs. J. R. Contee, Miss Mattie Overton, Mrs. H. V. Ray, Mrs. L. A. Peach, Miss Ida Young, and Mrs. S. C. Rogers. *Colored American*, February 14, 1903.

55. James P. Byrne, "The Genesis of Whiteface in Nineteenth-Century American Popular Culture," *MELUS* 29, nos. 3–4 (2004): 133–49.

56. *Colored American*, February 14, 1903.

57. Ibid.

58. Ibid.

59. Thomas L. Riis, "The Music and Musicians in Nineteenth-Century Productions of *Uncle Tom's Cabin*," *American Music* 4, no. 3 (1986), 272.

60. "Kentucky's State Song: 'My Old Kentucky Home,'" Kentucky Department for Libraries and Archives, http://www.kdla.ky.gov/resources/KYSong.htm (accessed August 27, 2010). Emphasis mine. On a side note, anecdotal evidence suggests that as late as the 1960s students at the University of Kentucky continued to sing the word "darkies" when the song was played at college football and basketball games.

61. Susan Key, "Sound and Sentimentality: Nostalgia in the Songs of Stephen Foster," *American Music* 13, no. 2 (1995): 155.

62. Ibid., 149.

63. Ibid., 157.

64. Lee Glazer and Susan Key, "Carry Me Back: Nostalgia for the Old South in Nineteenth-Century Popular Culture," *Journal of American Studies* 30, no. 1 (1996): 8.

65. Bruce and Davis, *Our Old Kentucky Home*, 12.

66. Ibid.

67. Davis to Bruce, April 30, 1916, John Edward Bruce Collection.

Midwest American Rural Landscapes and the Creation of a Unique Theatre Culture, 1870–1940

—RICHARD L. POOLE

Immigrants created this country, and agriculture developed it. This was especially true for the immigrant populations who settled in and eventually created the great breadbasket of America's vast middle. Small towns became powerful magnets that drew sprawling rural communities. These hubs nurtured an aesthetic that manifested itself in a unique theatrical culture, reinforcing specific ideas of what being an "American" meant. That culture produced many places of performance: opera houses, circle-stock theatres, traveling tent repertoire theatres, and airdomes. From 1870 to 1940, millions of people throughout the Midwest were entertained nightly by dramas, comedies, and vaudeville sketches that shocked, amused, titillated, or horrified. Farming communities convulsed in laughter to the antics of the Toby Show comedian, thrilled to the sensational drama *Jesse James,* and cringed at the immorality of *Saintly Hypocrites and Honest Sinners.* Don Carle Gillette, in an October 1927 *New York Times* article, claimed that that year an estimated 76,800,000 people saw 96,000 performances enacted by approximately four hundred tent repertoire companies.[1] By the twentieth century, technology advanced and radio, silent films, and talkies became available. Yet for many years rural communities embraced the older, live entertainment venues of tent repertoire, circle stock, airdomes, and opera houses.

Rural communities and the entertainments they enjoyed constituted a theatrical micro-community—a stable tradition that endured in one form or another for over seventy years. More than just showbiz, this theatrical tradition reflected local and national core values. These values, incubated within diverse immigrant populations, flourished in an agricultural structure and constructed a specific "American" identity, one that often conflated fundamental Christianity, hard work, gender role reinforcement, and distrust of urban life.

This essay explores that unique rural and small-town theatre culture by examining prominent plays and venues. It also examines the core values that allowed this culture to develop and, for a time, flourish. Theatre historians, a gender theorist, an elementary school educator, and an American president were key elements in the creation of this study.

Many factors affected rural values and gave midwestern rural culture its unique flavor and quality. The earliest was the impact of Jeffersonian idealism. America's third president was fascinated by many subjects. A Renaissance man, he was especially taken with agriculture. "From the age of twenty-three, Jefferson had maintained a 'garden book,' keeping track of flowers and plants at Monticello, and much of his only published book, *Notes on the State of Virginia*, was devoted to describing the plants of his native state. 'No occupation is so delightful to me . . . as the culture of the earth.'"[2] Further he wrote, "Those who labor in the earth are the chosen people of God, if ever he had a chosen people, whose breasts he has made this peculiar deposit for substantial and genuine virtue."[3]

In a January 18, 1803, letter to Congress, Jefferson declared that native peoples must be exposed to and become participants in "agriculture, to manufacture and civilization, in bringing together our settlements, and in preparing them ultimately to participate in the benefits of our government. I trust and believe we are acting for the greatest good."[4] Given Jefferson's beliefs, it was not surprising that farming was the first and most crucial activity native peoples needed to perform to fulfill his idea of civilization. Jefferson celebrated decency and democracy as inherent in the rural life of the yeoman farmer. Urban life was evil, morally debased, essentially corrupting, and inherently undemocratic. Such a view was "one to which he would hold for the rest of his life. It was, moreover, a formulation that would exercise a special influence on both popular and intellectual culture in America, long after the passing of its most distinguished exponent."[5] This philosophy would find expression in many plays of tent repertoire theatre, especially those that dealt with the character of Toby Tolliver, hero and driving force of the ubiquitous Toby Show.

By the 1870s "small town [and the surrounding rural society] was America's norm."[6] Immigrants seeking economic, political, and religious freedom created rural towns that developed and subsequently reflected a distinctively American rural ethos. Besides hard work, willing hands, and a grateful attitude, they arrived with a strong sense of family and an absolute belief in Christianity. The

Bible commands that man should "rule the fish of the sea, the birds of the sky, the cattle, the whole earth, and all creeping things that creep on earth . . . fill the earth and master it."[7] Those who developed rural America took that command literally. Many of these first- and second-generation farmers, primarily from western Europe, created a prosperous farm life. In Europe, most peasants could not own land. In America, anything was possible. Land was available, but life without strong values could support neither the land nor the people on it. Clearly, here was Jefferson's idealism in action. Other ideas, however, were also to have a substantial impact on rural American's developing core values, and some of them were contained in a series of little books known as the *McGuffey Readers.* Formal education had always been an essential aspect of American life, although for many, especially in rural areas, it was limited to a few years at best. Instructional methods were minimal as well as marginally effective. All of that changed in the nineteenth century when American education encountered William Holmes McGuffey.

McGuffey's early education in Youngstown, Ohio, revealed his extraordinary capacity for learning and spectacular ability to memorize, especially biblical texts, which he could recite verbatim. His education in Latin, provided by a Presbyterian minister, determined his future vocational choices. After graduating with honors from Washington College, he received a license to preach in the Presbyterian Church. For reasons unknown, he never held a position as a minister, yet it was claimed that he gave at least three thousand sermons. He held academic and administrative positions in Ohio and Virginia.[8] His background in education and his religious views supported much that appeared in his six little books, *McGuffey's Eclectic Readers.* Its publishing record is nothing short of astonishing. First published in 1836, "well over 122 million copies of *McGuffey's Readers* were sold." The series was translated into French and Japanese. "It is estimated that there were as many as 555 revisions and editions."[9] Further, "from 1836 until near the close of the century, [McGuffey] exerted the greatest influence, culturally, of any person in American History."[10] For over seventy years, the six *Readers* were the most successful, popular, and influential children's textbooks.

McGuffey was especially interested in the teaching of reading. He differed "from his American predecessors by his emphasis on the importance and beauty of the spoken language . . . he encouraged children to read stories aloud so as to reinforce the message. Memorization of content played a big role in McGuffey's philosophy of reading. . . . An understanding of materials and command of the spoken word joined print translation and memorization as goals."[11]

Using the *Readers* as an educational base, schoolchildren learned more than how to read and memorize. They became saturated with McGuffey's philosophy of life. Such a philosophy confirmed value-based citizenship as the bulwark of American democracy. McGuffey, like Jefferson, believed that "schooling in a democracy should include moral education. That is it should aim to improve students' morality and minds, so that they become both good and wise."[12] "Heavily moralistic and Protestant in religious preachment, the *Readers* were deemed to promote good character."[13] They did much more than that, however. Within their pages, rural life was exalted while big cities were reviled. Church and school were the crucial ingredients for the well-lived life of small towns. Family was paramount and motherhood idealized.[14] Such values were later reflected and reinforced by that quintessential tent repertoire play, the Toby Show.

Perhaps most importantly, the *Readers* "were the means by which a totally new class of people—the immigrants—were to become parts [*sic*] of nineteenth century society in America."[15] And they "played an important role in American education, and in American culture and helped shape that elusive thing we call American character."[16] What type of person could become an American? One who was a God-fearing, hardworking, decent Christian person, imbued with biblical values and rural sensibilities. Again, these were prominent values in all tent repertoire plays, especially those featuring the Toby character.

By 1870, an agrarian sensibility, mirroring Jeffersonian ideals, reinforced by the *McGuffey Readers*' morality became solidly entrenched in the minds and actions of millions of immigrant farmers and their children. Most immigrants had poor English skills. As a result, their children translated for them, spoke for them, and, most importantly, read to them. Two household books maintained a position of prominence: the always-present Bible and the *McGuffey Readers*. Within rural communities, however, other significant influences were at work; ones that especially affected rural women's (and, by extension, men's) sense of self, purpose, and position. Gender identities, culturally pervasive and maintained through behavior, were reinforced and continually supported by immigrants' desire for assimilation, rural myth, and the possibility of a strong and new self-definition.

Gender theorist Nan Johnson asserts that gender roles, especially rhetorical ones for women, were scripted and maintained through a series of conduct guides such as elocution manuals, letter-writing handbooks, and advice and etiquette literature.[17] She maintains that there were a "legion of conduct authors who overtly discouraged women from having strong voices, literally and culturally, and who reminded American readers that if happiness were to be preserved in American homes, women needed to reserve their rhetorical influence for their counseling and instructive roles as wives and mothers."[18] This ideal of womanhood maintained itself throughout the nineteenth and into the twentieth century. While Johnson references primarily urban experiences, there is no doubt that such influences extended into farm families who were familiar with *The Complete Home: An Encyclopedia of Domestic Life and Affairs* (1879), where the "salvation for the nation" consisted of "a happy, orderly, and beautiful home" structured and maintained by women.[19] Other influential publications included *Godey's Ladies Book* (1878); Sarah Hale's *Manners: or Happy Homes and Good Society All Year Around* (1868); James Henry Potts's *The Golden Way to the Highest Attainments: A Complete Encyclopedia of Life* (1889); and B. R. Cowen's *Our Beacon Light, Devoted to Employment, Education and Society* (1889).[20] With regard to communication, women were expected to confine their speaking and writing to the private platform of the home, while men were encouraged to develop their rhetorical skills in public. In short, men were public leaders, women, private hearth-keepers. Truly, God would be in his heaven and all would be right with the world. "A range of subtle evidence suggests that rhetorical genres such as orations, serious literary poems, and essays on intellectual and political issues were considered the province of men, and descriptive poetry and poems about marriage, children, or traditional female duties and virtues were considered appropriate for women to perform in the home and on community occasions."[21] Theatre, an unsubtle public rhetorical space, encompassed all of Johnson's contentions in terms of gender behavior. Public rhetorical space recognizes "those rhetorical situations that potentially have impact on the shaping of cultural opinion, whether locally or globally."[22] Clearly, rural theatre had the potential to shape and reinforce cultural opinions, attitudes, and behavior.

The most significant shaper and reflector of cultural attitudes in rural America was, according to Charlotte Canning, Circuit Chautauqua. As her book asserts, it was "the most American thing in America." It was a place where "American culture was made and remade" and occurred "almost solely in the nation's rural precincts."[23] It transformed people's lives by focusing on audience concerns, community development, and patriotic and community themes and became an accurate reflector and creator of what this country was all about. Christian socialist and labor reformer Richard T. Ely declared that "no one can understand the history of this country and the forces that have been shaping it . . . without some comprehension of the work of that splendid institution that was, and is, Chautauqua."[24] Circuit Chautauqua provided an immense variety of activities, from platform speakers and lectures to theatrical presentations, although, ironically, the latter were officially banned by the Methodist Church from 1887 to 1924.[25]

Chautauqua audiences were primarily white, rural, and Protestant. They believed that they could translate their "moral vision into the law of the land . . .

for them, Chautauqua was the highest expression of American democracy."[26] Further, "most of the rural (Protestant) church-going audiences believed that theatre was, according to one Chautauqua memoir, 'big city evil' and 'the handiwork of the devil.'"[27] Still, thousands of plays were presented on the Chautauqua circuit from the beginning of the twentieth century until Chautauqua's decline in the 1930s. The millions of people who attended its activities were the same audiences that attended other rural theatre venues such as tent repertoire, circle stock, airdomes, and opera houses. Performance activities and venues flourished side by side. Canning asserts that "the study of performance is a particularly useful approach" because it can be seen as "a reaction to and an embodiment of national and local experiences."[28] Because of her excellent study, we know what Circuit Chautauqua meant to rural audiences. What did other rural theatre forms and plays mean to those same audiences? What was it within rural America that allowed or created an atmosphere conducive to the plays, players, and performances of tent repertoire, circle stock, airdomes, opera houses, and that most ubiquitous of all rural forms, the Toby Show? Perhaps most importantly, why have such forms and venues been marginalized and ignored by theatre historians?

Parsing any culture is difficult, and the culture of rural midwestern America between 1870 and 1940 is extremely complex; however, as we have seen, several factors contributed to the development of a core Midwest rural culture: Jeffersonian democracy; massive immigration during the nineteenth century; agriculture workers who constituted more than one quarter of America's early-twentieth-century population;[29] gender inscription both male and female, asserted through various conduct and rural-focused journals; the *McGuffey Readers;* Circuit Chautauqua; potent Protestant Christianity; and finally, the typical and ever-present tension between country dwellers and city folk. It was within this atmosphere that rural and small-town theatre flourished for more than one hundred years. Plays created and performed for these rural and small-town audiences were uniquely audience-centered. As a result, the performers and their audiences enjoyed a special bond, maintained year after year, a bond reinforced and strengthened by dramatic themes that reflected basic ideals both groups valued.

Farming communities of the Midwest experienced periods of great prosperity during the late nineteenth and early twentieth centuries. During this period, money became available for the entertainment rural folks hungered for. They wanted to see the best from the big cities without actually having to go there and be subjected to the wiles of urban life. Further, they wanted to see their way of life, their ideals portrayed upon their American stage, their rural American stage. Theatre professionals were eager to oblige.

Figure 1. Opera House, Omaha, Nebraska. Image courtesy of the author.

In the early days of the Republic and well into the nineteenth century, structures that housed theatrical presentations were called by a variety of names (theatre practitioners have always had to contend with a segment of society that believed theatre was immoral and disreputable). One of the earliest mentions of such a subterfuge occurred in Philadelphia when "in 1787 a Philadelphia law prohibited theatrical performances" and "the Southwark Theatre was advertised as the Opera House Southwark."[30] Thereafter, theatres, especially in small towns, were euphemistically referred to as "academies of music" or "opera houses." The great irony, of course, was that opera houses were usually found in larger urban areas where grand opera actually was sung. Smaller towns wanted the cachet of big-city class and culture without having to confront what many rural folk thought were the "evils" of big-city life. So, many of their opera houses were multipurpose facilities and the largest public space in the town.

Finding sources for this essay that dealt significantly with opera houses was difficult but not impossible. These books were crucial sources for my understanding of rural opera-house social history and physical structure: William Slout's *Theatre in a Tent;* Jerry Mickel's *Footlights on the Prairie;* George Glenn and Richard Poole's *The Opera Houses of Iowa;* William Condee's *Coal and Culture: Opera Houses in Appalachia; The Opera Houses of the Midwest* (published by the Mid-American Theatre Conference); and Brian Leahy Doyle's *Encore: The Renaissance of Wisconsin Opera Houses.*

Both the Slout and Mickel studies cover the country, focusing primarily on the Midwest and South. Four books center on opera-house spaces in select states: *Opera Houses in Appalachia* focuses on parts of four states where the Appalachian Mountains served as a cultural and physical touchstone (Ohio, Pennsylvania, West Virginia, and Kentucky); *The Opera Houses of the Midwest* focuses on Iowa, Nebraska, and North and South Dakota; *Encore: The Renaissance of Wisconsin Opera Houses* highlights Wisconsin opera houses of various sizes and locations. Also of value was the *Directory of Historic American Theatres* by John W. Frick and Carlton Ward. It surveys extant theatres in the United States, but its scope is limited. There are a few other books that include opera houses and their effect on small-town life along with a few dissertations and theses that catalog opera-house entertainments. There is, however, no comprehensive listing of opera houses in Midwest rural and small towns, nor is there a definitive analysis of the effect that small towns and opera houses had upon each other. "Rural" is easy to define, but what does "small town" mean?

In terms of population, numbers that define a small town can be problematic and arbitrary. In *Main Street on the Middle Border,* Lewis Atherton defined "country town" and its synonyms in terms of function. "If a town has been primarily a service center for farmers it has been included although in general my examination has been limited to places of less than 5,000 population."[31] Of course, town populations change, depending on economic conditions and other factors. Some researchers do not specify population numbers for small towns but merely refer to those areas as small towns. Included in these designations as the smallest units are hamlets and villages.[32] Villages might contain as few as one thousand people; however, Atherton does not specify hamlet populations. In my research, small-town opera houses that served the town and the surrounding agricultural community (important with regard to circle stock and especially tent repertoire) ran the gamut between village-size and fifteen thousand, allowing for normal changes in population. Towns that did not have opera houses held performances in the largest available community space. Towns that did have opera houses constructed four distinct but related types: general utility halls, opera halls, opera houses, and grand opera houses. All were multipurpose facilities, but some had more stage and auditorium appurtenances than others. Variations included fixed or permanent seats, theatre location (first, second, or third floor), and movable or permanent stages. All but the general utility halls had stages of some kind, with grand opera houses having the most opulent auditoria and most complete stages and stage machinery. Opera houses were often named after the town or after the businessman who built the structure and

Figure 2. Opera House, York, Nebraska. Image courtesy of the author.

was responsible for booking shows. The "golden age" of opera houses occurred between 1870 and 1915.

There were many reasons why such structures existed. Small towns and rural communities did not want to think of themselves as unsophisticated backwaters. They wanted the cachet that came with such a structure. Although the agricultural economy went through boom and bust periods between 1870 and 1920, numerous opera houses were constructed during the prosperous times. Also, the railroads had a major impact on small-town theatrical activity. At the beginning of the Civil War there were approximately 30,600 miles of track throughout the United States. By 1900, mileage had increased to 199,000.[33] If a town was not on a main line, it was on a spur or close to one. Along with the increase of rail transportation came the increase in opera-house construction that "occurred in nearly every village, and hamlet and continued at a rapid pace (with the 1890s showing the greatest activity) into the first decade of the 20th century, creating the vast theatrical network known as 'the road.'"[34] There was plenty of work for all sorts of entertainers. But it didn't last.

By 1915 "the road" started to fade. The cheap entertainment known as motion pictures competed heavily with the more expensive shows on the road. Radio developed and was a major competitor. Better roads and more cars made it easier to leave small towns for more excitement in the county seats or even bigger cities. With American entry into World War I, transportation, especially railroads, focused on the war effort. Before the war, virtually everything—scenery, baggage, and performers—traveled by rail. Once the war started, road shows were left scrambling to find adequate transportation. The draft also took many performers. All these factors contributed to the demise of the small-town opera houses. They fell into decline in all but the larger towns. Many structures were converted into movie houses, storage facilities, and apartments, or they faced the wrecking ball and became parking lots or empty spaces. And then the Depression hit. It did more than just put people out of work. It dislocated millions and destroyed many small towns across the Midwest. Another traveling theatre structure, initiated at the beginning of the twentieth century, existed alongside traveling tent theatre and survived until the 1960s. This traveling show, however, was intimately tied to a specifically organized rural "road." As such, it also supported the aspirations and business needs of theatre people as well as supplying rural America with exciting entertainment. This was circle stock.[35]

Although circle stock is mentioned in a number of books about traveling theatre, the only comprehensive treatment of it is Landis Magnuson's *Circle Stock: Touring Small Towns, 1900–1960*. Magnuson chronicles the rise and fall of circle stock and analyzes its impact upon the communities in which it thrived. Even though it first began on the East Coast around 1901, it developed nationwide and into Canada, performing primarily in small towns, with its greatest impact in the Midwest. Unlike traditional repertoire organizations that played wherever they could, "circle stock followed a strict order of rotation. . . . The basic formula involved a circuit of six towns—seven if the company played on Sunday . . . one town . . . served as the 'base' or 'headquarters' for the troupe." Company members lived in the base town, from which they "toured to outlying communities roughly in a circle around their headquarters."[36] Initially operating in the summer, circle stock eventually "operated primarily in the winter months."[37] Locations for performances varied. They "often ranged from a platform in a simple meeting hall, to the small stage of a motion picture house, to the much larger stages in the old second-story opera houses."[38] As with all other small-town traveling shows, circle-stock companies—bowing to the march of technology, changing tastes, increasing competition from other entertainment forms, and lack of performers willing to put up with the rigors of the road—died a quiet death by 1960. Long before 1960, however, another unique, primarily small-town, Midwest entertainment venue had also disappeared: the airdome.

While there are histories on tent repertoire and circle stock, accounts of airdomes are very limited. In all the information available on American culture

Figure 3. Airdome, Fayette, Missouri. Image courtesy of the author.

and theatre, only five published sources deal with airdomes: Slout's *Theatre in a Tent* devotes two paragraphs, and Mickel's *Footlights on the Prairie* gives two pages. Magnuson's *Circle Stock* mentions airdomes on three pages, primarily focusing on their use by tent repertoire performers as a physical variant of the canvas tent. *The Cambridge Guide to American Theatre* (2nd ed.) has a brief entry on airdomes but no pictures of the structure. The latest and most complete study of airdomes is located in Landis Magnuson's 2009 *Theatre Symposium* article, "No Roof Except the Sky: The Rise and Fall of Airdomes in American Popular Entertainment."[39]

Airdomes "consisted of a covered stage and seating open to the sky, all enclosed by a high board fence."[40] Their heyday was before the turn of the century through 1915, although some airdomes operated into the 1920s. While there were numerous circuits nationwide, "the Bell and Olendorf and Crawford circuits operating out of Kansas City were the best known." They presented stock, vaudeville, and repertoire in the earlier days, and when movies achieved popularity they presented silent pictures.[41] Airdome circuits were developed and controlled by those who owned and booked opera-house circuits. Between 1893 and 1906, Midwest theatre magnate L. M. Crawford and his three sons (sometimes with partners other than family) owned, operated, or booked attractions for an extensive circuit of airdomes and other venues located in the Midwest, West, and South.[42] By 1906, other theatrical entrepreneurs owned and operated airdomes in Oklahoma, Texas, Kansas, Missouri, and the Indian Territory (later part of Oklahoma).[43]

By 1905, the elements of a successful airdome were established: show business entrepreneurs; established theatrical circuits; a novel theatrical space; summer; needy actors; willing customers; and primarily, but not exclusively, a small-town or rural marketing base. Eventually, airdomes existed in thirty-six states, Canada, and France. Between 1905 and 1915 they numbered at least 439, with the majority located in Kansas, Oklahoma, Missouri, Texas, Illinois, Indiana, Ohio, and Pennsylvania. When located on a town's outskirts, they usually stood alone. They could, however, be connected to another entertainment facility. Many times they were constructed as stand-alone units or in a downtown area close to business traffic.[44] A downtown location could also fill the empty lot between two buildings, thereby creating a potentially profitable source of income. Airdome amusements paralleled those provided by opera houses and theatres, which is not surprising since they were often created and controlled by theatre and opera-house managers and owners. A typical bill of fare included vaudeville, plays from stock or repertoire companies, light comic opera, minstrel shows, Chautauqua, illustrated songs, and movies. Sometimes there were daily performances—a matinee and two evening performances. Admission price could vary, but ten to twenty cents was typical.[45] Airdomes vied for public patronage with other structures with such exotic names as theatrette, vaudette, vendome, kinodrome, and nickelodeon. Airdome popularity spread not only at home but also overseas. In 1909 the *New York Dramatic Mirror* reported that "the popularity of the airdome is assured abroad and is on the increase on the Continent."[46]

By 1910 the larger cities of Dallas, Pittsburgh, and St. Louis/East St. Louis each had its own airdome circuit providing live entertainment and films.[47] Many airdomes booked independently while others booked exclusively with the national Sullivan-Considine circuit. Smaller towns usually booked together. By 1913 the *New York Clipper* advertised for a Texas, Arkansas, Oklahoma, and Louisiana airdome circuit comprising thirty-three towns.[48] Such growth, however, belied the earlier trend toward the airdome's demise.

By 1911, airdome advertising in the *Clipper* and the *Dramatic Mirror* began to decline and the airdome itself began its slow fade to obscurity. Iowa tent repertoire entrepreneur and Toby Show performer Neil Schaffner contended that "airdomes had become popular for summer theatre all over the Middle West beginning about 1910 and by the summer of 1911 nearly every town had one. They did enormous business until 1915, when the entire Midwest had a very wet summer; then most of them went broke and few came back."[49] At first airdomes were enormously popular as they were unique entertainment al fresco. They filled the

Figure 4. Garden Theatre Airdome, Abilene, Kansas. Image courtesy of the author.

gap between the spring and fall/winter theatre season utilized by traveling repertoire companies. The elements, air-conditioning, economics, and changing tastes conspired to seal the fate of this once enormously popular outdoor theatrical. Indoor repertoire companies, performing both repertoire and stock, were also experiencing difficulties. Traveling tent shows became increasingly popular and profitable, providing a singular source of entertainment. Who were the artists who filled the major theatrical venues and repertoire available to the small-town and rural audiences?

Traveling theatre companies and individual "entertainers" have been part of American theatrical history from colonial days. Shortly after the American Revolution, John Durang, minor player, dancer, utility man, and theatrical jack-of-all-trades, was a member of Lewis Hallam's company that reopened theatre in New York in 1785. He was a flexible, talented performer and theatrical entrepreneur. In addition to being a dancer, he "painted scenery, built playhouses, performed acrobatic and equestrian feats, constructed a puppet show, developed summer amusement parks, organized and directed companies."[50] When big-city theatres closed for the summer, he took to the road. His leadership qualities and his many talents were ones that theatre managers, especially those of theatres that played in small towns and tents, deemed crucial for survival. During the nineteenth century, especially after the Civil War, "the road" developed so that combination companies, and later repertoire troupes, toured towns of all sizes.

Repertoire companies played either stock or repertoire. In repertoire they often played a week or more, offering a different play each night. Playing stock meant staying in a town for an extended period of time, offering a variety of fare.[51] In both stock and repertoire, success meant the town might welcome the company back year after year. Small towns were a boon to business, especially for tent repertoire.

Theatre under tents (of varying fabrics) probably goes back to the time of ancient Rome.[52] Tent theatre in America could have occurred as early as 1825.[53] Robert L. Sherman in *Chicago Stage: Its Record and Achievement* claims that early circus entrepreneur Yankee Robinson (real name Fayette Lodavik) played in a tent in Rock Island, Illinois, around 1848 or 1849.[54] Records are unclear, but tent theatre, circus, and other performance forms became closely intertwined during the nineteenth and twentieth centuries.[55] Slout contends that there is little information available about companies touring under canvas prior to 1885. "Although the basic format of operation was the same among all repertoire groups, the small outfits are more representative of what the tent show was to become. . . . Many of these companies toured in the middle-western states from Ohio to Kansas."[56] However, "the repertoire tent show was basically a rural theatre and, as such, was influenced by attitudes of the agrarian class and by the agricultural economy."[57] By the turn of the century, "tent show activity . . . [was] more visible. By this time, shows were touring in large numbers and were evident in nearly every part of the country, although the largest concentrations were in the Midwest and the South."[58]

Slout, Mickel, and Magnuson detail popular plays and characters that made the rounds of rural theatre circuits operated by tent repertoire companies or opera-house managers. Many of these plays were performed in other venues, such as airdomes or on the circle-stock circuit; however, American theatre historians have never analyzed a tent's physical configuration and its effect. Such an analysis would include the tent's location in a town, its structural materials, its physical configuration, and its impact on the players and audience. These areas are generally described, not analyzed, and never considered as an area worthy of independent investigation. Only the most basic ideas can be introduced here, but understanding them allows the theatre historian to apply them to any theatre. Including them here gives rural theatre yet another perspective that contributes to and increases our understanding of that theatre form. The historian and theorist who most contributed to my understanding of these areas was Marvin Carlson. His two related texts, *Theatre Semiotics: Signs of Life* and *Places of Performance: The Semiotics of Theatre Architecture,* had a major impact on my thinking about physical structure and location of rural and small-town theatres. *Places of Performance* focuses on the meaning of a theatre's physical location as well as other aspects of theatre architecture that were not stage related. As Joseph Roach comments, "Carlson expands the performative context of the theatrical event itself outward to embrace the lobbies and foyers of the theatre building, then the façade and exterior, and finally the situation of the building in the urban space."[59] For the purposes of this essay, I would change urban space to rural space to accurately locate the structures in this study. Carlson's *Theatre Semiotics* focuses on the life of the multiple signs and their referents within the total theatre experience. As he says, "if we really wish to consider the semiotics of an actual theatre performance, we must of course bear in mind that the performance itself, while it is the central object of investigation, is only part of the total experience of attending the theatre and making sense of what happens when we undergo such an experience."[60] Tents and opera houses of various configurations are the two physical structures that lend themselves to the Carlson approach. What were the similarities and differences between them, and what types of cultural codes might be revealed through such an analysis?

Tents and opera houses were specific places of performance. Both presented theatrical entertainments. Tents were temporary structures that traveled from place to place. They, like the circus and Chautauqua tent, were circular. Everybody could see everybody. Womb-like, the tents were round, inviting, and safe. They produced a feeling of familiarity and comfort. Treats were sold during intermissions. Most times, the sellers were members of the cast and instantly recognizable. These pitchmen and pitchwomen communicated well with the audience, and many times the sweets box held coupons good for a variety of prizes lined up on the front of the stage. It was exciting! Also, because of the stage and auditorium configuration, the stage was close to the audience. Consequently, the actors were close to the audience. And since many of the companies employed actors who returned to the same locations year after year, the comfort of knowing these "friends" was palpable; however, company managers made sure their personnel didn't get too friendly. Actors, especially the single males, had to comport themselves with honor and graciousness, a necessary quality if the troupe was to be welcomed back the next season.

Tents were erected in a vacant lot after getting the necessary licenses, and town boys were given free tickets to the show if they helped set up the tent, the stage, and the chairs. That was another solid and familial connection with the locals. The tent was always located in the town. It was a part of the town—for a while. And perhaps that is what was most important about the structure of tents: they were temporary. They and their contents provided a much-needed relief from farm life, and then they were gone, only to reappear the next year

Figure 5. Audience laughing at a tent repertory performance. Image courtesy of Theatre Museum, Midwest Old Threshers, Mount Pleasant, Iowa.

Figure 6. View of a tent from the stage. Image courtesy of Theatre Museum, Midwest Old Threshers, Mount Pleasant, Iowa.

Figure 7: Slout players raise the tent. Courtesy of William Slout.

Figure 8. Setting up the tent entrance for the Slout Players. Courtesy of William Slout.

with promises of new shows bringing tears and laughter. Towns waited for them year after year with eager anticipation. Auditorium lights could not be dimmed, so audience members could see one another. A tent repertoire audience had few strangers within it, and audiences were really a smaller community within their larger community. Tent repertoire never advertised itself as a "theatre" or "showbiz." Those titles bespoke negative connotations from the big city. Tent repertoire was always advertised as "players" or "company." Similar euphemisms were also utilized for opera houses.

Opera houses were always named "opera house" or "academy of music," never "theatre." Designating a facility as a "theatre" always reflected a negative connotation connected with urban entertainments—risqué productions, and performers and audiences of questionable morality, all located within sleazy, disreputable neighborhoods. Truth did not matter. What mattered was belief. The opera-house building itself was a permanent structure. Depending on how much money was available and whether it was the town or an individual who was paying for its construction, opera houses varied in size. The shape always, in some way, mirrored that of the urban opera house. No matter how large or small, there were always dressing rooms, foyers, box offices, sometimes balconies and lower floors, and, of course, the usual backstage spaces. Audience members may have known the owner. The structure was created to mirror the opera houses of urban settings—minus the disreputableness. In the larger opera houses, there were spaces for other businesses, but the rectangular or square construction, plus the building's structure and exterior (brick, stone, or wood), gave them a very different feel when audiences viewed the opera house and when they encountered it. They were greeted not by an informal space but by a formal, more big-city-like space. Undoubtedly it changed the way they felt about what they were about to see. They were excited with just a touch of the naughty. Also, opera houses were often the largest community space in town; as a result, a variety of non-theatrical activities occurred there: speeches, debates, church services, service club meetings, and high school graduations. Sometimes, the internal configuration was altered to accommodate high school basketball games and dances. Despite their physical structures and subsequent psychological impact upon their audiences, opera houses and tent repertoire organizations were intimately connected by the companies that performed in them and the time of year the performances took place. In the winter, companies played in the marginally warmer opera house; in the spring and summer they took to the tents.

Between 1900 and 1940, tent repertoire companies produced numerous plays. Many of those same plays were performed in opera houses and airdomes and on circle-stock circuits. There were many popular tent repertoire characters, but the most endearing (at least to some) and enduring character was Toby, the rural Howdy Doody, he of the red hair, freckles, toothy grin, and the "ah shucks" attitude. The "silly kid" character, often with his sidekick, Susie Green, dominated tent repertoire for years. According to theatre historian William Slout, most plays presented in tents were old-fashioned, uncopyrighted melodramas; plagiarized New York hits; or comedy-dramas written by tent-repertoire performers or managers. Many of the old standbys were such favorites as *Kathleen Mavourneen, Camille, East Lynne, Caprice, Fanchon the Cricket, The Hidden Hand,* and *Jack Sheppard.* Another device tent managers used was dramatizing popular novels. Other plays utilized "local color themes [that] appealed to small town audiences, particularly 'rube dramas' tailored to rural tastes, portraying Victorian ideals of virtue, reverence for mother, home and heaven, suspicion of everything urban."[61] There is some controversy as to exactly when Toby appeared on the tent repertoire scene and who was the first to play him. Neil Schaffner claimed that he first appeared as a Toby character (Toby Haxton) in a play by W. C. Herman, *Clouds and Sunshine,* at a "popular priced resident stock company at the Magic Theatre in Fort Dodge, Iowa" in 1912. While Toby was not the main character, he provided laughs as a fun-making wisecracker together with his sidekick, Susie.[62] Tent-show historians Slout and Mickel place Toby's beginning in 1911 and credit comedian Fred Wilson as the originator. Eventually, "Toby proliferated all over the tent show world" and became "the feature role instead of the conventional leading man."[63] He became a stock character and "took on the manners of the regions in which he appeared . . . mid-western farm boy . . . western cow hand . . . or lackadaisical hill-billy."[64] However, Slout also claims the Toby character got out of hand and his character superseded all else in tent repertoire. Audiences began to demand that all tent repertoire plays feature Toby. Eventually "overworked and overdone," the Toby character "succumbed to a more exaggeratedly made up, a more grotesquely costumed, zany-acting clown who takes over the entire program, pushing the play and the performers into the background." In short, Toby wrecked tent repertoire.[65] Toby's performances and the plays in which he appeared became (at least for his character) more commedia and less literary. Rural audiences, however, didn't care, and Toby maintained his enormous popularity. What is interesting about Slout's analysis is that he was both a tent repertoire player (his father was an influential actor/manager on tent repertoire and other circuits) and an academician. It is likely that his Ph.D. and his tent repertoire experiences created an aesthetic conflict.

For rural audiences, Toby became "their Don Quixote, their knight in bib overalls."[66] In appearance and speech he was the country rube, hick, or hayseed

Figure 9. Toby scores a hit with the audience. Courtesy of Theatre Museum, Midwest Old Threshers, Mount Pleasant, Iowa.

who somehow managed, through sheer intelligence, to outwit the city slicker. He was a rural everyman who had power over both himself and those interlopers from the big cities. He exemplified rural values and achieved the impossible for millions of rural Americans. He not only faced rural enemies, but he defeated them with humor and brain power. He fooled them. And he was funny. He exemplified the mythic possibility of potent rural morality, stability, and hegemony, supported by Jeffersonian philosophy, the Protestant diaspora, *McGuffey Reader* sensibility, and gender reification. In the early decades of the twentieth century, he became an entire population's escape from their reality of rural existence, or maybe his antics were just fun and a welcome diversion from the rigors of farm life.

Of the thousands of tent repertoire shows that were written, pirated, or altered, four favorites were *Saintly Hypocrites and Honest Sinners* by Charles F. Harrison; *Girl of the Flying X,* also known as *Sputters,* by George J. Crawley; *Clouds and Sunshine* by W. C. "Cal" Herman; and *The Return of Aunt Susan: A Whimsical Comedy* by Neil Schaffner. These four examples are representative of the most popular types of tent repertoire plays, because the Toby character plays a prominent role in each. The plays, with simple plots, characters, and themes, also referenced Midwestern rural core values, especially Christian religious ethics, where the goodness of rural life consistently defeats evil.

All the plays that I mentioned, and hundreds if not thousands of others like them, were typical tent repertoire fare. They exemplified America's agrarian myth: decency; honor; good-heartedness; belief in Christian, especially Protestant, values; and suspicion of all things urban. These qualities were conflated with an unshakable faith that right would triumph over might. With tent repertoire, the city slicker always faced defeat at the hands of the smarter, decent, God-fearing, woman-honoring, good friend and gentle advocate for the rights of the oppressed, Toby Tolliver. Toby shows, as well as other types, were the province not only of tent shows but circle stock, airdomes, and opera houses. Unfortunately, these venues, plays, and performers have been systematically forgotten, ignored, or marginalized by the majority of advocates for theatre education and scholarly culture in this country.

Lawrence Levine provides significant insights into the nature of culture hierarchy in America. He contends that during the nineteenth century, powerful elites in the cities felt their culture threatened by the incursion of "strangers," people of color and immigrants, whose theatres reflected the richness of "public cultural life that took place daily on the streets of American cities." The elite responded to the threat by attempting to persuade the public that only the elite definitions of taste and discernment were worthy of consideration.[67]

Those ideas reflect two major assertions in this essay. The first is that pervasive tension between the city and the country has been ongoing from the beginning of the Republic—the city being the place of culture for all the arts and the country being the place for rubes, boobs, hicks, or hayseeds—take your pick. The only culture coming from that section of America must be acknowledged as "folk" culture, quaint but certainly not sophisticated, which of course means incapable of anything beyond the rudimentary. Clearly, those ideas reflect a profound lack of understanding about both rural culture and, especially, rural theatre. The second is that a palpable cultural hegemony controls the teaching and publishing of textbooks and play anthologies on American theatre history. In the thousands of college and university departments throughout this country, seldom, if ever, is there a significant section on rural theatre covering any of the topics or plays that I have mentioned. Even though, as I have shown, an enormous amount of theatre was happening in America's rural areas—especially in the Midwest—current, comprehensive, and thorough scholarship is needed.[68] Local histories might yield appropriate and sufficient data.

Pulitzer Prize–winning historian Michael Kammen reinforces the value of exploring local history because it allows researchers to make crucial connections within contexts: “It is the laboratory where we study the relationship of one town to another, to a state or region or even to natural history.”[69] Learning more about these marginalized or neglected plays and venues allows us to understand more about rural character and how it was reflected in a particular theatrical matrix. It allows us more insight and research possibilities into that complex world of late-nineteenth- and early-twentieth-century American Midwestern rural culture.

Finally, perhaps Brooks McNamara says it best when he asserts that it “might be that all forms of performance are serious and complex expressions of a culture’s most fundamental concerns, and that all are worthy of study . . . and no apologies needed.”[70]

Notes

1. Don Carle Gillette, “The Vast Tent Drama Industry: Facts and Figures about the Little Known Canvas Playhouses, Which Constitute a Bigger Business than Broadway,” *New York Times,* October 16, 1927, section IX, part 2, page 1.
2. Dayton Duncan and Ken Burns, *Lewis and Clark: The Journey of the Corps of Discovery* (New York: Knopf, 1997), 36.
3. Thomas Jefferson, *Notes on the State of Virginia,* in *The Portable Thomas Jefferson,* ed. Merril Peterson (New York, 1975), 216–77.
4. Donald Jackson, ed., *Letters of the Lewis and Clark Expedition with Related Documents,* vol. 1, 2nd ed. (Urbana: University of Illinois Press, 1978), 11.
5. Stanley Elkins and Eric McKitrick, *The Age of Federalism* (New York: Oxford Press, 1993), 195; Morton and Lucia White, *The Intellectual versus the City: From Thomas Jefferson to Frank Lloyd Wright* (Cambridge: Harvard University Press, 1962), chaps. 3 and 4; John Mack Faragher, “Open Country Community: Sugar Creek, Illinois, 1820–1850,” in *The Countryside in the Age of Capitalistic Transformation: Essays in Social History of Rural America,* eds. Steve Hahn and Jonathan Prude (Chapel Hill: University of North Carolina Press, 1985), 233.
6. Robert H. Wiebe, *The Search for Order, 1877–1902* (New York: Hill and Wang, 1967), 2.
7. Genesis 1:27.
8. “William Holmes McGuffey,” in *Dictionary of American Biography,* Base Set (American Council of Learned Societies, 1928–36). Reproduced in *Biography Resource Center,* http://galmet.galegroup.com/serlet/BioRC.
9. Ellen Greiner, “William McGuffey’s Readers: The Story of a Nineteenth-Century Best Seller for Children,” *Top of the News* 41, no. 1 (1984): 73, 74.
10. Hugh Fullerton, *Old Favorites from the McGuffey Readers,* ed. Harvey Minnich (New York: American Book, 1936), preface.
11. John Bayer Jr., “The Shifting Function of Rhetoric in Early Nineteenth Century American Education and Belle Lettres” (Ph.D. diss., St. Louis University, 1982), 80, 81.

12. John Snarey, "Moral Education," in *Encyclopedia of Educational Research,* 2nd ed., vol. 2 (New York: Macmillan, 1992), 856.
13. Daniel Tanner, "School Textbooks in the United States," in *Encyclopedia of Educational Research,* 6th ed., vol. 2 (New York: Macmillan Reference USA Thompson/Gale 2003), 2,555.
14. Lewis Atherton, *Main Street on the Middle Border* (Bloomington: Indiana University Press, 1984), 65–72.
15. "Unit 903: Approach to Grammar" (Minnesota University Center for Curriculum Development in English, 1968), 30.
16. Henry Steele Commanger, *The Commonwealth of Learning* (New York: Harper and Row, 1968), 102.
17. Nan Johnson, *Gender and Rhetorical Space in American Life, 1866–1910* (Carbondale: Southern Illinois University Press, 2002), 2, 75.
18. Ibid., 15.
19. Ibid., 29.
20. Ibid., 52, 178.
21. Ibid., 16.
22. Ibid., 175.
23. Charlotte M. Canning, *The Most American Thing in America: Circuit Chautauqua as Performance* (Iowa City: University of Iowa Press, 2005), 1.
24. Richard T. Ely, *Ground under Our Feet: An Autobiography* (New York: Macmillan, 1938), 79.
25. Canning, *The Most American Thing,* 192–93.
26. Ibid., 41.
27. Jean Hadley Adams, *Second Fiddle to Chautauqua* (1938), quoted in Canning, *The Most American Thing,* 187.
28. Canning, *The Most American Thing,* 5.
29. U.S. Senate, "Abstracts of Reports of the Immigration Commission," 61st Cong., 3rd sess., 1911, document no. 747, 799.
30. Arthur Hornblow, *A History of Theatre in America,* vol. 1 (New York: Benjamin Bloom, 1965), 172–73.
31. Atherton, *Main Street on the Middle Border,* xvi.
32. Ibid., 362.
33. George Brown Tindall, *America: A Narrative History* (New York: Norton, 1984), 625, 749.
34. William L. Slout, *Theatre in a Tent: The Development of a Provincial Entertainment* (Bowling Green, Ohio: Bowling Green Popular Press, 1972), 1–2.
35. Landis Magnuson, *Circle Stock Theatre: Touring Small Towns, 1900–1960* (Jefferson, N.C.: McFarland, 1995).
36. Ibid., 6–7.
37. Ibid., 12.
38. Ibid., 55.
39. Slout, *Theatre in a Tent,* 26; Jere Mickel, *Footlights on the Prairie* (St. Cloud, Minn.: North Star Press, 1974), 51–53; Magnuson, *Circle Stock Theatre,* 208–9; *The Cambridge Guide to American Theatre,* ed. Don Wilmeth, 2nd ed. (New York: Cambridge University Press, 2007), 57–58; Landis Magnuson, "No Roof Except the Sky: The Rise and Fall of Airdomes in American Popular Entertainment," *Theatre Symposium* 17 (2009): 39–55.
40. Slout, *Theatre in a Tent,* 25.
41. Mickel, *Footlights on the Prairie,* 51.

42. *New York Dramatic Mirror,* September 16, 1903.
43. *Billboard,* June 2 through December 15, 1906.
44. Slout, *Theatre in a Tent,* 25.
45. *Billboard,* April 17, 1909.
46. *New York Dramatic Mirror,* June 12, 1909.
47. *Billboard,* February 19, 1910.
48. *New York Clipper,* June 14, 1913.
49. Neil Schaffner, *The Fabulous Toby and Me* (Englewood Cliffs, N.J.: Prentice-Hall, 1968), 51.
50. Alan Downer, *The Memoir of John Durang* (Pittsburgh: University of Pittsburgh Press, 1966), xiii, 113, 116.
51. Magnuson, *Circle Stock Theatre,* 6.
52. Slout, *Theatre in a Tent,* 36.
53. Sol Smith, *Theatrical Management in the West and South for Thirty Years* (New York: Reissued by Benjamin Bloom, 1968), 40.
54. Robert L. Sherman, *Chicago Stage: Its Record and Achievement* (Chicago: Published by the author, 1932), 260. See also Robinson's personal statement in the *New York Clipper,* November 17, 1872, 384.
55. Slout, *Theatre in a Tent,* 36–39.
56. Ibid., 20.
57. Ibid., 52.
58. Slout, *Plays of Repertoire and Stock,* n.d., 2, available at the National Theatre Museum in Mount Pleasant, Iowa.
59. Marvin Carlson, *Places of Performance: The Semiotics of Theatre Architecture* (Ithaca: Cornell University Press, 1989), front flap.
60. Marvin Carlson, *Theatre Semiotics: Signs of Life* (Bloomington: Indiana University Press, 1990), 41.
61. Slout, *Theatre in a Tent,* 71–72.
62. Schaffner, *The Fabulous Toby and Me,* 2, 3.
63. Mickel, *Footlights on the Prairie,* 149–50.
64. Slout, *Theatre in a Tent,* 84.
65. Ibid.; and author's personal conversation with Dr. William Slout, April 18, 1996, Mount Pleasant, Iowa.
66. Slout, *Theatre in a Tent,* 84.
67. Lawrence Levine, *Highbrow/Lowbrow: The Emergence of Cultural Hierarchy in America* (Cambridge: Harvard University Press, 1988), 177.
68. For further research, historians are urged to contact the following: Texas Tech University's Museum Library and the Southwest Theatre Collection; the National Theatre Society's Museum and Library, Mt. Pleasant, Iowa.
69. Michael Kamen, *Selvages and Biases: The Fabric of History in American Culture* (Ithaca: Cornell University Press, 1975), 177.
70. Brooks McNamara in *Passing Show: Newsletter of the Shubert Archive,* Shubert Centennial Edition, vol. 22 (New York, 2002), B4, B5.

Ibsen's Unexpected Triumph

Peer Gynt at the Seattle Repertory Playhouse

—VICTOR HOLTCAMP

> One woman came a thousand miles from San Francisco just to see it. They came from all classes and walks of life—fishermen from up north, lumberjacks from the Grays Harbor Region. I recall seeing a day laborer, who had been working in the rain all day repairing the car-tracks in front of the theatre, go to the box office of The Playhouse at quitting time to buy a pair of seats. The same people came twice, some three, four and more times to see it.
>
> ALBERT OTTENHEIMER, "Seattle's 'Peer Gynt,'" June 1941

It is commonplace to consider Henrik Ibsen as one of the fathers of modern drama. Realistic pieces like *A Doll's House* and *Ghosts* practically defined the plays of the art theatre movement and linked him to box-set realism. Their subsequent widespread inclusion in dramatic literature anthologies further paints Ibsen as the playwright of the middle-class domestic drama. But before Nora and Torvald, Ibsen had written theatre pieces more closely akin to epic poetry. *Brand* (1866) tells the story—in verse—of a man of God who brooks no compromise from himself or others, and who dies, onstage, being crushed by an avalanche. Theatrically, *Peer Gynt* is even more challenging. Published in 1867 but not receiving its first production until nine years later, *Peer* clocks in, uncut, at five acts and thirty-eight scenes. It managed to put even Ibsen himself to sleep during an unedited performance of it in honor of his birthday. "I shall be satisfied," he is reported to have said, "as long as the piece is reduced to a proper length. Not to do this would spoil everything."[1] *Peer Gynt* is enormous, covering the picaresque wanderings of its titular hero as he runs from his village in the Norwegian hills, woos the daughter of the Troll King, sails the world as a slave trader and merchant, meets madmen and fools, comes face to face with his own mortality, and returns home as an old man to the woman he has always loved and who has always loved him. Like Goethe's *Faust* (one of Ibsen's inspirations), *Peer Gynt* focuses on a strong central character, addresses weighty issues of morality and identity, and blends the natural and the supernatural in a theology that is anything but orthodox.[2]

Both *Peer* and *Faust* held (and continue to hold) fascination and dread for theatre producers. As such, despite Ibsen's own significant popularity among the theatre cognoscenti of the early twentieth century, it did not have much of a life outside of Norway, and even there only received a major production once every ten years.[3] Vast in scope, difficult in staging, demanding in technical requirements, poetic in timbre, and lengthy in performance, *Peer Gynt* was enough to daunt even the most enthusiastic of theatre-makers. Infrequent might be too weak a word for the production history of *Peer*, which had somewhere between four and six U.S. productions prior to 1930, including a production by the Santa Barbara Community Players in the late 1920s and a rumored staging by a "Norwegian Workingman's Society" in Seattle sometime between 1890 and 1893.[4]

Yet it is *Peer Gynt* that Albert Ottenheimer describes in the above epigraph as one of the most popular shows he had ever been a part of. *Peer Gynt* was not only a landmark production for the Seattle Repertory Playhouse in the 1930s but also one of their biggest moneymakers, responsible, according to one account, for saving the fledgling theatre company from bankruptcy and dissolution.[5] Originally mounted in 1931, the play would be revived *four* times over the course of the next decade, earning notices in national publications as it enticed locals and visitors alike. *Peer Gynt* became one of the longest-running shows in Seattle until after World War II, seen by over twelve thousand people in its initial nearly three-month run; it had a rare combination of theatrical artistry and popular appeal, earning lauds in multiple papers and rave reviews in four languages. How did it happen? How did a struggling theatre group with one foot in the community theatre world and the other in the emerging modernist tradition manage to strike such a resonant chord with the city of Seattle, and beyond, with a play widely considered almost completely unstageable? In this essay I provide a performance reconstruction of the Playhouse's *Peer Gynt,* drawing heavily from the Seattle Repertory Playhouse Papers located in the Manuscript Division of the University of Washington Archives, and offer some informed speculation as to the particular elements that might have made this production so successful. I will also provide some historical context for the production and the Seattle Repertory Theatre in general.

The history of the Seattle Repertory Playhouse (SRP) is fascinating and significant in its own right, although a published full-length history of the company does not exist. The company began prior to the Depression, became affiliated with the Federal Theatre Project, and lasted until after World War II. In his dissertation on the SRP, Ron West states, "The Jameses and the Playhouse provide a linear correlation with Depression Era theatre's evolution. Their cultural, social and political development directly parallels that of more notable and influential figures and institutions."[6] This parallel extended beyond styles and programming, and the leaders of the SRP found themselves accused, like so many others, of Communist ties. In 1948, state senator Albert Canwell accused them of being Communists in hearings on "Un-American Activities." These hearings eerily anticipated the national House Un-American Activities Committee (HUAC) and McCarthy hearings, including denying the accused the opportunity to cross-examine witnesses, spurious and perjured "friendly" testimony, and demands—under threat of contempt of Congress—to know the political history and affiliations of the defendants. The accusations were disastrous to the company, making survival difficult, and eventually impossible. The state supreme court denied their appeal of contempt charges in 1949. The final SRP production, *Pygmalion,* closed in 1950, and by 1951 one of the two founders was dead.[7]

The Seattle Repertory Playhouse started life in 1928 in a storefront office in the university district, the brainchild of Florence and Burton James, previously instructors at the Cornish College of the Arts in Seattle. (Florence was actually a bit more than an instructor, serving as director of the drama department from 1923 to 1928.) Albert Ottenheimer, although not one of the original founders, quickly became a leader in the organization, serving as the in-house press agent as well as a sort of literary manager. Surviving letters between Ottenheimer and the Jameses attest to their closeness, and his record of the SRP activities in the playhouse log indicates his centrality in the running of the organization. The first SRP production—*Juno and the Paycock* —was performed at the downtown Metropolitan theatre, and they would continue to rent performance space until the *Peer* season of 1930–31.[8] That year they arranged the lease of a plot of land at the corner of Forty-First and University Way and began construction of an "ultra-modern"—in the newspaper parlance of the day—theatre building. The theatre still exists. It was acquired by the University of Washington in 1951 and has undergone numerous renovations, the most recent, as of this writing, completed in 2009.[9]

In addition to *Peer,* the 1930–31 season included Shaw's *Major Barbara;*

an original comedy about the film industry called *Leading Man; Our American Cousin* (advertised somewhat gruesomely as the play Lincoln was attending when he was assassinated); and Tolstoy's *The Living Corpse. A Christmas Carol* was offered outside the normal subscription season as a holiday bonus. Even without the stress of overseeing construction of a new theatre building this was an ambitious schedule, but it was in keeping with the ideals and philosophy of the company. The SRP was committed to doing "important" plays, and this season was clearly no exception. *Peer Gynt* was originally set to open in December but was switched for *Leading Man.* According to an SRP newsletter, the switch was due to a delay in crafting the acting edition of the text, although it is possible that other aspects of the production—and a wish for lighter fare during the holiday season—influenced the decision to postpone. In addition to adapting the script, there were a number of other logistical challenges to address. The desire to include Grieg's music necessitated musicians. A chorus of dancing girls likewise meant additional personnel and expenses. All told the initial production's cast alone totaled over forty,[10] and the number would climb in subsequent remountings to close to one hundred.

It is useful to recall that the operations of the SRP were not those of today's regional theatres, and their process much more closely followed a community theatre model. Most of the performers were unpaid, as were many of the laborers involved in building the production, and lots of people wore multiple hats. The set designer, Robert Mahaffey, was also the house manager, and he had performed in the previous season's *Six Characters in Search of an Author.* Ottenheimer recalls that Mahaffey had expressed a desire to design, even though "Bob had never designed a set before."[11] The Mary Ann Wells School of Dance—supplier of dances and dancers for *Peer Gynt*—had received special thanks in the program for *Six Characters* as well. Virginia Opsvig (costumes and masks for *Peer*) was also the assistant house manager; Walter Shaw (mask design and "execution") played the Steward and was an assistant stage manager. Shaw had been stage manager on the preceding production (*Leading Man*) and would find himself back on stage as an actor in *Our American Cousin.* In short, this was an organization that relied on an extended family of theatre workers to fill all the tasks necessary to produce any show, especially one as demanding as *Peer Gynt.* This is not said to denigrate their accomplishment but rather to help keep in perspective the success they managed to achieve.

Overseeing *Peer Gynt* was Florence herself.[12] While there was a great deal of give-and-take between Florence and Burton, it seems clear that Florence was the ultimate arbiter of artistic decisions regarding *Peer.* In one instance, recorded in her memoir, Florence and Burton were trying to dissect what was going wrong in a given scene:

> "What does it need, Bill?" Burton asked Florence, using her nickname.
> "You've got the poetry, Burton," she explained worriedly, "but no salt, fish and cheese."
> From then on the cast tried to work into the Ibsen all the "salt, fish and cheese" flavor of Norwegian village life.[13]

Throughout the production process Florence navigated between "salt, fish and cheese" on one hand and the highly imaginative world of Ibsen on the other, seeking to bring clarity to a play that could confuse even those working on it. Freely admitting that there was much to be bewildered by in the script, she writes, "We sometimes felt as Peer says of Begriffenfeildt, the madhouse keeper, 'A remarkably learned man, almost all he says is beyond comprehension.'"[14] Florence's success at bringing clarity to the confusion is evident in the reception of the piece and can be traced back to her earliest work on the show: the adaptation itself.

Taking Ibsen at his word that the play needed to be "reduced to a proper length," Albert and Florence worked on cutting the mammoth text down to something approaching an appropriate size, a task that took them roughly nine months.[15] From the original sprawling mass they distilled three acts and sixteen scenes organized by the age of Peer Gynt: "Youth," "Middle Age," and "Old Age."[16] Even with this cutting the settings list in the program runs the gamut from "By the Mill-House, in the mountains near Gudbrandsdal, Norway" to "Near the village of Gizeh, in Egypt, by the great Sphinx," and the named characters total over forty, exclusive of the uncredited "Wedding-guests, Trolls, Madmen, etc." listed in the program. Florence and Albert consulted various acting editions at their disposal, as well as a copy of a prompt book from the National Theatre of Norway at Oslo. This unusual source had come to them from Miss Helga Lund, who would play Solveig. She had gone to Norway on vacation the previous summer, arranged an audience with the king of Norway, and made a connection with the National Theatre. Florence recalled consulting five different editions, "some of which left out scenes that we thought necessary for the development of our script."[17] Of particular note is the somewhat infamous "onion scene" in which a destitute and aged Peer forages for wild onions to eat. As he sits peeling his mediocre treasure, he philosophizes about the nature of a man's life relative to the construction of an onion: "You're not an emperor, you're an onion! / Now my dear Peer, I'm going to peel you, / However little you may enjoy it . . . It's nothing but layers, smaller and smaller."[18] While this scene was originally deleted from Florence and Albert's adaptation, a supposed "outcry from some of the audience" led to its reinstatement. Florence later noted that no less a luminary than George Bernard Shaw, under the belief that any actor worth his salt would jump at the chance to "peel the onion," once criticized Sir Henry Irving for not producing *Peer Gynt*,[19] and perhaps Burton's desire for the opportunity helped bring back the scene.

Perhaps the easiest thing to understand about the entire process is the SRP's decision to produce *Peer* in the first place. Florence, Burton, and Albert all loved the play. "Ibsen's *Peer Gynt* had occupied our attention since our student days," Florence recalled. "Most actors dream of plays and parts they would like to play, and my husband, I am sure, had for a very long time dreamed of the day when he would play 'Peer.' So in the spring of 1930 we decided that one of the plays to be produced early in the theatre would be *Peer Gynt*."[20] Florence indicated her own attractions to the script, likely speaking for herself, Burton, and Albert: "We were charmed by the fantasy and poetry in our first production. . . . The high romance, flights of fancy, Peer's braggadocio and impudence, his love of his mother, combined with the half-understood mythology, intrigued us."[21] Beyond their love of the specific text there were other factors influencing their decision. The SRP had produced Ibsen's *The Wild Duck* and *The Master Builder* in prior seasons, so there was an audience expectation of an Ibsen piece (although the difference between those pieces and *Peer Gynt* is vast, as is indeed the gulf between *Peer Gynt* and most modern drama). Moreover, Seattle was home to a large Scandinavian immigrant population for whom Ibsen and *Peer* were more familiar fare. In a 1973 essay titled "Ibsen in Seattle" for the journal *Norwegian-American Studies*, Sverre Arestad asserts: "It can be assumed that *Peer Gynt* was familiar to most Norwegians in the region, and it can be demonstrated that Ibsen had been known to the general public for several decades through performances in Seattle and other cities."[22] As a final Scandinavian bonus, the wife of the editor of the *Washington-Posten*, the "largest Norwegian Newspaper in the Northwest," was a board member of the SRP.[23] Beyond Ibsen, Grieg's suite of songs enjoyed popularity independent of the script, and Burton confessed that the play "had been shrewdly chosen with an eye to the large Norwegian population and the universal knowledge of Grieg's music."[24]

And so, on February 7, 1931, the houselights dimmed and *Peer Gynt* began in front of a sold-out audience. While the original prompt script seems not to have survived, there is enough archival evidence to get a good sense for what the production would have looked and sounded like to that first group of spectators. Descriptions of the sets, costumes, and lights are frequent in the surviving papers of the SRP, and publications as diverse as the *Christian Science Monitor* and *Theatre Arts Monthly* joined with the local Seattle papers in running articles and production pictures.

When word got out that *Peer Gynt* was going to be produced, a recent immigrant asked the theatre if they would like him to "paint the barn as the Norwegians would have painted it."[25] The SRP politely declined, as their concept for the production meant that there wouldn't *be* a barn to be painted in Norwegian style. For all of the tradition associated with Ibsen, the SRP decided to go in a different direction with the sets and lights, which are closely linked in most contemporaneous descriptions. Like the new theatre, they are "ultra-modern," meaning a scrim backdrop and abstract set pieces rather than a series of fully realized settings replete with lifelike detail. No lighting designer is credited in the program, although Burton is listed as technical director (in addition to playing Peer). Pre-opening publicity from the SRP indicated that one attraction of *Peer Gynt* was "the newest and most remarkable of modern settings and lighting, including a revolving scenic basis, never before seen in Seattle."[26] A reviewer for the *Seattle Times* described the settings as "stark and startling in their simplicity, utilizing various combinations of levels against a limitless blue sky, combined with lighting effects of unusual beauty."[27] Florence was aware of prior production practice, which had favored detailed, realistic settings, but indicating an awareness of the need for playability she remarked, "No matter what may be said for or against scenery of this kind, it must have lengthened the playing time."[28] She felt strongly that in order to make the play work, the scene changes would need to be smooth, fluid, and, above all, fast. "Our settings were presentational, rather than representational, and ideally suited to a production of this type. Scenes were changed in one minute, the longest taking three minutes." Even with drastic editing and fast set changes the production ran over two and a half hours, including an intermission between parts one and two during which complimentary coffee and cigarettes could be enjoyed in the lobby.[29]

To set a specific scene a particular item might be brought on, while other set "pieces" would be nothing more than projections: "A rickety fence, a little hut, a sphinx projected in the sky, an exotic palm tree, bed coverings which cascaded over the stage for Ase's [*sic*] death scene—these were some of the devices used to create the illusion of realism."[30] From the photographic evidence available, the "rotating basis" appears to be a series of platforms stacked ziggurat-like, reaching a height of approximately four feet off the stage floor. More than one of these platforms could move, and Ottenheimer relates that when the set was rebuilt for the revival it was improved by the addition of "rubber-tired casters on both the upper and lower portions, making them silent, where before they

Figure 1. Horned Woman: Likely the daughter of the Troll King, whom Peer nearly marries in the first section of the play (actress unknown). Note the platforms and background set pieces against the scrim. University of Washington Libraries, Special Collections, UW 29358z.

were very noisy."[31] Judging from the photographic evidence, it seems that for some scenes the platforms were covered in a fabric of some kind to break up the hard edges of the lumber, while in others they are bare. Similarly, in some of the photos the backdrop is augmented with rectilinear shapes rising up behind the action. These were solid, although most were likely flats painted to look three-dimensional rather than sculptural units (see figures 1 and 2).

While the sets and lighting were abstract, many of the costumes were nearly antiquarian in their attention to detail. Although there was no barn to paint in

Figure 2. One man and two women in black clothes. Most likely a shot of Peer (Burton James) interacting with two of the Saeter Girls on the mountainside (actresses unknown). University of Washington Libraries, Special Collections, UW 29359z.

Norwegian style, there were plenty of outfits to re-create. A number of the characters wore "authentic dresses imported from Norway or loaned by leading residents of the Norwegian colony of Seattle."[32] Surviving production photos attest to the verisimilitude attempted by the SRP in costuming Peer and the villagers. But not every character is Norwegian—or even human—and another design element that garnered much critical attention and praise was the "weird, modernistic masks" used for the Troll King, his followers, and some of the characters in the madhouse scene toward the end of the play.[33] Curiously, *Theatre Arts Monthly* ran a caption for an image indicating that "a Japanese actor in a traditional Kabuki make-up played the part of a Troll King in the Seattle Repertory Playhouse production of this fantastic play which was directed by Mr. and Mrs. Burton James."[34] Leaving aside the issue of directorial credit, this is the only indication I have found for the use of Kabuki makeup in the show, although Ottenheimer indicates that the troll dancers used "grotesque makeups" instead of masks.[35] None of the other surviving pictures indicates that the makeup was specifically Kabuki in design, although it could be argued that the masks and makeup were Kabuki-inspired.

They are correct, however, that an actor of Japanese descent played the Troll King. Twenty-eight-year-old J. T. "Joe" Hirakawa played both the Troll King and the Boyg (although "voicing" the Boyg would be more appropriate, as the Boyg is a formless mass that speaks to Peer following his escape from the trolls and the scene was performed in total darkness). Hirakawa's participation in the production is likely why Japanese was one of the four languages in which the play was reviewed, with English, Swedish, and Norwegian being the other three.[36] Hirakawa's work with the SRP was not isolated to *Peer Gynt.* His name appears on a list of "Junior Members" in the December 1930 edition of the SRP newsletter, and after *Peer* Hirakawa played the artist Petushkov in Tolstoy's *The Living Corpse.* That same year Hirakawa graduated from the University of Washington with a degree in dramatic arts—the first person of Japanese descent to earn a drama degree from the University of Washington—and moved to Hollywood to seek his fortune in motion pictures, although he remained in contact with the SRP.[37] In subsequent stagings the parts of the Troll King and the Boyg were taken over by Bertram Boog, a utility player from the first production.[38] Hirakawa was later tapped to translate a version of *Chushingura* for Ottenheimer to adapt and the SRP to stage, but this project never fully materialized, nor did a proposed tour of *Peer* to Tokyo that Hirakawa had helped initiate.[39]

Two other production areas are noteworthy: dances and music. Mary Ann Wells is credited with "devising and executing" the dances in the play. As previously mentioned, she, too, was a friend of the SRP, and her School of Dance would give a concert at the new playhouse that June. Her corps de ballet is credited only with "Anitra's Arabian Dance" in part 2, scene 2, but given the photographic and textual evidence, her dancers would have been onstage for the wedding dance at the beginning of the play, the Saeter Dance where Peer meets the wild women of the hills, and the Troll Dance. A picture from the 1931 production was published in the *Seattle Times* showing the three "Saeter Girls . . . in eccentric dance," credited as Jayne Garvin, Louise Hastert, and Sally Sue White, "who are appearing in the current production of the Ibsen masterpiece by the Seattle Repertory Playhouse Company." (see figure 3).[40] Jayne Garvin was apparently "jobbed in" from nearby Tacoma for the part, as evidenced by an article in *Drama Magazine:* "An interesting Newspaper Announcement concerns one of Tacoma's Little Theatre players. One is Miss Jayne Garvin who was engaged to take an important role in the Seattle Repertory production of *Peer Gynt.*"[41] Jayne is also credited with "Bird-Cries" during the Boyg scene, and it can be safely assumed that she was also one of the unnamed "dancing girls" that comprise the

Figure 3. Peer Gynt in Chains: Peer (Burton James) is chained to the "rotating scenic basis," calmly facing yet another antagonist. The actor wielding a trident is not credited in the photo. University of Washington Libraries, Special Collections, UW 29360z.

Mary Ann Wells dancers. Based purely on the surviving photographic record, the dances themselves seemed to match the sets' and lights' "modernity" and were not traditional ballet.

Grieg's music was another selling point—and expense—for the SRP. Part of the advertising campaign for the play was based on the chance to see it "with the Grieg music, which plays such an important part in the Continental productions of this play."[42] The conductor, Myron Jacobsen, led a chamber group of two violins, one viola, one cello, one bass, one harmonium, and one piano. Jacobsen was a gifted musician who was active in the nascent Seattle music scene, but like others working on this production he was also a friend of the Jameses, whom he met while they were all teaching at Cornish. And like many of the others, this was not his only job for the SRP. Jacobsen is listed as the SRP's musical director in the newsletter, and he had collaborated with Florence on productions prior to *Peer.*

Grieg's full orchestral composition has over twenty movements, and for underscoring, his smaller "*Peer Gynt* Suite" is more commonly used. This was advertised in the SRP newsletter as a reason to see the show, as was the fact that Myron Jacobsen would conduct the orchestra.[43] Jacobsen also did the arrangements used by the SRP, and the program's "musical synopsis" lists nine pieces: three overtures ("Morning," "Arabian Dance," "Peer Gynt's Homecoming"), two dances ("In the Hall of the Mountain King," "Anitra's Dance"), two postludes ("Aase's Death," "Solveig's Cradle-Song"), and one "scene" ("Solveig's Song"). These match up in most cases to Grieg's own suite of music, although Grieg gave Solveig only one song, rather than a "song" and "cradle-song," and "Aase's Death" is not in the traditional suite.

All in all the SRP was taking a tremendous risk with *Peer Gynt.* The production cost a great deal of money, even with the support and dedication of the friends and accomplices the Jameses had enlisted, and this was money that was needed to continue financing their newly constructed theatre. While devoting a tremendous amount of energy to the adaptation, conception, and rehearsal of the production, the SRP did not neglect the cornerstone of any good marketing campaign: advertising. "Teaser" pieces appeared prior to opening in a number of local and regional outlets. Arestad notes, "Before the play opened, national and even international interest was created in the forthcoming performance. . . . News items appeared on the progress of the preparations for staging, and interviews were published with actors and actresses."[44] Professors Glenn Hughes and Sophus Keith Winther (University of Washington professors of drama and English, respectively) gave Sunday-afternoon talks on Ibsen and *Peer Gynt* in the weeks before opening to further prime the pump and provide their subscribers with some context for the production.[45] In addition, other company members gave talks and speeches at a variety of venues throughout the city. Helga Lund "talked on 'My Day at Court' [about her trip to Norway] . . . to numerous Seattle audiences. . . . Local audiences, particularly women's and service clubs, were saturated with lectures on *Peer Gynt* by university professors and members of the cast, but particularly by Burton James, who for a time became identified throughout the Seattle area with Ibsen's hero."[46] Ottenheimer, before going to work for the SRP full time, had been employed at the *Town Crier,* one of Seattle's local papers, and he put his contacts in the newspaper trade to good use. Florence indicated that the "first announcement of production of the play came in the *Town Crier,* a weekly, in September 1930."[47] This would be the first announcement of many, which were printed in as many of the Seattle papers as they could reach.

The primary points of interest about *Peer Gynt* were established early and reiterated with remarkable focus and intensity. *Billboard* magazine's "Seattle Players Attempt Ibsen's Poetic Fantasy," while not published until a week after opening, was clearly penned beforehand and emphasized the selling points that can be found in other articles about the production: a unique opportunity to see a legendary play, seasoned with spectacle and innovation, and a dash of Scandinavian authenticity. "As far as is known this is the first time it has ever been produced by a little theatre. Incidental music, written for the play, is being interpreted by an orchestra recruited from the Seattle Symphony under the direction of Myron Jacobson. According to reports the play is being presented with new settings and lightings, including a revolving scenic base, never before seen in Seattle. Modernistic masks have been designed and executed especially for this production. Many of the costumes have been imported from Norway . . . a *corps de ballet* has been arranged by Mary Ann Wells."[48]

The points about the innovative set and lighting, the use of masks and dancers, and the inclusion of Grieg's music can be found nearly verbatim in most local articles as well. Compare the above with this selection from the Seattle paper *The Argus* that ran three weeks prior to the *Billboard* piece: "More than sixty actors are required. The regular Playhouse Company will be reinforced by a ballet corps of the Mary Ann Wells dancers. . . . Robert E. Mahaffey, Jr. has designed many of the settings for the fifteen scenes of *Peer Gynt.* Walter Shaw, property director, said that a revolving scenic basis will be used, upon which the fantasy will be played against an expanse of blue sky. Modern masks will be used in one scene."[49] The local *Jewish Transcript* summarized these same points: "Drama, music and the dance all play vastly important parts in the notable production of Henrik Ibsen's epochal poetic fantasy, 'Peer Gynt,' one of the unique dramatic spectacles of the world."[50] The SRP put its connection with the *Washington-Posten* to good use as well. Special thanks went out in the newsletter prior to opening thanking the editor "Mr. Gunnar Lund . . . [for] material aid in bringing our presentation of 'Peer Gynt' to the attention of the great number of Ibsen's compatriots in Seattle and the vicinity."[51]

The SRP made these same points in their newsletters to subscribers, but they were naturally far more forceful in their salesmanship. "THEATRICAL EVENT OF THE DECADE AT PLAYHOUSE—'PEER GYNT'!" screamed one headline. This was followed by a list of not ten but eleven reasons to see *Peer*

Gynt, ranging from the familiar points about the dancing, masks, sets, and costumes to the size of the cast and the rarity of seeing *Peer* performed. For those who might feel nervous about committing to such an epic evening, the newsletter assured that "*Peer Gynt* has a well-nigh universal appeal. It is of consuming interest to the lover of the theatre, the student of literature, the musician, the dancer and the artist. Make certain that you see it and that everyone you know who might be interested comes and sees it, for it is an opportunity that comes but rarely."[52]

While confident in their product and hopeful for a success, most of the cast and crew were relatively modest in their expectations. Ottenheimer remembered that most participants expected the show to run for about twelve performances, which had been the previous SRP long-run record. "With great good luck, some brave souls thought, it might run as many as fifteen [nights]. And then things began to happen."[53] First, whole nights began to be pre-sold, then whole weeks. Once the show opened, the reviews were ecstatic and the audience response incredible. From California to Canada, from Montana to the Pacific Coast, people came to Seattle to see *Peer Gynt.* "It was as though a dam of newsprint had suddenly burst," Florence wrote. "Pictures, interviews, rave reviews, which seemed to reflect amazement at the magnitude of the undertaking—all of this giving our company an emotional lift beyond imagination."[54] A review from the *Seattle Times* exemplifies the general tone: "There is Burton W. James. He plays Peer Gynt. No, he is Peer Gynt. . . . J.T. Hirakawa enacts the Troll King. His portrayal deserves the highest of praise. The Mary Ann Wells Dancers execute an amusing and fascinating routine. . . . Yes, the Repertory Playhouse has done exceedingly well by *Peer Gynt*!"[55]

Other papers spoke of the production in similarly laudatory terms, and the production was extended past its original booking again and again. In the Japanese-language *North American Times,* Florence is quoted as saying, "Never before have we had such an outstandingly complete 'hit' as *Peer Gynt.*"[56] The run was extended so long that the next edition of the quarterly SRP newsletter could quote from glowing reviews in the *University District Herald* of the production that had opened in February, and mention that it was still possible to see *Peer Gynt* in April. "All who love beautiful and classical music . . . interpreted by artists, all who enjoy the humorous, the fantastic, whose eyes feast on color and effect, will live again, thrill, laugh and weep, surprised and delighted with *Peer Gynt.*"[57] It was so popular that *Our American Cousin* was forced to play in repertory with *Peer,* taking the stage on Wednesday and Thursday nights, leaving Friday and Saturday free for continuing performances of their unexpected success. The original run finally closed in May, having enjoyed thirty-nine performances and a total audience count of between twelve and thirteen thousand.

In a post-opening interview, Florence paid tribute to the Scandinavian community for their support of the production: "Our greatest source of pleasure is that our Scandinavian patrons, our most exacting critics in a production of this sort, have assured us of their complete satisfaction with our presentation of what is to them the most revered in drama."[58] But it wasn't only the Scandinavians who made the production a success. "They came from everywhere," runs the brochure copy for the tenth anniversary season, "throughout the state of Washington, from Oregon, British Columbia, Idaho and Montana, and one woman made the trip from San Francisco to see it."[59] Florence describes the audiences in her memoirs in much the same terms as Ottenheimer used in his National Theatre Conference address: "Audiences filling the theatre were not only of the intelligentsia or the socialites, during the run of the play a man fixing street car tracks in front of the theatre came to the box office for tickets. 'I want my kids to see this.'"[60] Clearly, the combination of elements and actors, visuals and story, struck a chord with Seattle and beyond. But despite the best talents and intentions of the members, the SRP never quite managed to create another production that matched *Peer Gynt* for popularity and artistry.

This was not for lack of trying. *Peer Gynt* naturally became the yardstick for all future productions. *Our American Cousin* was said to be "a worthy successor to [our] greatest achievement, *Peer Gynt*," and a special lecture by Professor Edward McMahon of the University of Washington history department on President Lincoln was added to the schedule of events.[61] But *Our American Cousin* was a quick failure, unable to be sustained playing in rep against *Peer*.[62] Tolstoy's *The Living Corpse*, the final play of the season, was promoted as "a production, in scope and power, its spectacular staging and acting opportunities, in its deep dramatic worth, fully as great as *Peer Gynt*." While the two plays might seem at first "totally different in theme, treatment, and presentation," they offered "a number of remarkable parallels." Both were "unique masterpieces . . . difficult, spectacular productions . . . rarely staged." In addition, the Playhouse production of *The Living Corpse* would include incidental music, just as *Peer Gynt* included the Grieg suite: "stirring, glamorous Russian gypsy songs, said by many to be the most beautiful music in the world." Finally, both shows were large, with *Corpse* having an advertised cast of over forty.[63] *The Living Corpse* did all right for itself, even earning a revival of its own, but it did not achieve the long-run status of *Peer*.

The following year they tried their hand at one of Ibsen's literary progenitors and staged *Faust* as part of the Goethe centennial. The company considered that production as good as or better than *Peer,* and while it did well, it did not bring in the ticket sales of its predecessor.[64] In their 1933 production of Hauptman's *The Sunken Bell* they tried to re-create all the elements of *Peer Gynt.* Like *Peer, Bell* had been done infrequently in the United States. The set would utilize a revolving stage, which this time would also include an "18-foot high mountain." The Mary Ann Wells dancers would return, along with Myron Jacobsen and a chamber group for live music.[65] Professors from the University of Washington were enlisted to provide lectures to the public. Their pre-release materials stated, "Your Civic Theatre has again achieved the notable heights of its epoch-making productions of 'Peer Gynt' and 'Faust,' which brought Seattle and its Playhouse international fame."[66] But these heights were not to be scaled so easily, as *The Sunken Bell* was widely considered a dismal flop. In Florence's words, it was "beautiful to look at but a crashing bore . . . a complete failure in acting and directing."[67] They tried doing other works by Ibsen, other poetic works, other works by Scandinavians (e.g., Bjornson's *Love and Geography*), works with dancers and musicians, rarely done works by literary masters, and they tried wrapping the trappings of *Peer Gynt* around any and all of these. Yet *Peer Gynt* remained, stubbornly, the production against which all others were judged. For the next decade the story of a young Norwegian adventurer exploring the world against a "limitless backdrop of blue" would be revived again and again, and managed to find an audience each time.

The first revival was in 1932 for a summer Ibsen festival. Not only could visitors watch *Peer Gynt,* but they could also see *The Wild Duck* and *A Doll's House* playing in rep. The festival earned a review in the *Christian Science Monitor,* proclaiming, "'Peer Gynt,' with the incidental music written for it by Grieg, is proving the best attraction of the festival, and will have to its credit 50 performances in 13 months—more if the festival time is extended, as is probable."[68] The review indicated that while the sets remained "modern settings on a revolving stage, with a spacious background of blue," some of the blocking and acting had been sharpened. "In the group scene for Ingrid's wedding which formerly was its weakest spot in Seattle each individual now moves with purposeful direction. Miss Helga Lund, a young Norwegian-American, is well suited in features and in temperament to play Solveig. Her work during the winter as Juliet . . . and as Margueriete ("Faust") has made her portrayal richer than her first appearance. . . . Miss Sophia Rosenstein's Aase, too, has mellowed and gained balance in pathos and humor. Casting for other parts is uniformly good."[69] The play was revived again in 1936, then in 1938, and again in 1941. The year 1938 also saw a most unusual "revival," for in addition to the stage show a version was created and performed as radio drama to help inaugurate a new 50,000-watt transmitter for local station KIRO. It was revived one final time in 1948, in the waning days of the company.

Burton James—Peer Gynt himself—analyzed the aftermath of *Peer Gynt* from the perspective of a decade after the original opening: "It seemed that we had achieved our first objective—a play of great literature, interpreted in the modern manner, actually making money. And we concluded that the fine things in the theatre would pay their way. Yet the play's success was the source of much puzzlement. Its popularity exceeded our wildest dreams. . . . The spectre of this success dogged us for many a month. Fight against it though we did, we were always looking for another 'Peer Gynt,' striving to arrive at the exact combination that had produced it, and never fully realizing that the world was sweeping on."[70] Despite Burton's assertion that "they" hadn't realized that the world had moved on, the later history of the SRP indicates, as West points out, a close parallel to the dominant theatrical trends of the period. The SRP moved into a phase of more contemporary social awareness and activism, staging plays such as *Waiting for Lefty* and *The Hairy Ape*.[71] The SRP would also participate in the Federal Theatre Project, with Florence staging the Seattle production of the Living Newspaper *Power* and notably working with the local Negro unit on an infamous production of *Lysistrata,* which was closed after one performance for charges of lewdness.[72] Such activities, along with a trip to Russia that Florence made in 1934 to see Soviet theatre firsthand, would prove fodder for the Canwell Committee in the late 1940s, when Burton, Florence, Albert, and others were accused of being Communists. Convicted of contempt of Congress, all were sentenced to jail. Florence's sentence was suspended, but Albert served ninety days.[73] Burton's health had not been strong prior to the accusations, and his eventual sentence did not include jail time in deference to his physical condition. Burton died in 1951, and Florence moved to Canada, continuing to work as a theatre professional and educator, passing away in 1988.[74] Albert continued to work as a writer and actor in the United States, although he was called before HUAC in 1955 and spent time on the federal blacklist.[75] A death notice in the *New York Times* indicates that he passed away "unexpectedly on January 25 [1980], in Cincinnati, Ohio, while rehearsing *The Cherry Orchard.*"[76]

What made *Peer* such a hit? As Burton indicated, the SRP never quite identified the unique elements of its triumph. In the same article for the National Theatre Conference that I quoted in the epigraph, Ottenheimer sounds a similar note of confusion: "What, then, is the secret of this phenomenal success? We wish we knew. . . . If we could isolate and concretize the formula of its success, we'd be doing ourselves and like theatres in America a very utilitarian service.

But the worst of it is, we can't. We've studied the matter for ten years now, and we're not much nearer the solution than we've even been." Ottenheimer goes on to describe the usual suspects: the revolving set, the expansive blue backdrop, the inclusion of Grieg's music and the Mary Ann Wells dancers. He pays tribute to Ibsen's text, which, "though often badly translated and still more frequently not wholly comprehended by the audience, nevertheless sweeps the listener along with its music." But he also paid tribute to the director and gave due credit to her husband as well. "But most of all, I think, [it is] Florence Bean James' truly brilliant direction and the acting of the cast . . . particularly Burton W. James, executive director of The Playhouse, in the exacting, exhausting title role."[77] Florence, modestly downplaying her directorial achievement, echoed Burton's centrality in her memoir: "In all my years at the Repertory Playhouse I would say the most oft-repeated query from audience members was 'When is Mr. James going to do "Peer Gynt" again?' It was never just a question about the play; it was always associated with him, first and last."[78]

While an entire accounting of a hit or failure is necessarily impossible in such an ephemeral form as live theatre, it is possible to offer some informed speculation to augment the comments of Ottenheimer and the Jameses. As a programming choice, *Peer Gynt* was not so surprising as it might originally seem. The SRP had been associated with Ibsen since their founding season. West has estimated that fully 25 percent of the SRP offerings from their founding till 1932 were Ibsen plays.[79] And it is quite true that there was (and is) a sizable Scandinavian population in Seattle that might be inclined to see this rarely produced piece by a favorite son. The casting of J. T. Hirakawa also broadened the potential audience base by encouraging members of the Japanese community to see the show. The overall publicity campaign was also noteworthy, with the actors speaking at meetings across the city and Ottenheimer putting his newspaper skills to work as a press agent to build excitement and demand. Given the presales, it seems clear that this investment paid off.

Additionally, as former instructors at Cornish College, the Jameses had built a following of people interested in "modern" artistic expression. This was the same institution, after all, that had hired the relatively unknown Martha Graham to teach in the summer of 1930. Her popularity led to a successful solo concert in the same theatre where the SRP first performed.[80] The SRP tapped into their patrons' desire to experience "great art," which practically seemed to define this production of *Peer.* Ottenheimer noted this in 1933, writing in the logbook, "Most theatres of our kind are under the necessity of producing an interminable series of light, modern comedies or revivals done in broad, burlesque fashion. With us, the lighter the play, the lighter the B.O. [box office] and vice versa."[81]

Given the success of *Faust* in the 1932–33 season it seems clear that a significant portion of their potential audience in the early 1930s valued the SRP's handling of classical and "academic" texts. In an article titled "John Public Goes to the Art Theatre," the *Seattle Times* offered a humorous morality tale of Mr. and Mrs. John Public discovering that art theatre (specifically the SRP) could actually be entertaining. "Fear of Boredom Fades as Mr. and Mrs. Average Person Explore the Works of Great Dramatists and Find New Amusement Thrills," reads a subtitle. Certainly part of this appeal was in celebrating Seattle as a place where cultured art could thrive, as indicated by a vignette about a representative from the Theatre Guild arriving to see the SRP. "At the first glance she dropped her Manhattan skepticism about the theatres of the hinterland and exclaimed, 'Oh, I had no idea you had anything like this out here! This is by far the most interesting little theatre in America.'"[82] But the appreciative spirit of Seattle boosterism would not be reason enough for the long-term success of the production. Going to *Peer* was a chance to go to the theatre, see modern dance, and hear live music all in one evening, and the totality of this experience seems to have contributed to its appeal, with the scope of the spectacle drawing audiences into the story rather than distancing them from it. Further, because of its initial popularity, a virtuous cycle was formed where each subsequent revival was able to feed on the previous successes. Ottenheimer noted in the Playhouse log in 1937 that "from the way [ticket buyers] talk on the telephone, asking about the balcony, etc. it is apparent that many of the people reserving seats for PEER GYNT have never been in the theatre before, which is a good sign."[83] If, by the latter half of the decade, *Peer Gynt* had become in some senses a museum piece, it could still be appreciated for its particular combination of elements and style, even if that style was no longer what the SRP was pursuing.

Although all these are contributing factors, I also believe that there was a very real congruence of talent, ability, and desire among the company—particularly between Florence, Burton, and Albert—and that this contributed materially to the success of the show. Their sincere and palpable love of the text gave them a solid foundation on which to build the production. Florence and Albert's care and dedication to crafting an acting version that would suit the theatre and the company, a process lasting close to nine months, was clearly beneficial.[84] Florence proved herself an exceptionally talented director, and Burton, playing Peer, found a role that matched his strengths as an actor and performer extremely well. Aside from the testimony of Florence and Albert to Burton's particular success in the role, evidence for this synchronicity can be found in a review of the 1932 revival in the *Christian Science Monitor:* "Mr. Burton W. James who plays Peer has the needed fire and poetic feeling for the part. People come not once or twice but over and over again to get that something which the Peer Gynt of Mr. James gives them."[85] All the advertising in the world would not have made the show a success unless it was, at its core, satisfying theatrically for the audience, and it is clear that this production was.

While the Seattle Repertory Playhouse might never manage to create another *Peer,* the one they did craft served them long and well, and it left an indelible mark on the company. It seems only fair to give Florence the final word, and one final anecdote from her memoir epitomizes the ubiquity of the production: "Twenty years later, on the night my husband died, my daughter was being driven to the hospital. She said, 'My father, Burton James, died tonight.' 'Burton James,' replied the taxi-driver, 'I saw him in *Peer Gynt.*'"[86]

Notes

Much of the material used in this essay is drawn from the Manuscript Division of the University of Washington Archives. In particular, accession no. 1556-3 covers much of the holdings for the Seattle Repertory Playhouse, and accession nos. 2117-1 and 2117-2 contain the Florence B. James Papers. The Florence B. James Papers also contain the manuscripts for Florence's memoir "Fists Upon a Star," the authorship of which is somewhat confusingly rendered as either an autobiographical work or in partnership with a Robert Johnson. For simplicity, since the vast majority of the text is in first-person narrative form, I have attributed it to Florence James in this essay.

1. *Playhouse News,* January–February 1931, 7, Box 33, Folder 3, Seattle Repertory Playhouse Papers [hereafter SRP Papers].
2. "*Peer Gynt* parodies *Faust* even as it does Shakespeare," writes Harold Bloom in *The Western Canon: The Books and School of the Ages* (New York: Riverhead Books, 1994), 216.
3. The original program notes say, "Ibsen admits, in another letter, that it was written with no thought of its ever being produced. Ten years after its publication, in February 1876, (fifty-five years ago almost to the day of the opening of our production) it was produced in Christiania (now Oslo) with Edvard Grieg's now famous incidental music, which will be heard in its intended setting in our presentation. It has been done approximately every ten years in Norway ever since." *Playhouse News,* January–February 1931, 7, Box 33, Folder 3, SRP Papers.
4. "Andrew Nerland, later a prominent citizen of Fairbanks, Alaska, was in Seattle from 1890 to 1893. He was a charter member of the short-lived but vigorous Norwegian Workingman's Society, which, despite its name, actually was a cultural and dramatic organization. Nerland recently informed the writer that in the early 1890's this society put on numerous plays, including Holberg's *Jeppe on the Hill* and Ibsen's *Peer Gynt.* This production of *Peer Gynt* is, as far as is known, the first performance of an Ibsen drama in Seattle and one of the very first in the United States." Sverre Arestad, "Ibsen in Seattle," *Norwegian-American Studies* 25 (1972): 167–85, quote on 173.
5. "The production of 'Peer Gynt' the first year at the Playhouse and the some fifteen thou-

sand dollars which it earned, averted a very precarious financial crisis." Talk given by Burton James about SRP history, Box 31, Folder 8, SRP Papers. The amount of money actually taken in by *Peer Gynt* is not clear, nor are the actual number of seats sold, as regular records were not kept until later in the company's history, but it is clear that *Peer* took in more money than had been anticipated and that this helped to cover the costs of the new building.

6. Ronald Oakley West, "Left Out: The Seattle Repertory Playhouse, Audience Inscription and the Problem of Leftist Theatre during the Depression Era" (Ph.D. diss., University of Washington, 1993), 296.
7. Barry Witham, "The Playhouse and the Committee," in *The Performance of Power: Theatrical Discourse and Politics*, ed. Sue-Ellen Case and Janelle G. Reinelt (Iowa City: University of Iowa Press, 1991), 146–61.
8. Early SRP history derived from Florence Bean James's unpublished memoir "Fists Upon a Star" in the University of Washington special collections holdings, as well as Ronald West's dissertation.
9. The means by which the University of Washington gained control over the building were not without controversy, as it followed their legal battles with the Canwell Un-American Activities Committee. See Witham's "The Playhouse" for more details. Also see note 45 below.
10. The program for the initial production names just over thirty individuals as cast members, but it does not name dancers or any "extras" that might fill out the various crowd scenes. Advertising copy for the production puts the initial cast at over sixty people, but it is difficult to know with certainty whether that number was padded for effect or is an accurate representation of the total number of performers involved.
11. Log, p. 230, Box 32, Folder 6, SRP Papers.
12. While Burton was occasionally mistakenly given credit as a codirector—see *Theatre Arts Monthly* citation in note 34 below—the initial program and all available evidence make it clear that Florence alone served as director (though Burton did serve as technical director).
13. Florence B. James, "Fists Upon a Star," 90, Box 4, Folder 8, Florence B. James Papers [hereafter FBJ Papers].
14. Ibid., 21. Incidentally, Ottenheimer played the role of Begriffenfeildt in the original production.
15. Log, p. 230, Box 32, Folder 6, SRP Papers.
16. While the program lists only fifteen scenes, the true number is sixteen. Ottenheimer draws attention to this in the SRP log: "For some reason, the listing of the scene marked * [Part 1, scene 8—Peer confronts the Boyg] has never been listed in any program, nor is it in the continuation of the Troll scene in my original cutting. In rehearsal, after the first program went to press, it was found necessary to draw the curtain and make it a new scene. The error has been perpetuated from program to program. Consequently there are 16 scenes, rather than 15." Log, p. 229, Box 38, Folder 6, SRP Papers.
17. James, "Fists Upon a Star," n.p., Box 1, Folder 12, FBJ Papers. It is perhaps unsurprising that Florence highlights her own work on the script, while Ottenheimer's recollections from the middle of the decade emphasize his own work. "I consulted [the prompt book from Norway] together with the Richard Mansfield and Theatre Guild adaptations and several translations. I followed none exactly, making an acting version which omitted

some the others left in but which, on the whole, included more of the story than many of the others. This took nine months work. In the end, I used a combination of the Sharp and Archer translations, the former predominating, using the latter whenever the readings were more dramatic." Log, p. 230, Box 32, Folder 6, SRP Papers. While I cannot say for sure, my hunch is that—given Ottenheimer's continued career as a writer—he did the bulk of the actual typing and rough-draft adaptation, and that Florence oversaw the work and provided suggestions and feedback on what to include and what could be discarded. The working relationship between Albert, Florence, and Burton was quite close throughout the SRP's existence, so I do not attach any malice to the competing narratives, simply the viewpoint of each narrator.

18. The "onion" line is taken from a radio version of the *Peer Gynt* script, p. 1, Box 37, Folder 10, SRP Papers.
19. James, "Fists Upon a Star," 20, Box 1, Folder 12, FBJ Papers.
20. Ibid.
21. Ibid., 21. Here again Albert's own narrative is slightly different. "Some years before I had read R. Farguharson Sharp's translation in the Everyman library of PEER GYNT. The scene of Aase's death did what only one other passage in fiction, the scene of the Bishop's candlesticks in 'Les Miserables' (read in French), had ever done—brought tears to my eyes. I started talking about PEER GYNT. Mr. and Mrs. James grasped the idea and developed it to include Grieg's music, ballets, and scenic spectacle." Log, p. 230, Box 32, Folder 6, SRP Papers.
22. Arestad, "Ibsen in Seattle," 169.
23. *Playhouse News,* January/February 1930, SRP Papers.
24. Burton James talk about SRP history, Box 31, Folder 8, SRP Papers.
25. James, "Fists Upon a Star," Box 2, Folder 1, FBJ Papers.
26. *Playhouse News,* January/February 1931, SRP Papers.
27. *Seattle Times,* February 22, 1931, 22.
28. James, "Fists Upon a Star," Box 2, Folder 1, FBJ Papers.
29. Program, 1931 production, *Peer Gynt,* Box 1, Folder 2, SRP Papers.
30. James, "Fists Upon a Star," Box 2, Folder 1, FBJ Papers.
31. Log, pp. 231–32, Box 32, Folder 6, SRP Papers. The revival set also sported a better braking system for the set, whereas the original means of securing the upper platform was to use wedges.
32. *Seattle Times,* February 22, 1931, 22.
33. Ibid.
34. *Theatre Arts Monthly,* December 1931, 1043.
35. Log, p. 239, Box 32, Folder 6, SRP Papers.
36. *Playhouse News,* April 1931, SRP Papers.
37. Correspondence, University of Washington Office of the Registrar, December 4, 2008.
38. The SRP newsletter indicates that "[Boog] carried off the palm as the busiest actor in 'Peer Gynt'; played four different roles, all of them in different make-ups and costumes and spent his odd moments aiding others to get dressed." *Playhouse News,* April/May 1931, SRP Papers.
39. Hirakawa's own career is noteworthy. After leaving Seattle, Hirakawa lived in Hollywood until 1937. He met and married his wife in Los Angeles, and both returned to Japan as the political situation deteriorated. Because of his command of English and performance

skills he got a job with the Broadcasting Corporation of Japan, and U.S. servicemen could hear him over the airwaves as part of Radio Tokyo (although he drew a sharp distinction between reading the news and seeking to undermine morale à la Tokyo Rose). Notably, it was his English translation and voice that announced the emperor's message of surrender. Following the war he earned a cult following as the host of a radio program designed to teach Japanese citizens English conversation skills. Known as "Uncle Come-Come" from the first line of the theme music, he hosted his program for nearly a decade, gaining the admiration of hundreds of thousands of fans and earning millions of yen in royalties from the accompanying workbooks. Japanese tour proposal found in Log, p. 27, Box 3, Folder 3, SRP Papers.

40. *Seattle Times,* February 15, 1931, 30.
41. *Drama Magazine,* March 1931, 39.
42. *Playhouse News,* September 1930, SRP Papers.
43. *Playhouse News,* January/February 1931, SRP Papers.
44. Arestad, "Ibsen in Seattle," 179.
45. James, "Fists Upon a Star," n.p., Box 2, Folder 1, FBJ Papers. Relations between the SRP and Hughes soured in later years, as Hughes, in his position as head of the University of Washington theatre program, clashed with the Jameses, culminating in what seemed the ultimate insult: the takeover of the theatre building itself by the university. Professor Winther, ironically, ended up as a "friendly witness" to the Canwell committee. See Witham, "The Playhouse."
46. Arestad, "Ibsen in Seattle," 179.
47. James, "Fists Upon a Star," n.p., Box 2, Folder 1, FBJ Papers.
48. *Billboard,* February 14, 1931, 36.
49. *The Argus,* January 24, 1931, 5.
50. *Jewish Transcript,* February 8, 1931, 8.
51. *Playhouse News,* January/February 1931, SRP Papers.
52. Ibid.
53. "X Marks the Spot," Box 31, Folder 10, SRP Papers.
54. James, "Fists Upon a Star," Box 2, Folder 1, FBJ Papers.
55. *Seattle Times,* February 7, 1931, 2.
56. Arestad, "Ibsen in Seattle," 179.
57. *Playhouse News,* April/May 1931, SRP Papers.
58. *Seattle Times,* February 15, 1931, 30.
59. Tenth Anniversary Season Brochure, Box 31, Folder 10, SRP Papers.
60. James, "Fists Upon a Star," 14–20, Box 2, Folder 1, FBJ Papers. West addresses the issues of class and class expectations in "Left Out."
61. *Playhouse News,* April/May 1931, SRP Papers.
62. Logs, Box 32, Folder 6, SRP Papers.
63. *Playhouse News,* June 1931, SRP Papers.
64. West, "Left Out," 193.
65. Ibid.
66. *Playhouse News,* January/February 1933, SRP Papers.
67. Quoted in West, "Left Out," 193–94.
68. *Christian Science Monitor,* July 9, 1932, 6.
69. Ibid.

70. Burton James talk about SRP history, Box 31, Folder 8, SRP Papers.
71. This was not without risk. The SRP's production of *Lefty* cost them the support of the *Seattle Times*, which waged a one-paper boycott against the company until its dissolution. See West, "Left Out," 222–28.
72. See Barry Witham's *The Federal Theatre Project: A Case Study* (Cambridge: Cambridge University Press, 2009), especially the chapter "A Negro Theatre."
73. West, "Left Out," 251.
74. Witham, "The Playhouse," 156, 161.
75. Milton Bracker, "Actor, Once a Red, Accuses 8 Others; 5 Assail Inquiry," *New York Times*, August 18, 1955, http://www.proquest.com (accessed May 12, 2011).
76. "Death Notices," *New York Times*, January 27, 1980, http://www.proquest.com (accessed May 12, 2011).
77. Albert M. Ottenheimer, "Seattle's 'Peer Gynt,'" *National Theatre Conference Quarterly Bulletin* 3, no. 2 (1941): 19–22.
78. James, "Fists Upon a Star," 85, Box 4, Folder 8, FBJ Papers.
79. West, "Left Out," 187.
80. Richard C. Berner, *Seattle 1921–1940: From Boom to Bust* (Seattle: Charles Press, 1992) 249–50.
81. Quoted in West, "Left Out," 191.
82. Betty Stewart, "John Public Goes to the Art Theatre," *Seattle Times*, February 22, 1931, 3.
83. Logs, pp. 239–40, Box 32, Folder 6, SRP Papers.
84. Ottenheimer, capturing the history after the fact in the SRP logbook, writes, "No one knows, to this day, what element or elements it was that built PEER GYNT into the phenomenal success it became. Many reasons have been assigned for it—the Grieg music, the large Scandinavian population, a first-rate publicity campaign, but none of these, or all taken together, it has always seemed to me, sufficiently explain what took place. The most reasonable answer, I think, is that it is a superlative show. We had lavished a good deal of care on it." Log, p. 230, Box 32, Folder 6, SRP Papers.
85. *Christian Science Monitor*, July 9, 1932, 6.
86. James, "Fists Upon a Star," Box 2, Folder 1, FBJ Papers.

BOOK REVIEWS

Stage Money: The Business of the Professional Theater. By Tim Donahue and Jim Patterson. Columbia: University of South Carolina Press, 2010. 173 pp. $18.96 paper.

The project of Donahue and Patterson's book is to study the structures of and approaches to producing professional theatre in the United States. The book's organization is slightly unusual, consisting of seven numbered chapters separated by "intermissions" that explore topics related to the overview chapters in greater depth. The volume begins with a study of Broadway, off-Broadway, and Broadway tours; the final two chapters examine nonprofit theatres and their relationship to commercial theatre. The authors struggle openly with defining "professional theater," which is problematic given the book's subtitle. Perhaps a better subtitle would have been "The Business of the Commercial Theater," which is the focus of all but one chapter.

The greatest strength of the book is its richness in relevant data. Each chapter contains hundreds of relevant facts and figures, as well as definitions of terms such as "options" and "subsidiary rights," explaining them simply and lucidly. The authors also perform risk analysis on for-profit theatre, concluding that it is no more or less risky than other types of investment in relationship to potential returns, and supporting their conclusion comparing data from recent Broadway seasons with data from other types of non-theatrical financial investments. This sort of comparison is innovative and creative, a real strength of the authors' perspective on theatre as a business. The chapter on ticket pricing is succinct, with a number of useful figures for visual reference, and explains the vagaries of variable pricing models and how and why they generate extra revenues. While the season-specific information the book provides will eventually grow dated, it is still immensely helpful to have a thorough portrait of a single Broadway season in terms of hits, flops, revenue, and origination of the work.

One small quibble is that the authors define "Commercial Theater" only in terms of Broadway, off-Broadway, "the road," and Las Vegas, which leaves out a number of for-profit theatres across the country. Dinner theatres, for example, are only mentioned briefly in the first chapter. Their modest size and variety of geographical locations would make their business models and financial data potentially relevant to theatre practitioners, since for-profit theatrical production might be subsidized by similar business partnerships such as bookstores, coffeehouses, or bars.

The intermissions provide useful case studies of specific approaches to theatrical production, such as Disney on Broadway and the "chitlin' circuit." The intermission section speculating on the "actor glut" is somewhat out of place in the volume, however. The authors' goal seems to be to apply general economic theories on labor to the acting profession, and they apply such theories with success and insight elsewhere in the volume. In this section, however, their avoidance of deeper discussion of the acting spectrum from "amateur" to "professional" is problematic. Their consideration of why actors choose to perform as "discounted labor" fails to take into account many reasons beyond the range of economic theory, and they do not incorporate current theories about creative economies and artistic capital that would be relevant to the questions they raise but leave unanswered.

By including a chapter on nonprofit theatres, the authors make the effort to touch on an area of research that certainly merits further scholarly attention. Their nonprofit theatre chapter focuses primarily on large regional nonprofit 501(c)3 theatres. By working with the data available to them through organizations such as TCG and LORT, the authors must ignore nonprofit theatre companies with budgets below TCG's $50,000 membership floor. This section gives a number of brief descriptions of nonprofit companies but not much in the way of a general picture of the nonprofit sector. Challenges such as board management and balancing earned and unearned revenue receive a few paragraphs at best. There is no tracking of "the life of a production" similar to that in the for-profit chapters, so there is no mention of the tangled web of nonprofit new-play development processes. The last few pages of the chapter are given to imposing a "business life cycle" onto nonprofits that is largely irrelevant when mapped onto actual nonprofit theatre companies unless they have issues with leadership transition.

The authors do not mention theatre management structures alternative to the 501(c)3, such as fiscal sponsorships or low-profit limited liability corporations (L3Cs), which have social impacts as a primary goal and profit making as secondary. Since much of the business model innovation in the theatre sector is happening in emerging theatres with small budgets, this book omits such innovations completely. This omission is understandable, since easily accessible data are scarce from smaller companies, but it limits the scope of discussion in a way that does not accurately reflect all the business models available to theatrical producers. As a result, this work is valuable as a snapshot of current for-profit theatre business practices but is less valuable as a handbook for those seeking to decide between competing production models for a new theatre.

In several places the authors reinforce stereotypes without further comment, as in "Some [nonprofit] theaters are professional versions of community theaters, whose seasons comprise unchallenging classics, musicals, and comedies that middle-class Americans are said to favor" (123). Which theatres? Which classics are unchallenging? And who determines what middle-class Americans favor? Such occasional broad generalities distract from their larger goals in relation to contextualizing the business of theatre.

The final chapter, on the possibilities and relationships between commercial and professional theatres, provides a number of case studies for the reader. Here, the authors return to their strength in analyzing the complex relationships that have grown up between nonprofits and commercial theatrical production in New York. This volume is a strong addition to the literature for those teaching and working in arts administration and may also be relevant for young artists who seek to know more about the current terrain of commercial theatrical production.

—**HEATHER A. BEASLEY**
Arts administrator, Boulder, Colorado

New Directions in Renaissance Drama and Performance Studies. Edited by Sarah Werner. New York: Palgrave Macmillan, 2010. x + 226 pp. $80 cloth.

In the introduction to *New Directions in Renaissance Drama and Performance Studies,* Sarah Werner establishes the focus of the volume: to give legitimacy to the study of performance of Renaissance drama. This book represents a third shift in Renaissance drama scholarship: a move beyond the first generation's naive assumption that performance practices and responses remain stable and consistent regardless of time, location, or culture and a rejection of the second generation's assumption that performances reveal modern theatre practice but reveal little about the text. The essays included explore a multiplicity of new approaches to studying Renaissance drama and performance, giving space to explore what has been omitted from the field of scholarship. The authors look at what can be learned in Renaissance drama through various methodologies and lenses ranging from semiotic and phenomenological analyses of performances to case study and analogous exploration of text and film.

Werner provides an excellent history of Shakespeare scholarship within her introduction and frames it in terms of "Shakespeare," not Renaissance drama, which exposes a central question of the book: How does one look at Renaissance drama without looking at Shakespeare? How can scholars move beyond the Bard? Several of the chapters explore this question and suggest opening the field to other relevant Renaissance drama. Thomas Middleton's *The Revenger's Tragedy* is one such play for examination. Considering that the play surfaces as either a reference or a focal point in nearly half of the eleven chapters, it would seem that the play is quite prominent as a viable means of circumventing Shakespeare. Werner sets forth several probative questions in her introduction, but the book seems to return to a singular overarching one: In what ways can scholars continue to seek out worthwhile inquiry within the study of performance of Renaissance drama?

The organization of the book is broad, divided into four major sections, but considering the various essays and perspectives, the divisions are fitting. The first section explores the ephemeral "dilemma" of performance and demonstrates scholars' struggles with "liveness." In "Replaying Early Modern Performances," William N. West explores the assumptions of an event's time and space and the concept of theatre as "replaying" rather than "loss" through an engaging analysis of The Wooster Group's *Hamlet.* The second section explores lessons gleaned from the intersection of literary and performance criticism. Overall, this was one of the more engaging sections, which includes critiques of self-fulfilling historiographic scholarship and of self-propagating performances and performance reviews. While the heading is inclusive, the topics explored in each chapter are quite varied. The third section of the book, "Resituating Shakespeare," attempts, through a variety of approaches, to decenter Shakespeare within the realm of Renaissance drama, suggesting that Renaissance drama is in need of a Derridean overhaul. The final section of the book, "Postscript," is a single chapter by Courtney Lehmann exploring Alex Cox's 2002 screen adaptation of Middleton's *The Revenger's Tragedy.*

Several chapters are noteworthy. In "Page and Stage Again: Rethinking Renaissance Character Phenomenologically," Andrew James Hartley uncovers the phenomenon of audience participation in the creation of character: we as audience fill in the gaps of a character, so that regardless of discontinuity of character, using the actor's body and our own experiences, we, the audience, create a whole character. Hartley argues that regardless of some scholars' perspectives of modern treatment of character as historically alien to Renaissance performance, the connection between actor and audience is the same whether past or present. Paul Menzer's "The Spirit of 76: Original Practices and Revolutionary Nostalgia" critiques original practices (the New Globe and others) and historiographic scholarship that values the architecture, or the trace, over the performance. He suggests that scholars should seek out the gaps or blanks of history rather than clinging to the material traces, imaginatively exploring the empty spaces. In many ways, Menzer and other authors in this book seem to be encouraging the employment of more creative scholarship similar to the creative approaches of theatre practitioners. Ayanna Thompson's essay, "'Ay, there's the rub': Race and Performance Studies," is a fascinating introduction to her broader work regarding race in/as performance in early modern drama. In this chapter, she explores race in/as performance through two contemporary plays, Neil LaBute's *This Is How It Goes* and Suzan-Lori Parks's *Venus,* and their use of Renaissance drama, in particular *Othello,* as moral or social barometers. Thompson argues quite eloquently that these contemporary plays imply behavior regarding race is already scripted, and that classical narratives limit our ability to act and react regarding race both on- and offstage. She also calls for a more rigorous and ethical analysis of race by Renaissance drama scholars, practitioners, and reviewers. While her strategies for negotiating race in/as performance may seem obvious, their importance cannot be overlooked.

Although the book has several worthwhile and engaging chapters, the highlight of the collection is Jeremy Lopez's "Spreading the Shakespeare Gospel: A Rhetorical History of the Academic Theatre Review," which provides an insider view and critique of valuing the building of audiences over producing theatre of quality. The colonialist tactics of both theatre and reviewers ensure more performances, which in turn propagate more performance reviews, which in turn propagate more performances, ad infinitum, guaranteeing security for both theatres and reviewers alike. The essay provokes the reader to reflect on his or her own participation in or resistance to building audiences over creating quality productions.

As one can see from the selected essays, the perspectives and approaches are quite varied. Werner notes that the book is not meant as a "univocal manifesto" on Renaissance drama, but rather the beginning of a debate that she hopes will continue with her readers (11). The variety of approaches sets the stage for a new shift in Renaissance drama and performance studies, demonstrating quite successfully that the study of performance is, as Andrew James Hartley argues, "a potent critical tool for exploration and discovery" (91).

—SHAWNA MEFFERD CARROLL
SUNY Plattsburgh

Reading the Plays of Wendy Wasserstein. By Jan Balakian. New York: Applause Theatre and Cinema Books, 2010. x + 244 pp. $19.99 cloth.

Feminist scholars do not easily embrace Wendy Wasserstein's plays. Written about wealthy, educated, heterosexual women living on the Upper East Side, her commercially successful plays smack of a conservative culture while doing little to interrogate the sexist power differential holding such culture in place. Wasserstein's is not the edgy theatre of feminist playwrights Megan Terry, Caryl Churchill, or Maria Irene Fornes, who used experimental techniques to critique stereotypes and normative ideology. That her characters associated their confusion with the increased opportunities feminism offered, sometimes speaking cynically of feminism without being aware of their own positions of privilege, irked many feminist scholars. *The Heidi Chronicles* in particular sparked a significant debate: Helene Keyssar, for example, found the narrow perspective of the play's frame disturbing, and Jill Dolan disparaged Wasserstein's liberal feminism as flawed.

In *Reading the Plays of Wendy Wasserstein,* Jan Balakian does not address the contentious position Wasserstein holds among feminist writers; rather, she sidesteps the criticism altogether by acknowledging that Wasserstein never claimed an identity as a feminist playwright. Instead, her plays reveal the historical, social, and political forces that have shaped women's identities in America since the liberation movement of the late 1960s. Balakian's book is not so much an argument as it is a well-researched reading of each of Wasserstein's seven plays; as such, it makes the case for contextualizing the personal issues of the characters within the political and economic setting of each period. Through this reminder that the personal is also political, Balakian proves that Wasserstein's ability to keep women's issues at the front and center of mainstream American theatre was itself a successful and significant feminist gesture.

No one would teach John Osborne's *Look Back in Anger* without situating the play in the leftist political climate and class animosity prevalent in 1950s England, yet few critical studies place Wasserstein's works within the political milieu that engendered them. By assembling the various cultural allusions within the plays and painstakingly researching the college handbooks, newspaper and magazine articles, television shows, commencement speeches, and song lyrics to which the characters refer, Balakian paints the ideologically charged landscape against which Wasserstein's female characters define themselves. Acting similar to a sociologist, Balakian examines the plays as cultural artifacts, studying how these flawed but realistic characters respond to their vexed environment by the choices they make and the challenges they overcome. In other words, each play acts as a barometer of feminist politics.

With each chapter, Balakian demonstrates how Wasserstein's plays are a "snap-shot" of their time. Her detailed historical reading of *Uncommon Women* (1977), set in 1967–71, shows a moment in time when women shifted from identifying with the conventional roles of their mothers to envisioning themselves as equal to men in careers and life choices. From today's vantage point the play strikes many as a quaint "period piece," but Balakian emphasizes the too easily forgotten personal turmoil these women experienced graduating into such a transitory world. As she cites an article from *Ms.* magazine advising how couples should split everything equally, or mentions Gloria Steinem hypothesizing if men could menstruate, or provides the lyrics from the Holyoke song in which women promise to "save" themselves for Yale alum, or quotes a 1968 commencement speech that advises putting careers on hold to raise a family, Balakian illuminates the conflicting pressures these characters responded to, endowing their anxiety with gravity. Throughout Wasserstein's plays, women are enjoined to be exemplary, "uncommon" women, while simultaneously reminded that their choices could leave them feeling lonely, exhausted, and unfulfilled.

The book delineates each play against the historical backdrop of its time: *The Sisters Rosensweig* against the collapse of the Soviet Union or *An American Daughter* as an allegory of the retracted nomination of Zoe Baird for attorney general. Balakian adroitly incorporates reading material from each period or itemizes key milestones and upheavals of the feminist movement. Her reading of *Isn't It Romantic,* a play about two young women searching for romantic and professional fulfillment, historicizes the women's concerns by pointing to particular referents of 1982–83: the Census Bureau's tabulation of unmarried people; an article about "corporate feminism" in *The Nation; Sex and the Single Girl* by Helen Gurley Brown; and the increasing number of psychological studies indicating how men and women relate differently to relationships, money, and careers. Seen through this lens of societal cues and media messages, the characters' concerns represent meaningful attempts at self-actualization.

This study is remiss in minor ways: the book lacks theatrical reviews contemporaneous to the productions, which could have lent support to the issues Balakian perceives, and the final two chapters about the plays *Old Money* and *Third* are notably underwritten. *Old Money* is Wasserstein's comparative portrayal of America's two Gilded Ages, with the actors playing characters eighty years apart, from turn-of-the-century New York to the late 1990s; while Balakian quotes from Henry James, Edith Wharton, and Thorstein Veblen to underscore the values of the early characters, she provides no corresponding cultural references to augment the later period. Similarly, the chapter on *Third,* Wasserstein's appraisal of liberal self-righteousness, could have been amplified by contextualizing the country's culture wars, but it is less than half the length of the other chapters—perhaps indicating future directions for scholars to pursue. Finally, Balakian does not theorize how Wasserstein's dramaturgy might be developed in performance to evoke the meanings behind these cultural references intrinsic to her plays. For example, when characters refer to a Eugene McCarthy rally in *The Heidi Chronicles,* Balakian notes the 1969 protest outside the Miss America pageant or the founding of the National Abortion Rights League to historicize the characters' experiences; however, she does not suggest ways this symbolic overlay could be conveyed in performance.

As Balakian traces the political and social zeitgeist of each work, she provides an invaluable teaching aid for third-wave feminists who might be ignorant of the battles women fought and the terrain they achieved. Wasserstein's characters cannot articulate the political pressures under which they operate because they represent human beings, not political sound bites, and they inhabit moments of valid, conflicted choices that reveal their humanity, whether it is the plight of a single woman or a doctor denied a political appointment due to a legal infraction. As time capsules, these plays are about the people caught within polemics, not the polemics themselves. Where each play ends is where the cultural analysis begins, and as Balakian rightly notes, "it is the critic's job to fill in the play's context, not the characters" (70).

—**MIRIAM CHIRICO**
Eastern Connecticut State University

Cooperation and Conflict: GDR Theatre Censorship, 1961–1989. By Laura Bradley. Oxford: Oxford University Press, 2010. vii + 312 pp. $99.00 cloth.

Laura Bradley takes her reader to a world as tense and treacherous as a John le Carré thriller; in fact, her astonishing account of the byzantine, arbitrary, and perilous process of theatre censorship in the German Democratic Republic (GDR) is like unsealing a top-secret file locked away for decades. Yet the cloak-and-dagger clichés of spy novels have nothing on the remarkable case histories of those infamous productions that dared express criticism, political opposition, or any deviation from party-line socialist realism. In a cultural climate where a single scene might kill a playwright's career—or ill-judged audience laughter could send a director to play the coal-mine circuit—the constant threat of excisions, bans, and punishment made "sacrificing for your art" take on a whole new meaning.

A lecturer in German at the University of Edinburgh, Bradley is the author of a previous monograph employing a near-microscopic focus on *Die Mutter*, the only play Brecht directed at all three stages of his career: Weimar, exile, and the GDR. Her latest project takes a macro approach, encompassing GDR history, cultural life, theatre companies, playwrights, and politicians. She also includes production photos, a useful map, and a list of abbreviations defining the myriad federal and state institutions that shaped East German theatre. Covering Berlin and the provinces from the building of the Wall to reunification, Bradley trains a wide-angle lens on her subject to capture the most complex—yet clearest—image of German theatrical censorship to date.

Of course, what complicates the picture immediately is the irony that state policy actually forbade censorship; after all, the "D" in "GDR" stood for "Democratic," signifying a government open to the free exchange of ideas. As confirmation of GDR tolerance, Bradley's introduction goes right to the source—quoting chairman of the Council of State Walter Ulbricht, who, in reaction to Alexander Dubèek's abolition of censorship (during the short-lived Prague Spring), blithely declared that the GDR had no censorship to abolish. From the outset, then, the author connects control of the theatre to the highest level of government and captures the sly, schizophrenic tone that characterized East German cultural policy. What follows is a fascinating exploration of the GDR's attempts to create and control a model socialist theatre yet maintain the appearance of democratic freedom; Bradley's trenchant analysis of this consistent divide between the overt and covert, the ostensible and real, gives the book its force and unity.

Bradley divides her book in two, devoting the first half to examples of censorship in East Berlin and the second to examples of censorship in important theatre capitals like Bautzen, Schwerin, Leipzig, and Dresden. She prefaces the whole with a short history of the East German theatre until 1961, where her case histories begin. The author anchors her approach in Bourdieu's theory of censorship as an act of compromise—an apt description of the GDR's peculiar position: to get the world-class theatre they avowed, culture ministers had to compromise; to earn commissions, state support, and travel to the West, theatre artists had to cooperate. Yet as Bradley's research shows, the dynamic was seldom that simple, nor the power evenly divided. To facilitate negotiations, the government evolved a rhetoric of compromise, what the author calls "a euphemistic code" that she breaks down into "four distinct strands" to "reveal how officials presented, justified, and conceived of their activity" (11). In an excellent and subtle analysis of bureaucratic doublespeak, Bradley explains how the four strands reflected East German buzzwords related to the planned economy, administrative language, cultural protection, and education. No matter how they were disguised, though, terms like "ideological clarification" and "administrative measures" were transparent stand-ins for coercion and punishment (12–13). Altogether, Bradley's examples of government surveillance, intervention, and sanctions demonstrate the extent, power, and regional variations in theatre censorship. Especially noteworthy are sections regarding the authorities' negotiations with theatre practitioners over political crises like the Wall, Prague Spring, the defection of luminaries such as Wolf Biermann and Adolf Dresen, and the political tsunami of perestroika. Bradley also presents moving examples of how the taut theatrical climate affected dramatic genres and performance practice, causing playwrights and directors to self-censor, stifling and distorting their works, in hopes of avoiding punitive measures.

Bradley draws on a wealth of sources: interviews, state and party papers from regional and federal archives, and new material from various theatre collections: prompt books, rehearsal notes, set designs, photographs, and correspondence. Of particular interest—and what makes her study so current—are revelations from the Stasi files. Bradley's thorough research into the Stasi's covert operations reveals extensive infiltration of theatre companies and an elaborate hierarchy of informants: strategically placed dramaturgs, "mentors" to guide playwrights and directors, and all manner of theatre artists. Some informers were true believers, while others sought promotion or informed out of spite;

some wretched souls were blackmailed into spying as atonement for past transgressions. In any case, this intricate, fluid network of covert communication adds a mind-boggling layer of complexity to the problem of censorship—but does much to explain the intense suspicion that informed "negotiations," the capricious reversals of ministry officials, and the ever-shifting alliances between theatre practitioners, cultural ministers, federal authorities, regional administrators, district managers, municipal leaders, judges, and journalists. As the author points out, all of these groups had a hand in censorship and were often at odds. Trying to navigate such bureaucratic chaos was a nightmare for dramatists and artistic directors. Bradley describes how playwright Christoph Hein, speaking at the Tenth Writers' Congress in 1987, "asked those of his colleagues less familiar with theatre to imagine a printed, bound book being checked again by the authorities in every region, district, and town to see if its sale should be permitted in local bookshops" (2). Even when approval was granted, it was never guaranteed; authorities could censor, restrict, or even cancel a production at any point in the rehearsal or performance process. Moreover, theatre's mutability and sheer number of variables gave bureaucrats so much more to object to: Bradley cites example after example of changes imposed on lighting, costumes, scenery, music, staging, gestures, audience behavior, and program design.

Bradley's thesis culminates in a finely nuanced portrait of GDR censorship, an ongoing, ambiguous process of "cooperation and conflict" that characterized administrators and artists alike. Neither theatre practitioners nor party apparatchiks were monolithic or immovable, but the state was fixed and absolute; it refused to give up both the covert practice and the public denial of censorship. Even in the final months before reunification, with federal authorities frantically trying to survive by suppressing change, denying it, or granting concessions, the GDR still insisted on its policy of freedom, rooted in its obsession with democracy and fear of scandal. Yet the "freedom" that allowed GDR officials to disguise censorship as "negotiation" also allowed theatre practitioners to disguise their unlawful assemblies as legitimate performances and their protests as public forums. Not without justification, Bradley's conclusion points with pride to East Germany's theatre community as leaders in the peaceful rebellion that brought down the Wall. Their theatres were the meeting halls and recruitment centers for the massive demonstrations that drove out their rulers and shamed the government into dissolution.

—STACEY CONNELLY
Trinity University

Queer Theatre and the Legacy of Cal Yeomans. By Robert A. Schanke. New York: Palgrave Macmillan, 2011. xxii + 229 pp. $85.00 cloth.

Fifteen years ago, while in the midst of a campus "culture wars" controversy over a production of Tony Kushner's *Angels in America* at Wabash College, I received from a student a poem intended as an expression of support. Its last lines are directed at an anonymous gay man living in the year 2040—"You are Unafraid and Unashamed and Young. Your Body is unfettered, your voice strengthened by all our Anonymous, Unchronicled Wars"—words that came rushing to mind while reading Robert A. Schanke's absorbing *Queer Theatre and the Legacy of Cal Yeomans.* In his preface, Schanke offers a 1979 quote from Yeomans ruminating in a tone similar to my student's: "Perhaps in years to come some young queen will find [my writings] in an old trunk bought at an auction, will read [them] and say, 'My God! Was that the way it was? Times sure have changed.' Let us pray for that anyway" (xv). Yeomans's prayer for changing times is much closer to reality in 2011, a fact that stands out in bold relief to a reader of Schanke's scholarly yet highly readable book on the "Unchronicled" life and career of Cal Yeomans.

Many iconoclastic artists are likely to lead lives filled with contradictions, and Yeomans is no exception. Raised by a conservative Christian family in Florida, he also had a mother who exhibited strong feminist proclivities, which allowed him to experience from an early age the deep cultural divisions of mid-twentieth-century America. The deeply conflicted (and bipolar) Yeomans ultimately emerged as a pioneer of early 1970s gay theatre. In that period he was nearly singular in his radical exploration of explicitly sexual subject matter, radical in that its frank depictions of same-sex relations were controversial even within the gay community. Despite considerable accomplishment in off- and off-off-Broadway theatres, Yeomans is little known today, even to those with knowledge of LGBT theatre history. Schanke's book goes a long way to rectify this omission.

Arguing a convincing case for Yeomans's place among that first wave of bold, gay dramatists whose plays kicked open the closet, Schanke stresses Yeomans's centrality among his peers. Better-known Yeomans contemporaries including Lanford Wilson, Robert Patrick, Doric Wilson, and Robert Chesley have received somewhat more scholarly attention to date (if, as yet, too little), but Schanke also reveals much about the movement as well as the plays of Yeomans, the specific themes he explored, and what his turbulent life represents. Without question, the overtly sexual aspects of Yeomans's plays, some of which were nurtured under the guidance of Ellen Stewart at LaMama, kept his work out of the mainstream limelight, a fact true of much gay-themed drama prior to the 1980s. However, Schanke makes clear that Yeomans's achievement merits a more central place among his peers.

To understand Yeomans's work, it is essential to understand his life within the context of his work. Troubled by erratic mental health, Yeomans found his way to the stage while a business student at Florida State University, gaining experience in summer stock and at Atlanta's Pocket Theatre. Once in New York, Yeomans labored in various capacities at LaMama, but in this period his bipolarity damaged professional and personal relationships. He ultimately moved to San Francisco and there began writing plays, including his 1979 Cable Car Award–winning *Richmond Jim*, produced by Theatre Rhinoceros and during the first New York Gay Arts Festival. Robert Chesley called it the "first genuinely gay play" (93), and it generated considerable controversy, even within the gay community, at the time. Along with his subsequent plays, it represents only part of his creative legacy; Yeomans was also a poet and an accomplished photographer. Following a 1996 diagnosis of AIDS, he spent his final years focused on philanthropic activities, including the establishment of a professorship in his mother's name at the University of Florida, where his papers are housed. When unearthed by Schanke, this treasure trove of play scripts, poetry, extensive journals, various records of performances, photographs, and other personal effects provided an essential and invaluable foundation for this book.

The book succeeds on many levels, but most directly as a result of Yeomans's papers and most admirably in Schanke's incisive scholarship. Reconstructing a mercurial life and a career carried out away from the bright light of mainstream American theatre and society, Schanke, who has amassed an impressive résumé of publications on gay and lesbian theatre (including major biographies of Eva Le Gallienne and Mercedes De Acosta), makes the most of the opportunity presented by Yeomans's collected legacy. Interviews with scores of Yeomans's friends and coworkers, and, most significantly, his own incisive analysis, permits Schanke to define Yeomans's achievement and the meaning of his life within the broader cultural evolution of gay culture in America. Schanke unspools Yeomans's life and times in engaging and intimate prose, illuminating that extraordinary era in the process. For those interested in LGBT theatre and its history, or in the personalities of a still too-little-known era, this book is a page-turner. The recovered accomplishments of Yeomans strengthen our common understanding of a complex, rapidly changing period in which gay artists and writers challenged American society to reconsider its values and its means of expressing them. If nothing else, Yeomans symbolizes the necessity of the stage in that reconsideration that has resulted, without question, in titanic social and aesthetic change in America, including progress toward the sexual liberation and true equality of a significant portion of the population.

In short, Schanke's book is an essential volume in the ongoing and still incomplete reconstruction of the LGBT foundation of contemporary American theatre and its meaning in creating the "Unafraid and Unashamed" society that my former student, like Yeomans, imagined for a faraway future that seems in reach.

—JAMES FISHER
The University of North Carolina at Greensboro

The Empire Actors: Stars of Australasian Costume Drama, 1890s–1920s. By Veronica Kelly. Sydney: Currency House, 2009. xii + 212 pp. $64.95 cloth.

Theatre historians face many challenges. Perhaps the greatest is to convince the wider community of scholars that their work is more than a footnote to "real" history; incidental at best. I recall, from my childhood, *Mad* magazine's satire on the U.S. Mail's dead letter office and how history might have been different if the following postcard had been delivered: "Dear Abe, saw *Our American Cousin.* It's a turkey. Stay home." Many accounts of that terrible event continue to ignore the imagined narratives played out in the minds of postbellum Americans, starting with John Wilkes Booth. As François Jost noted in *Modern Language Notes* (1978: 503–5), Booth, who once played Shakespeare's Brutus, shouted from the stage after firing the fatal shot, "Sic semper tyrannus!" He, at least, thought life would imitate art; though, like Caesar's assassins, he misjudged the willingness of the people to rise up in support. Perhaps they were busy reading *Uncle Tom's Cabin.*

Veronica Kelly is preeminent among the second generation of Australasian theatre historians who, from the 1980s, moved beyond the excavatory efforts of those who first drew attention to the long tradition of live performance in Australia and New Zealand and, while continuing to dig, started to analyze in an increasingly theorized manner the major professional live theatre industry in those countries before it was almost entirely wiped out by silent and then sound movies, by radio and the Great Depression, and wiped too from popular memory. This leads to another challenge: to introduce readers to texts they have never heard of and demonstrate that plays that survive today are not necessarily those that the societies that first saw them discussed and in part modeled their lives on. A theatregoer between 1890 and 1930 would be astonished that the plays of Ibsen, Wilde, Shaw and (to them) unknown women are staged today, while *The Sign of the Cross, The Prisoner of Zenda, A Royal Divorce, Monsieur Beaucaire,* and *Chu Chin Chow* are (although operatic and musical versions have lasted better: *Tosca, The Girl of the Golden West, The Merry Widow,* and *Kismet*). Long before Kurosawa, audiences knew about Japanese samurai culture *(The Darling of the Gods),* thrilled to *Pirates of the Caribbean* equivalents *(The Spanish Main),* and suffered with gladiators played by Geelong-born, London-acclaimed Oscar Asche, "probably the boofiest bloke before Russell Crowe to perform masculinity in the [Australasian] region," as Kelly colloquially notes (112). Inevitably, the theatre historians have much basic story and character explaining to do and more, if they are to try to convey in writing and still images the effect of movement and dance, colorful sets, lights, and makeup, swirling costumes, and resonant voices.

Empire Actors is written with immense scholarship and wit and much of it is done superbly, including reproducing a rich array of visual evidence. It is an account of some of the major actors who, condemned to be in the limelight only in the regional touring companies while Irving, Tree, et al. held sway in the metropolis, toured the world in the years after steamships made it safe and before film undercut their preeminence. It is understandable that in 1912 the *Wellington Post* in most distant, most lonely, most loyal New Zealand would see them as evidence of the British Empire's cultural reach (15), but in fact many were American, including Minnie Tittell Brune (see Kelly's article in *Theatre History Studies,* 1995) and the impresario who brought her to Australia, J. C. Williamson, both prominent in this book. Kelly is well aware of this and twists the phrase around to mean "an empire *of* actors" (15), but they were more precisely cultural manifestations of what on both sides of the Atlantic was called, when occasion suited (e.g., the London *Times* on September 21, 1881, after the assassination of another president, Garfield), "the English-speaking race"—white, of course.

The subtitle refers to one major genre, costumed historical melodrama, to which Kelly devotes serious attention—she knows her frocks, furs, spangles, wigs, gauze, and wire. Chapter 7, "Gendered Bodies in Glad-Rags," on Asche's and Lily Brayton's oriental fantasy spectaculars, powerfully makes the case for including such seeming superficialities as central to cultural imagining in the years around the Great War, as "preservation of history as moral or social exemplum; as a private locus of self-recognition; or as a complacent survey of subjectivities deemed to be exotically unlike 'us'." (24), although some of her empire of actors did little in this genre (e.g., Daisy Scudamore and Roy Redgrave, parents of Sir Michael, in chapter 9 with Maud Jeffries and others). *Julius Caesar,* as well as being a star vehicle for Asche (Brutus, of course), lurks behind many stories of heroic resistance to tyranny in more recent epochs and behind more innocent pastimes. (See page 42 for Kelly's riff on the public enthusiasm for dressing up in bedsheet togas and effortlessly incorporating Caesar into British history.)

The opening chapters on costume drama culminate in a study of Julius Knight, well-ranked London player and, south of the equator, crowd-stopping "prince of romantic actors," who spent twenty years in Australasia playing Marcus Superbus in *The Sign of the Cross.* Knight in fact gets two chapters (4 and 5), written in very different styles: the first addresses "cultural memory," while the second is a more orthodox stage biography. Here and elsewhere, Kelly's two somewhat different goals of reclaiming undeservedly forgotten actors, including women (Brayton, Jeffries, Scudamore, Brune), and explaining the power of historical melodrama unfortunately sometimes leads to essential information about a subject being provided long after its first mention or, conversely, being repeated several times in almost exactly the same words. One of that endangered species, a good editor, would have helped; but this is small criticism of a major and invaluable cultural history.

—RICHARD FOTHERINGHAM
University of Queensland

Holocaust Drama: The Theater of Atrocity. By Gene A. Plunka. Cambridge: Cambridge University Press, 2009. vi + 447 pp. $102.00 cloth. $45.00 paper, on demand.

Gene Plunka has written a wide-ranging survey of Holocaust drama, combining historical background, description of major dramatic works, accounts of theatrical reception, and broad moral interpretation. The more than thirty plays he discusses and the book's thirty-six-page bibliography offer all a teacher might need to design a course on the subject. With this comprehensive reach, Plunka's book, despite its flaws, is likely to become the standard text in the field for some time to come for an English-speaking readership.

Plunka builds on the anthologies and criticism of several predecessors: the pioneering work of Robert Skloot, beginning with *The Theatre of the Holocaust,* volume 1 (1982); my own international anthology, *Plays of the Holocaust*

(1987); Edward Isser's *Stages of Annihilation* (1997); Vivian Patraka's *Theatre, Fascism, and the Holocaust* (1999); and the criticism and commentary of many others. These works in their different ways examine dramatic form, national styles, particular authors, and especially the ethical and critical issues that must be stirred by attempts to stage the unstageable. For Plunka, a generation later, Holocaust drama is less a problem to be wary of or a contradiction to be reconciled than it is an established field; in a sense, the "aura" surrounding the subject has been dispelled. Aiming for comprehensiveness, Plunka seeks to include and categorize every "salient" play on the subject and, through the prism of drama, to sketch the entire story of the Holocaust—its emergence, its aftermath, and its moral and cultural implications. His multi-pronged, deeply researched approach, which one might describe as historico-thematic, is both valuable and, in some ways, ironically limiting.

In his introduction Plunka describes his double role as historian, "alerting the reader when the playwright deviates from the historical record or manipulates the Holocaust for artistic purposes," and theater critic of the works he discusses, examining "form, content, and stage techniques to make sure that they mesh effectively," as not every Holocaust play "works on the boards" (19). Words like "deviate" and "manipulate" may make the reader uneasy, but in practice Plunka welcomes a wide range of dramaturgical experimentation, and his interpolations of documented fact enrich his discussions. The criteria of theatrical salience, effectiveness, and workability, however, are more questionable. Plays may be "salient" here because they have drawn the attention of respected critics, but also because they were written by a well-known author, or because they earned some commercial cachet on the West End or Broadway, or because they created a furor. For what "works" in the theater no objective standards are offered, and none can be. The result is a bumpy book, frequently admirable as it unfolds the great moral eclipse of the Holocaust through the dramatic form, but sometimes backed by this very effort into questionable categorization or ham-handed interpretation.

In chapter 4, "The Holocaust as Literature of the Body," Plunka lays out the Third Reich's obsession with the physical superiority of German youth, the passage of the Nuremberg Laws that identified the Jewish body as contaminated, and the cultivation of systematic physical debasement in the camps. He enlists here the accounts of Agamben and Terrence Des Pres and the analysis of historians Goldhagen and Wistrich. This background comprises a sobering introduction, for instance, to Charlotte Delbo's concentration camp play for a cast of all-female actors *(Who Will Carry the Word?)*, and helps the reader cut through the play's formal poetic diction to a visceral sense of inmates' suffering in the camps. Other fine discussions include Plunka's absorbing accounts of Gilles Ségal's little-known *All the Tricks But One* and the more familiar *The Deputy* by Rolf Hochhuth in the two chapters titled "Aryan Responsibility during the Holocaust," I and II (peculiarly so titled, I might add: If "Aryan," why not responsibility *for* the Holocaust, and if *during*, then why the loaded Nazi term "Aryan?").

Yet, early in the book, a problematic aspect of Plunka's thematic approach also comes into view. His second chapter, "Staging the Banality of Evil," summons the notorious Eichmann trial, citing Hannah Arendt's delineation, in *Eichmann in Jerusalem*, of a Nazi character type (one who displayed the "banality of evil") that was to become iconic. Plunka illustrates this theme with a discussion of four plays, including Peter Barnes's one-act farce, *Auschwitz*, the second half of his 1978 diptych, *Laughter.* In the play's epilogue, Barnes startles his already shaken audience with a pair of concentration camp victims in prisoners' uniforms, Bimko and Bieberstein (the "Boffo Boys of Birkenau"), who enact a Borscht-belt vaudeville routine that wrings outrageous comedy from the moments before asphyxiation in the gas chamber ("This act's dead on its feet"). Coordinating his play discussion with Arendt, Plunka adopts a misplaced psychological realism. Bimko and Bieberstein become *real* camp inmates who, about to be gassed, do not see that "joking about the problem is futile, an excuse to avoid confronting the brutal reality of their fates" (38). His shaky argument continues, "[T]he comedy suggests their complacency and inability to act" (38). The audience's laughter similarly exposes its own failure to "confront the seriousness of genocide" and reveals the spectators as "little Eichmanns" (39). The play has been made to conform to the historical analysis and moral interpretation it was enlisted to illustrate.

Barnes intends to teach his audience the "need to assume responsibility, rather than laugh at the banality of evil," Plunka concludes (38). But the unbearable pathos of the scene may arise from another source, the entrapment of the audience in a peculiarly British form of psychic contradiction, in this case stirred by the mix of wrenching subject matter and the studied detachment of the popular performance types that influenced Barnes's work—*The Goon Show, Monty Python,* and the black comedies of Joe Orton. The audience is not so much educated into morality as stripped of pretensions to it.

In another example, shoehorning Liliane Atlan's play *Mister Fugue* into a chapter on "Culture and the Holocaust," Plunka reads the title as a reference to musical form, and the fugue form itself as a stand-in for European culture under assault by Nazi barbarism; however, the "fugue" of Atlan's title in French, *Mon-*

sieur Fugue, refers to flight and running away, and in both languages it refers to the psychoanalytic idea of the "fugue state," meanings appropriate to the Dr. Korczak–type figure, Krol, who on a whim accompanies Atlan's trapped children to the "Valley of Bones." Continuing the theme of music as culture, however, Plunka piles on another misreading, calling the stories Krol tells the children and the children tell each other as they travel to certain death (a game sequence in which they play out to adulthood the lives they will never be able to live) a "polyphonic cacophony of tales" (70). The theme of the degeneration of culture is thus served, at a price.

Note the Jack Sprat marriage here of "polyphony" and "cacophony." The carelessness of Plunka's writing is astonishing, given both the gravity with which he regards his subject and the gravitas of his publisher, Cambridge. Mendelssohn did not write violin "concertos" (31) but only one. Lawrence Langer did not coin "l'univers concentrationnaire" as is implied here (13). There are mind-boggling verbal confusions, "invoked" for "evoked," "eternal" for "constant," "spurned" for "spurred," "personified" for "epitomized," "infer" for "imply," "endearing" for "inuring," "irresolute" for "unresolved." There are myriad "ill phrases," as Polonius would scold. Is using babies as footballs merely "mistreatment"? A character succeeds in delaying some Nazi actions against the Jews, or, as Plunka writes, succeeds in "*stultifying* the atrocities" (192). Plunka inadvertently courts a Barnes-like black laughter at the description of a camp victim who is "*replete* with dysentery." (Wait, it gets worse.) "Her spirit is broken because her dysentery is draining" (78–79). Do academic publishers no longer employ copy editors?

Though marred by poor writing, wobbly criteria, and occasionally questionable interpretation, this book makes a substantial contribution to the ever-widening literature on the dramatic representation of the Holocaust. It helps to expand the boundaries of Holocaust drama beyond the ghettos, camps, gas chambers, and tribunals. Four chapters deal with survivor trauma into the next generation. Throwing a wide net, Plunka even includes plays that may not have been intended as Holocaust dramas at all, such as Tony Kushner's parable play set in 1930s Berlin, *A Bright Room Called Day,* about progressives' failure to stop Reagan's election and his disastrous AIDS denial, and Harold Pinter's *Ashes to Ashes,* which never alludes directly to the Holocaust. Yet on balance Plunka's wide embrace helps to expand the realm of moral, political, psychological, and spiritual inquiry associated with this compelling field.

—ELINOR FUCHS
Yale School of Drama

Women on the Stage in Early Modern France, 1540–1750. By Virginia Scott. Cambridge: Cambridge University Press, 2010. ix + 325 pp. $95.00 cloth.

This fascinating volume explores both the lives of actresses and some broader historical topics connected with their profession. The main focus is on questioning the disreputable social position of actresses, what constituted stardom, how women came to adopt their profession, what early modern audiences and critics considered good and bad acting, and how the talents of individual performers influenced playwrights. The discussion is limited to actresses in the leading Parisian troupes or in Italian troupes that performed in Paris during the early modern era.

Scott is determined to rehabilitate the leading actresses of the early modern French stage by treating them as serious and talented professionals. This resolution also extends to terms of address: she chooses to avoid the use of the definite article "la" preceding an actress's surname, traditionally a form of denigration. Scott provides a history of this usage, noting that several important critics protested against the practice and that members of the profession insisted on the more respectable "mademoiselle."

Perhaps the most remarkable chapter concerns the reliability of available anecdotal evidence for performers' biographies. Scott is rightfully critical of much previous scholarship for taking such stories at face value rather than questioning the identity and credibility of an author's sources, examining the author's motives, and seeking external confirmation. She examines a sampling of anecdotes from such standard sources as gossip collectors and police archives and shows that much of the material about actresses is dubious, and some of it is blatantly false.

The history of actresses is not limited to a review of the scanty extant documents. Scott speculates about what repertoire women might have played and how their presence in a troupe could have influenced the selection of plays or even the types of roles composed for them. For example, the frequency during the 1630s of plots where women dress as men, and in some cases engage competently in duels or warfare, suggests the presence of svelte and robust actresses. Her study of the lead female roles in three of Pierre Corneille's early comedies leads her to hypothesize that they were tailored to sophisticated actresses capable of rendering complex emotions and delicate nuances of expression.

Scott notes the profession of actresses' parents and spouses, showing that most had respectable middle-class backgrounds. Before 1700 the majority of

French actresses, like most of their Italian counterparts, came from theatrical families and/or married actors, although that would change. Financial records suggest that many members of the Parisian troupes lived comfortably, while statements made by or about the actresses concerning their private lives indicate that most were exemplary wives and mothers, with only a minority taking lovers or otherwise involved in scandal. Starting in the 1630s, theorists and playwrights contested the assumption that actresses are immoral in their private lives.

Scott convincingly argues that theatrical stardom developed during the second half of the seventeenth century. Tracing the careers of several actresses who would qualify as stars by modern definitions and of several others who did not quite achieve that rank, she demonstrates that a combination of genuine professional talent and of notoriety in private life (whether or not the accusations of immorality were well founded) was required. In each case, Scott examines (or conjectures on) the roles they performed and in which they were deemed to have excelled, their looks, their versatility or areas of specialization, and their special aptitudes, plus their documented or alleged love affairs. In some cases, an actress's detractors may have simply confused the woman with the roles she played. Scott argues that Racine's coaching of Mlle Champmeslé for the lead roles in his later tragedies was primarily due to his wish to create a new style of tragic acting based on melodious declamation.

The grand merger of Parisian theatrical companies in 1680 led to the creation of a system of typecasting known as *emplois*. Scott gathers together what information is available about the expectations for each category, in both tragedy and comedy and for both male and female roles, while noting that some performers held contrasting specialties simultaneously or changed specialties over the course of a career. She attempts, relying both on historical dictionaries and on documents of the period, to determine the precise meaning of some of the notoriously tricky terms used to describe an actor's performance, such as simplicity, naturalness, fire, and soul. While referring to theoretical treatises on acting, she prefers to quote non-theorists, especially playwrights and performers, who described and critiqued what they saw. In engaging the thorny question of the conflict between two acting styles that were simultaneously featured at the time, the more "natural" and the more singing or declamatory, Scott tries to determine what precisely these terms meant, while cautioning against imagining an unbridgeable chasm between them or automatically assuming that the former approach was superior.

During the eighteenth century the private lives of actresses tended to become more scandalous, with some remaining unmarried and a fair number known, or rumored, to have had liaisons with wealthy and powerful men. Scott suggests causes for this change: a much smaller proportion of the actresses came from theatrical families and/or were married to fellow performers; actresses started their careers at earlier ages, often with no adult supervision; with expenses onerous and salaries not always generous, they needed extra income. Scott examines both the professional and financial difficulties they faced (due in part to increased interference in troupe affairs by royal administrators) and the contribution they made to keeping the company afloat (their sex appeal was central to the success of plays featuring persecuted heroines and delicate ingenues). She concludes with a review of some of the sensationalized accounts of Ancien Régime actresses' lives in plays and films of the last two centuries, faulting them for underestimating the stars' intelligence and professionalism and following questionable stereotypes.

This book is a delight to read and should prove extremely useful to anyone interested in French theatre history. The one significant flaw concerns proofreading: several of the typos involving dates or proper names are embarrassing.

—**PERRY GETHNER**
Oklahoma State University

New Women Dramatists in America, 1890–1920. By Sherry D. Engle. New York: Palgrave MacMillan, 2007. x + 276 pp. $74.95 cloth.

American Women Theatre Critics: Biographies and Selected Writings of Twelve Reviewers, 1753–1919. By Alma J. Bennett. Jefferson, N.C.: McFarland, 2010. vii + 186 pp. $45.00 paper.

Both of these books illustrate the point that women's history in the theatre is still fertile ground for excavation. Roughly ending at the same historical point, 1919–20, both texts examine early American women writers who specialized in theatre. While American female playwrights are increasingly a presence in drama anthologies, many remain unknown. *New Women Dramatists in America, 1890–1920* provides a window into the lives and works of five Progressive Era female playwrights: Martha Morton, Madeleine Lucette Ryley, Evelyn Greenleaf Sutherland, Beulah Marie Dix, and Rida Johnson Young. Engle's primary contribution in this work is to demonstrate that these five women had ongoing, long-term, successful careers as playwrights.

The first playwright examined, Martha Morton (1865–1925), was quite well known in her time. Her work today, however, is largely forgotten. Morton was born in New York City into an affluent, theatrically literate family. Engel provides the plots of several Morton plays, including *His Wife's Father, A Fool for Fortune, A Bachelor's Romance* (her biggest hit), and *Her Lord and Master.* Engle closes each chapter with a bibliography of the author's work. In the chapters on Morton and Ryley she adds another primary document to each account.

Madeleine Lucette Ryley (1858–1934) enjoyed success on both sides of the Atlantic. Born in England, she later moved to the United States. In 1897, Ryley had three plays running simultaneously on Broadway, an impressive feat for any playwright. Engle's analysis of the differing receptions offered by English and American critics helps the reader place the work in a historical context. Ryley's most successful work was *Mice and Men,* a work that Engle claims foreshadows Shaw's *Pygmalion.*

One of the most interesting parts of this book is the chapter on the collaboration between Evelyn Greenleaf Sutherland (1855–1908) and Beulah Marie Dix (1876–1970). Sutherland worked as a drama critic for several Boston newspapers before she began writing plays, while Dix wrote plays and novels during her years at Radcliffe. They began their collaboration in 1901, eventually creating nearly twenty plays, most of which were historical romances or "costume" plays. *The Road to Yesterday,* featuring Minnie Dupree, was Dix and Sutherland's most successful collaboration and ran on Broadway for more than a year. This section on collaboration is a strength of the book, since little research has been done on women collaborators.

Rida Johnson Young (1875–1926) is probably the best-known playwright included in the book, most likely due to her prodigious output. Born into a respectable, middle-class family in Baltimore, Young persuaded her parents to allow her to go to New York when she turned eighteen to pursue a career in the theatre. Her most enduring comedy, *The Lottery Man,* opened at the Bijou Theatre in 1909, but it is her work with operetta composer Victor Herbert that remains her greatest legacy. Young and Herbert wrote *Naughty Marietta,* which was a critical success if not a financial one, and is still frequently revived by light opera companies throughout the country.

Engle's scholarship is thorough and appropriate. Her primary sources are the works themselves, and Engle is diligent in providing source locations. Collections of the plays, both in America and England, are conscientiously noted. She provides an appendix, "New York Plays and Musicals by Women, April 1885–June 1925," that adds to the historical context. The chapters include a comprehensive list of each playwright's works, organized chronologically. The lists at the end of each chapter include the date and length of most significant American and English productions, source material, collaborators, leading performer(s), publisher, and, if not published, where the typescript may be located.

This is a valuable book, but at several points in my reading I wished for better editing. Several typographical errors are present, the most egregious of which is the confusion regarding the renowned actress Mae West, referred to in the book as both Mae and May. But this is a minor problem. Engle's book is an important contribution to women's studies and theatre studies and reminds us that women's history still needs to be excavated and explored.

Bennett's equally slim volume, *American Women Theatre Critics: Biographies and Selected Writings of Twelve Reviewers, 1753–1919,* follows a similar thematic structure. This anthology provides a brief description of the women's lives, their working conditions, samples of their writing, and supporting analyses. Bennett covers twelve women writers, breaking them down into three major time periods: eighteenth century (Charlotte Ramsey Lennox and Judith Sargent Murray), nineteenth century (Kate Field, Olive Logan, Mildred Aldrich, Dorothy Lundt, Emma V. Sheridan, Amy Leslie, and Lucy Monroe), and twentieth century (Ada Patterson, Annie Nathan Meyer, and Dorothy Rothschild Parker). Bennett is careful to give a contextualized historical approach to each section, allowing the reader to place the women into a larger portrait of theatre and society. She makes a convincing argument that in books dealing with American critics and criticism, including Tice Miller's *Bohemians and Critics* and Moses and Brown's *The American Theatre as Seen by Its Critics, 1752–1934,* women critics before 1920 are conspicuously absent. Further, when women critics are mentioned, as in Carolyn Latta's essay "The Lady Is a Critic" (in Chinoy and Jenkins's *Women in American Theatre*), they start with Rosamund Gilder or Olive Logan. Bennett points out that one reason for this may be that women frequently did not sign their names to early criticism, preferring to hide under the anonymity of unsigned articles or to use male pseudonyms.

Essays in this book provide a critical focus that reflects a female view of the plays covered in the reviews, the social context of the theatre of the time, and a female perspective of the larger social sphere. Moreover, many of the essays offer detailed analysis of female performers. These reviews offer a fresh perspective on the acting of noted actresses, as so much acting criticism is from the male perspective. For example, Kate Field's review of Ristori's second appearance as Medea, in the *New York Tribune* on September 24, 1866, offers a fascinating comparison of the acting styles of Ristori and Rachel. This offers a different perspective through which to process theatrical experience by women. It is also very interesting to read Annie Nathan Meyer's fresh critical take on the importance of Ibsen for women.

The two earliest writers discussed—Charlotte Ramsey Lennox and Judith Sargent Murray—give additional information to a feminist reader of how difficult it was to establish a writing, much less a theatrical, career in the eighteenth century. Both women had tried to forge careers in theatre as actresses and playwrights, with varying degrees of success. Ramsey Lennox's contribution to criticism rests on her *Shakespeare Illustrated,* which offers a feminist perspective of Shakespeare's female characters. Sargent Murray's critical essays published in the *Massachusetts Magazine* under the pseudonym "Mr. Virgilius" offer a refreshingly feminist perspective on the plays of Mercy Otis Warren and Hannah Cowley.

I wish there had been a more careful editing process in Bennett's book. Bennett reproduces the many typographical errors in the primary source materials included in each section, which interferes with the reader's enjoyment of the material. It would have been helpful to have editorial corrections to these documents. However, both of these volumes offer fresh perspectives on previously overlooked American women writers.

—HELEN HUFF
City University of New York

Enacting History. Edited by Scott Magelssen and Rhona Justice-Malloy. Tuscaloosa: University of Alabama Press, 2011. 240 pp. + 10 illustrations. $19.96 e-book, $24.95 paperback.

These ten essays clearly trace "ways recent performance practices have been used to select, devise and perform narratives of the past to their participants and audiences" (1). Rather than attempting an all-inclusive collection, the editors have done well to choose a short list of contributors who deftly tease out "the contours of contemporary performance practices that bear witness to a moment or a set of moments of the past, whether actual or imagined" (3). From this approach emerges a focused, sophisticated "conversation about the *kinds* of knowledge these performances do a good job of producing, even if the jury is still out on whether the knowledge they produce is beneficial to all parties" (5).

In "Present Enacting Past: The Functions of Battle Reenacting in Historical Representation," Leigh Clemons suggests that the Battle of Coleto Creek/

Goliad Massacre reenactment and the alleged Texas history on display "are trapped together in a symbiotic relationship of progressive clarification and determination" (10) with the primary goal being commemoration rather than "authentic" re-creation. Dealing, too, with powerful sites of remembrance, Lindsay Adamson Livingston explores Mormon cultural memory and the production of space both in Palmyra, New York, and Nauvoo, Illinois. She argues that spatial or embodied performances found here work to connect tourist-spectators to a site via "echoes of events and personalities associated with the spaces" (37). Equally, "Tourist Performance in the Twenty-first Century" recounts Scott Magelssen's experience as an "illegal migrant" in Parque EcoAlberto's *Caminata Nocturna*. He asserts that by "participating bodily in tourist performances that invite visitors to take on the personae of those who have been made abject by violent or oppressive forces," tourist-performers construct embodied knowing beyond that of print sources (175). Magelssen does concede, though, that considerable slippage "is found between the meanings intended by the producing bodies" and "the bodies that perform them" (175). Taken together, these three glimpses into the complexities of constructing both public memory and communal identity—national, religious, ethnic, or otherwise—are quite absorbing.

Amy M. Tyson, Aili McGill, and Catherine Hughes offer fresh perspectives on historiographic performance. Tyson, writing as a participant-observer at Historic Fort Snelling in St. Paul, Minnesota, analyzes "quality control" practices at the site in order to get at the "hives of subtlety that surround how enacting history affects workers' subjectivities" (47). She finds that gendered "authenticity" encourages a "culture of surveillance wherein *co* workers monitored one another's behavior" both in the past and present (61). McGill's "Defining Museum Theatre at Conner Prairie" turns from institutional policing of "authenticity" to creating successful guest experiences that not only "inspire creativity and foster learning" (91) but also include "emotional engagement, artful story development, and skilled character development and interaction" not always in use with first-person interpretation events (110). Encompassing both notions of "authenticity" and affective response, Hughes uses reception study data to propose that a "sense of realness can emerge" from theatrical performance at places like the Kentucky History Center and the Museum of Science, Boston, particularly when "the spectator is invited into the play frame" (149). The ways that these authors discuss institutional approaches to enacting history point to intricate layers of connection for both workers and guests as they seek a present connection with a past community.

Richard Poole uses "History, Archive, Memory, and Performance: The Lewis and Clark Bicentennial Play as Cultural Commemoration" to remind readers that dramatizing history "offers considerable challenges, among them many possible interpretations of history" (81). Although Poole's analysis does not always offer novel findings, the way he queries his decision-making processes as writer/director/producer forms a telling case study. Patricia Ybarra also handles issues of commemoration and re-membering. Using her experience as director for . . . *And Jesus Moonwalks the Mississippi,* she contends that the production's inherent "performance of difficult history" regarding slavery (117) "produced a necessary supplement not only to dialogue but also to monuments as memorialization of slavery on the Brown campus" (128). Ybarra closes by insisting that "ambivalences of performing difficult history" (132) might open paths for productive rage "within histories and historiographies" of our slaveholding past (131). Collisions of enacted past with scripted present are at the core of "*Dinner: Impossible*—'Medieval Mayhem' at the Maryland Renaissance Festival." Here Kimberly Tony Korol-Evans unpacks what happens when, in 2007, the *Food Network* takes on sixteenth-century meal-making for reality television. Deploying the intrastice, "a place that is both here and there, now and then" (153), she concludes that the "needs and desires of these two forms of performance produce differing results with regard to the history portrayed" (172). Rhona Justice-Malloy closes the collection by recounting the process of devising and developing "Secret Histories: Oxford" with Ping Chong and Company writer/director/performer Leyla Modirzadeh. This case study of sorts bears witness to "moments remembered: private, personal moments of individual histories" (221).

Squarely situated at the intersection of American studies, popular culture, and theatre history, *Enacting History* will undoubtedly "encourage scholars and practitioners alike to think in new ways about enacting history" (9).

—SCOTT R. IRELAN
Augustana College (Illinois)

Historical Dictionary of French Theater. By Edward Forman. Lanham, Md.: Scarecrow Press, 2010. xxviii + 308 pp. $85.00 cloth.

Medieval Roles for Modern Times: Theater and the Battle for the French Republic. By Helen Solterer. University Park: Pennsylvania State University Press, 2010. xii + 287 pp. $80.00 cloth.

These two books of French theatre history—one a wide-ranging reference work and the other a close investigation of a specific endeavor and its long-term repercussions—treat both medieval and twentieth-century theatrical manifestations. Beyond coverage that includes those distinct historical eras, the two books have little in common. Yet both make important contributions to understanding a national theatre that is, as *Historical Dictionary* series editor Jon Woronoff acknowledges in his foreword, second only to the English tradition in terms of world theatre. He adds that "French theater has never been exceeded . . . in its passion" (ix).

That passion surfaces on virtually every page of Helen Solterer's *Medieval Roles for Modern Times,* both in her diligence at exploring all aspects of a little-known story and in the passions driving the major figures of that story. Gustave Cohen (1879–1958) is a name well known to scholars of French literature but, as Solterer's study demonstrates, unjustly ignored by theatre historians. Cohen's messianic devotion to staging medieval plays with student actors—the Théophiliens, a company Cohen founded and named for their first production, *Le miracle de Théophile,* by the thirteenth-century minstrel Rutebeuf—gratified audiences hungry for reaffirmation of French values and patrimony in the wake of the Great War. By the 1930s, surprisingly, the Middle Ages had become ardently contested territory for a French citizenry ideologically torn between socialism and conservatism.

Cohen had already published major books on medieval French religious drama as early as 1906. But it was as a lieutenant on the battlefield in the Great War that the Jewish, Belgian-born Cohen committed himself heart and soul to being French, through the war wounds he suffered for France and by embracing a medieval concept of patriotism bound up with religion. Not until 1943 did he go through with his long-desired conversion to Catholicism, a step delayed by various complications attending a public figure after he attained the prestigious position of chair of French medieval literature at the Sorbonne in 1932.

In founding Les théophiliens in 1933, Cohen was also partly motivated by "'la rage à faire vivant,' the passionate need to make something come alive" (23). Staging medieval dramas was a way of embodying Frenchness. In the original company, a young Syrian Jewish actor named Moussa Abadi (1908–97) played Salatin in *Le miracle de Théophile* and went on to play the devil in *Le jeu d'Adam et Eve* and Judas Iscariot in *Le mystère de la Passion.* Solterer contends that it was the role-playing that Moussa Abadi learned with the Théophiliens that enabled him to adopt the persona of Monsieur Marcel in Nice in 1942 and to save more than two hundred Jewish children from Nazi-ordered deportations. He used skills acquired under Cohen to coach the children at role-playing new personae so that they could be placed in non-Jewish homes for safety.

Medieval Roles for Modern Times is a compelling story that spans the first half of the twentieth century up to the disbanding of Les théophiliens in 1952, when the company had a track record of eleven productions and more than five hundred performances. The study is supported by forty halftone illustrations and copious documentation in footnotes that often occupy a third of the page. While the book focuses on the one amateur company, its contextual framing draws in such major figures as Nikolai Evreinov, Jacques Copeau, Charles Péguy, and Louis Jouvet. Helen Solterer has given us an important book for understanding French cultural vicissitudes in the twentieth century.

There is little overlap between Solterer's and Forman's work. Copeau and Jouvet get short entries in the *Historical Dictionary of French Theater,* as do Adam de la Halle (author of the Théophilien-produced *Jeu de Robin et Marion*), *La farce de Maître Pierre Pathelin* (the seventh play in the Théophilien repertoire), Pierre Gringoire, Les Enfants sans souci, La Basoche, Farce, Fabliau, Morality Play, and Mystery Play. The final entry incorporates three play titles, but it does not include the important author Arnoul Gréban, nor is there any entry for Miracle Play or for Jean Bodel or Bodel's *Jeu de Saint-Nicholas.*

The *Historical Dictionary* series from Scarecrow Press follows a standardized reference-book format within which various readerships may be targeted. This French theatre volume appears to serve those who might be oriented to French literature with minimal grounding in theatre, given the use of such nonstandard terms as "defamiliarization" (for alienation, distanciation, or *Verfremdungseffekt*), "multiple set" (for simultaneous setting or *décor simultané*), and the erroneous definition of *le manteau d'Harlequin* as "proscenium arch" (131), instead of the theatre term "teaser," for the border across the top and inside the proscenium opening. Indeed, the two works listed under dictionaries of terms in the bibliography should probably have been supplemented with André Bataille's *Lexique de la machinerie théâtrale,* Agnès Pierron's *Dictionnaire de la langue du théâtre,* and Joel Trapido's *International Dictionary of Theatre Language.*

There is certainly much that is fresh, interesting, and useful to researchers in Forman's *Historical Dictionary of French Theater.* The entry for Alexandrine verse provides excellent examples. The Artaud entry is strong on specifics. The complicated history of the Hôtel de Bourgogne is traced in a clear trajectory. The real names of numerous seventeenth-century actors are cross-referenced with their stage names. My reservations about this volume proceed partly from knowing how good the series can be, as may be inferred from my review of *Historical Dictionary of Russian Theater* in *Theatre History Studies* 29 (2009). Although French theatre history got a four-century head start over Russian (which did not begin until 1672), the Russian *Historical Dictionary* is li + 553 pages as opposed to only xxviii + 308 for the French. For a theatre history as rich as that of France, this is a serious limitation on the volume's usefulness. A few examples of missing names and terms are Jean Bérain, *la décentralisation* (or the Centres dramatiques created in 1947), Robert Lepage, Werewere Liking, *négritude, Les plaisirs de l'île enchantée* (or Versailles as a performance venue), Salle du Petit Bourbon, Salle des Machines, George Sand (mentioned in the Odéon entry without specifying that she was a playwright), Daniel Sorano, and *théâtre de société.* Many entries for playwrights offer a list of plays as "key works" but maddeningly often omit a major work; for example, the Jean Giraudoux entry makes no mention of either *Ondine* or *La folle de Chaillot*, and Émile Zola is dismissed as a failed playwright with no mention of his important theatre essays or his defense of Dreyfus. There is also a question of proportion when the nineteenth-century Mauritian singer and opera director Léon Carvalho gets a fifteen-line entry while Jacques Rouché gets only five lines, Henry Bernstein gets six, and Edmond Rostand gets seven.

The strengths of the *Historical Dictionary of French Theater* are the music-related entries on composers and other theatre artists who crossed over into opera, abundant allusions to and cross-referencing of seventeenth-century theorists, entries on a good selection of Paris theatres, and the incorporation of strong influences from the German and Italian theatres. The chronology begins in 1283 and culminates in highlights of Paris theatre for each year from 1998 to 2009. The forty-page bibliography includes works on francophone theatre of Canada, Africa, and the Caribbean.

—FELICIA HARDISON LONDRÉ
University of Missouri–Kansas City

Bulldaggers, Pansies, and Chocolate Babies: Performance, Race, and Sexuality in the Harlem Renaissance. By James F. Wilson. Ann Arbor: University of Michigan Press, 2010. ix + 260 pp. $49.50 cloth, $27.95 paper.

James Wilson's compelling study maps the intersection of race, identity, and sexuality (including gay and lesbian identity) in Harlem Renaissance performance using socio-historic and performance criticism to contextualize the individuals and the performances within their respective social, historical, and cultural milieu. Wilson cogently argues that depictions of race and gender in performance were "often highly ambiguous, ambivalent, and bewildering" throughout the 1920s and 1930s (3). His clear, accessible historical analysis considers interviews, newspaper accounts, and reviews to illuminate forgotten but once-popular scripts, songs, and performances of the 1920s and 1930s.

Although his justification for his selection of representative case studies is not fully articulated, Wilson finds a cohesive structure to unify his five chapters and conclusion with titles inspired from the lyrics of period jazz and blues songs. Acknowledging the era's inherent contradictions (and consciously refusing to resolve them), the author frames each chapter as an "expository snapshot" revealing the "social and professional connections between artists, audiences, and critical observers" (8).

While I largely admire the vast terrain of the study, I have a few minor quibbles regarding the book's organizational structure and its particular pairings of chapter subjects. Chapter 1 focuses on the rent parties and the gay and lesbian demimonde. Chapter 2 highlights Wallace Thurman and William Jourdan Rapp's melodrama *Harlem* (1929). Chapter 3 treats drag balls and the influential Broadway melodrama *Lulu Belle* (1926). Chapter 4 traces the careers and critical response to the subversive work of Florence Mills and Ethel Waters and their allegiance to the homosexual community. Similarly, chapter 5 turns to Gladys Bentley and follows the same model as the previous chapter. Although the author wants to draw parallels between the subjects that divide his chapters, their connections are not always clear. This reader would prefer more explicit pairings, particularly in the first two chapters. Chapter 2, for example, seems the least cohesive; its trajectory departs from the author's central vision.

Chapter 1's dual purpose investigates the rent parties of the 1920s as a "crucial site of inquiry" in the Harlem Renaissance (12) and attends to the dynamics of "public/private spaces and racial/sexual identity within the shifting political and cultural geographies" of New York (29). These topics share common ground, as the author maintains that rent parties supported an alternative network for gay men and lesbians and offered a supportive environment for performers to nurture new material. Yet the second half of this chapter shifts somewhat abruptly to focus on the gay and lesbian presence in Harlem and in performances. Wilson hits his stride providing an overview of responses to homosexuality, including the virulent homophobic accounts in the tabloid *Broadway Brevities,* which frequently named homosexuals in the industry and revealed the stomping grounds of gay men and lesbians.

Chapter 2 is concerned with the complicated tensions in representing and defining an authentic African-American identity. Wilson sets out to illustrate how *Harlem* embodied contradictory attempts to "define the 'real' Harlem" (44). The best part of this chapter provides a persuasive analysis of the work and its impact on identity and finds "not a fixed cultural identity but one that is constantly transforming" (78).

Chapter 3 is one of the book's finest contributions, focusing on the divisive melodrama *Lulu Belle* by Edward Sheldon and Charles MacArthur, which indirectly galvanized the queer community. Wilson focuses on how the production sparked great controversy in its day and marshaled both support and criticism from the African-American community for its illustration of race and sexuality. Although Wilson's connections linking *Lulu Belle* with the drag balls are at times somewhat forced, his readings of *Lulu Belle* and the annual masquerade competitions are provocative and rich. He persuasively writes of Harlem's drag balls as providing a safe space for homoerotic desire and enabling "social commingling" of different classes and races (86). Moreover, as Wilson makes clear, these masquerades provided sanctioned opportunities for same-sex attraction and interracial socializing during a time when Harlem's notorious nightspots were segregated.

Despite a lack of critical evidence on how members of the gay community would have read and reviewed *Lulu Belle,* Wilson's deft analysis invokes significant critical response from black periodicals and the white press. Wilson contends that the play was a touchstone for the community because of Lulu Belle's transgressions against propriety, race, and class; she threatened Harlem's dominant institutions: the church and the family (98). His interesting argument suggests a link between "visible homosexuals and the lascivious black women such as Lula Belle . . . because of their 'moral depravity'" (97–98). He also proposes that "Lula Belle's parodic appeal to the drag subculture stemmed from her defiance in the face of attempts to conform to her religious and social expectations" (111).

In chapter 4, Wilson notes how renowned performers Florence Mills and Ethel Waters were embraced by racially mixed audiences and "exposed the contradictory yet intertwined elements of blackness and whiteness" in their revues, developing a culturally "pluralist art form" (116). Wilson argues that while Mills's performances illustrated the tensions between savagery and civilization and primitivism and modernism, Waters distanced herself from stereotypes and images even as she pushed the boundaries of eroticism and sexuality with her double entendres and suggestive movement. Both women, to use Henry Louis Gates's term, signified on minstrelsy and deeply entrenched stereotypes.

Chapter 5 charts the career of singer/entertainer Gladys Bentley, but it does not deliver the same deep analysis and description of the previous chapters. This chapter largely consists of biographical material and critical response. Wilson notes that the negative criticism leveled at Bentley's vulgarity, immorality, and sexual preference reflected the era's social tensions and discomfort with homosexuality. As attitudes grew even more conservative in the 1940s and 1950s, Bentley attempted to domesticate herself and toned down her butch lesbian image.

Wilson's well-researched, strongly articulated critical study charts new ground and is an excellent addition for scholars of American theatre, African-American theatre, and queer studies. *Bulldaggers, Pansies, and Chocolate Babies* offers a vital contribution to the field.

—ADRIENNE MACKI BRACONI
University of Connecticut

To Broadway, To Life! The Musical Theater of Bock and Harnick. By Philip Lambert. New York: Oxford University Press, 2011. pp. xvi + 361. $35.00 cloth.

The Broadway songwriting team of composer Jerry Bock and lyricist Sheldon Harnick has rightfully earned its place in the pantheon of the American musical. Collaborating between the transitional years of 1957 and 1970, this team wrote seven Broadway shows, the most successful of which, *Fiddler on the Roof*, is one of the most beloved and most frequently revived in the musical canon. The seven shows they created (in collaboration with many other Broadway masters too numerous to name) run the gamut from the virtually forgotten *The Body Beautiful* (1958) to the Pulitzer Prize–winning *Fiorello!* (1959) and the cult classics *Tenderloin* (1960), *She Loves Me* (1963), and *The Apple Tree* (1966) to the disappointing *The Rothschilds* (1970) as well as the career-defining *Fiddler on the Roof* (1964). Their shows garnered seventeen Tony Awards and inductions into the Theater and Songwriters Halls of Fame, as well as honorary degrees, awards, and productions from around the world.

Their collaborative years on the Broadway stage fell directly within the transition from the Rodgers and Hammerstein era to the concept and rock musicals of the late 1960s and 1970s. Philip Lambert's *To Broadway, To Life!* demonstrates how the evolution of this creative duo parallels the seismic shifts happening on the Broadway stage and in U.S. society at large during this time. As Lambert observes, "Bock and Harnick stand right on the bridge between the old and the new: their second show and first big success, *Fiorello!,* shared a Best Musical Tony Award with *The Sound of Music,* and their last major effort, *The Rothschilds,* opened on Broadway the same year as Stephen Sondheim's innovative *Company*" (xii). With close readings of each work from the collaborators' oeuvre, this first full-length monograph dedicated to the work of Bock and Harnick is a fascinating study not only of the subjects but also of the reception of their works and their contributions to the evolution of the American musical.

The book is not a biography in the traditional sense, but rather a scholarly approach to the subjects' collaborative life together. The first two chapters provide parallel biographies of each artist's early life with appreciatively more attention paid to their artistic development than to their personal lives and relationships. These chapters give a picture-postcard view of a bygone era when adult summer camps in the Catskills provided theatrical training for up-and-coming artists and when television variety shows were nurturing future musical and theatrical talent. The intersection with other rising stars at this time, such as Chita Rivera, Charlotte Rae, and Beatrice Arthur, make for entertaining and informative reading about Broadway's so-called Golden Era.

Each succeeding chapter focuses on a different Bock and Harnick musical in chronological order with a comprehensive, if sometimes formulaic methodology: genesis, collaborative creation, musicological and dramaturgical analysis, production process, reception, and revivals or further productions. Through these close readings, Lambert illuminates Bock and Harnick's unique style, providing further evidence as to why their creations are significant contributions to the musical canon. To Lambert, Bock's compositions "demonstrate a particular flair for tailoring musical style to dramatic setting," which helps to explain why virtually all of their musicals cross countries, time, and culture from 1890s New York to an Eastern European parfumerie to a Russian shtetl (35). Likewise, Lambert characterizes Harnick's lyrics as "razor sharp, all-too-relevant social commentary" inviting obvious comparisons with Yip Harburg and Harold Rome (27).

In addition to his consideration of their Broadway musicals, Lambert also gives sufficient attention to other, less-defining works, such as songs written for revues, film and commercial work, the made-for-television *The Canterville Ghost* (1966), and even a one-act puppet show (1963). What emerges from each of these descriptions is Bock and Harnick's indefatigable striving for experimentation and innovation. Although Lambert describes *Fiddler on the Roof* as a work "mark[ing] the end of a storied period in the evolution of the Broadway musical," he fails to acknowledge how this work breaks with convention as much as reifies it (180). Likewise, he alternately praises Bock and Harnick's "customary standards for Broadway-style melodic grace and lyric eloquence" while critiquing their overly sentimental portrayals (93). Although this approach delivers a fairly balanced estimation of the team's musical contributions, it somewhat undermines their innovation and commitment to risk. The political-mindedness of *Fiorello!*, the social commentary of *Tenderloin*, and the formalistic innovation of three musicals comprising the plot of *The Apple Tree* are testament to their experimental spirit. Lambert's critique may be attributable to his specialization in musicology, which may have led him to overlook theatrical merit.

The book is an important addition to musical theatre scholarship, not only because of the significance of the subjects but also because Lambert details the collaborative process between the two, allowing the challenges and personality conflicts their due place but generally honoring the difficulties of collaborating within the Broadway system. This book is especially useful for musicologists, with pages of detailed descriptions and analysis of Bock's musical motives and inventions, although for non-musicians this analysis can become tiring. The work is equally impressive and useful dramaturgically, citing additions and changes to shows as they moved from creation to rehearsal to tryout to Broadway, delineated by clear outlines. The analysis of each show also includes some brief history regarding further productions beyond the initial Broadway run, which is rare for musical theatre chronicles.

The final chapter of the book explores the dissolution of Bock and Harnick's creative relationship without providing a definitive reason why they eventually stopped working together. One might assume that the pressure from the success of *Fiddler*, along with Harnick's desire to work in opera and other genres, created the final rupture, although this is not explicitly stated in the text. The book concludes with a synopsis of the artists' work since the split. Perhaps Lambert's conclusion regarding *The Apple Tree* is the best summarization of Bock and Harnick's legacy: "sometime in the 1960s . . . the musical, like the American society it was designed to entertain, lost its innocence" (212). The work of Bock and Harnick "stands at the crux of this shift, on the one hand reaping the fruits of the Garden, on the other confronting the daunting complexities of fame and happiness" (212).

—CHRIS M. MCCOY
University of California, Davis

The Universe of Oz: Essays on Baum's Series and Its Progeny. Edited by Kevin K. Durand and Mary K. Leigh. Jefferson, N.C.: McFarland, 2010. vi + 252 pp. $35.00 paper.

This book focuses on the progeny of Baum's series—four of its seventeen essays discuss the 1939 Hollywood film, two *The Wiz,* one Gregory Maguire's *A Lion among Men* (a sequel to his *Wicked*), one the musical made from *Wicked,* one Tina Landau's gay-themed play *1969,* one a hypertext called "Patchwork Girl," and two a television miniseries called *Tin Man;* only three essays discuss *The Wizard of Oz,* and one Baum's whole Oz series. In the introductory essay, Durand argues that the 1939 film should take primacy over Baum's book because most people who come to Oz come via the film, and many never go beyond it to Baum's books. Moreover, it is the film that inspired *The Wiz, Wicked,* and other spin-offs. He elaborately establishes a canon of the "Oz-verse" (12), using an analogy with establishing the canon of the Christian Bible, and concludes that "the movie *is* the first piece of the Baum Oz canon"(19). I question, however, whether its being more generally known makes the film a more significant achievement than the book; for as clever and engaging as the film is, to my mind it cheapens Baum's creation.

Agnes B. Curry and Josef Velazquez compare *The Wizard of Oz* to a traditional fairy tale, "Cinderella." They point out that both stories feature a good and a bad mother figure but that Dorothy, unlike Cinderella, must fend for herself without a prince to rescue her. The reason would seem to be obvious: a child does not require a mate, and, being a particularly capable, self-reliant little girl, Dorothy sets out to solve her own problems rather than waiting for someone to rescue her. Baum pointedly replaced the standard passive fairy-tale heroine with a female who did not have to be validated by a man. Hence the authors' labored explanations and far-fetched comparisons are not needed to explain the absence of a prince in *The Wizard of Oz.* Although this absence might be more significant with regard to the pubescent Dorothy of the film, which is the authors' primary concern, even the film presents Dorothy as a child. Charity Gibson argues that *The Wizard of Oz* is a modernist work because it reflects Baum's time—but doesn't every author's work reflect his or her time?

Randall Auxier raises a very interesting question at the beginning of his essay: Why is it that the Oz world is constantly reimagined, often in versions radically divergent from Baum's original? Many essays in this book discuss writers who were sufficiently intrigued by Baum's work to create Oz stories, yet they radically changed his characters, values, atmosphere, and meaning. What inspired Maguire to transform Oz into a land of guilt and repression, where the Witch of the West is sympathetic because she is rebelling against an unjust order? I would like to know, but Auxier does not enlighten me. Instead of answering his question, he describes the elaborate intellectual constructs of Maguire's third Oz book, *A Lion among Men,* without showing how it relates to Baum's work.

The authors, many of them philosophers, tend to bring in heavy philosophical arguments to elucidate the commonsense points made by Baum or the 1939 filmmakers. Gail Linsenbard enlists St. Augustine, Sartre, and de Beauvoir to ground the plain, wholesome lesson of *The Wizard of Oz:* that Dorothy and her companions succeed by banding together in friendship, with each friend generously making up for the weaknesses of the others. Durand brings in Kant to indict the Wizard for deceptiveness and unscrupulous schemes to save his position rather than recognizing that he is presented with indulgent humor in both book and film as a harmless con man just trying to save his skin.

"While researching feminist perspectives of *The Wonderful Wizard of Oz,* it became painfully clear" to Paula Kent that "not much has been written specifically about L. Frank Baum's Dorothy Gale from a feminist standpoint" (179). This is a peculiar observation, considering that several critics, including me, have demonstrated Baum's strong feminism. Ignoring the powerful evidence of feminism in the book, Kent resorts to a less pertinent and forceful strategy: painstakingly matching Dorothy's journey to the pattern described by Joseph Campbell in *The Hero with a Thousand Faces.* It does not help that she calls Dorothy a heroine when *hero* would be the appropriate term in this context.

Kevin Tanner has at least read a reasonable amount of Baum scholarship, although not precisely: I did not say that Maud Baum possibly believed that her niece Dorothy "was the reincarnation of her recently departed mother," nor would I (211 and note 22). He goes on to find an elaborate religious allegory in *The Wizard of Oz,* with Dorothy as a little Eve type and her three companions representing different aspects of Christ; for example, in Denslow's illustration, the Scarecrow on his pole looks like Christ on the cross, and Dorothy takes him down on the third day after his creation, as Christ rose from the dead on the third day (212).

Jason M. and Jessica Bell sensibly outline Baum's persistent concern for emancipation throughout the Oz series. The Wicked Witch of the East, slaveholder of the Munchkins, is crushed by Dorothy's house; and Dorothy goes on to free the Scarecrow from his pole, the Tin Woodman from his rusted immobility, and the Winkies from the Witch of the West. They trace this theme through the entire series, describing, for example, the emancipation of the Patchwork Girl, who was made to be a humble servant. Less convincingly, they relate these elements in the Oz books to the emancipation of American black slaves during Baum's childhood and his general belief in the evils of racism. Actually, Baum did write a hilarious satire of racism; but it was in a non-Oz fantasy, *Sky Island*.

It is disturbing to find, in a collection written by teachers of the humanities, so many examples of awkward, ponderous style and imprecise choice of words. The latter include "the *demise* of the Wizard" (meaning his exposure or embarrassment) (Kent, 185), "teaches him *of* his worth" and Friedan's *Feminist Mystique* (Williams, 194, 197), "Asian religions . . . that appealed to *intellects*, reformers . . ." (Tanner, 216), "the social *contexture* of Baum's youth" and "such characters *like* Johnny Dooit" (Bell 225, 228), restrictive nineteenth-century ideologies that "were only beginning to be *absolved*," Baum's narrative that "elucidates the United States *downfalls* by creating Oz as superior," and "Dorothy's *loyalty* to remain home" (Gibson, 112, 116).

—KATHARINE M. ROGERS
City University of New York (Emerita)

Enacting Others: Politics of Identity in Eleanor Antin, Nikki S. Lee, Adrian Piper, and Anna Deavere Smith. By Cherise Smith. Durham, N.C.: Duke University Press, 2011. ix + 307 pp. $89.95 cloth, $24.95 paper.

Art historian Cherise Smith offers a close reading of four contemporary artists whose works occupy seminal moments in the historicization of the politics of identity. Smith examines how Eleanor Antin, Nikki S. Lee, Adrian Piper, and Anna Deavere Smith occupy "liminal spaces," or moments in which their dual identities as "self" and "other" are simultaneously present in their art. While such factors as age, gender, class, politics, and sexuality inform her analysis, Smith is principally interested in how these artists manipulate their corporeal presences through such visual signs as passing, minstrelsy, cross-dressing, and drag in an effort to slip between boundaries of race and ethnicity. Considering how power dynamics between artist and audience are complexly negotiated, Smith points to Antin's, Lee's, Piper's, and Deavere Smith's art as evidence of work that occasionally reinforces identity as a "fixed" and "stable" concept but also productively illuminates the "arbitrariness, constructedness, and fluidity of identity and identifications" (10).

Smith's study begins with Adrian Piper's *Mythic Being* project, in which Piper performed a fictionalized male persona, the "Mythic Being," from 1973 to 1975. Smith situates Piper's work within the liberation movements that followed the black freedom struggle of the late 1950s and 1960s. In this context, Piper's work straddles communal identification, which these liberation movements promoted, and individual identity. Donning an afro, facial hair, and sunglasses, and often seen smoking a cigar, the Mythic Being personified stereotypes of black masculinity and challenged his audience to confront their feelings of hate and fear. In one incarnation of the project titled "The Mythic Being: Getting Back" (1975), Piper staged an assault by the Mythic Being on a white man. Captured in a series of photographs, the visual images reveal Piper's dual identities of "other" (the Mythic Being) and "self" (the artist). Indeed, Smith interprets Piper's simultaneous presence of "self" and "other" throughout the *Mythic Being* project as evidence of an artist who "can use the politics of identity to her advantage by assuming the authority to make art and identity" (77).

Eleanor Antin's *Antinova* project of the late 1970s dabbled in feminist art traditions of the 1970s, often described as "essentialist and biological-determinist," as well as the "theory-oriented and intellectually heady art" of the 1980s (83). In October 1981, Antin assumed and lived the persona of Eleanora Antinova, the Russian ballerina, by darkening her fair skin so as to appear black, wearing stereotypically feminine apparel and makeup, attending art gallery showings, and displaying fake production photographs of Antinova in a public museum. Antin's utilization of the politics of identity is most clearly articulated in *Being Antinova,* a published collection of the project's photographs and the artist's self-narrative. Antin acknowledges exploiting stereotypes of blackness, whiteness, Jewishness, and femininity as a means of demonstrating how identity is "open to manipulation" (109). This "openness" divided critics, Smith notes, who debated whether Antin embraced or rejected her own Jewishness, and how, if at all, her work linked Jews and blacks historically. Smith maintains that by constructing herself as "doubly 'other,'" enacting both the "ultrafeminine ethereality associated with white womanhood" and the "power, sensuousness, and glamour . . . of the black woman" (132), Antin was able to challenge racial, ethnic, and gender stereotypes, assert her own Jewish identity, and reinforce the historic link between blackness and "otherness."

Turning to the 1990s and the demise of "multiculturalism" in American culture and the art world, Smith studies the 2000 film *Twilight: Los Angeles* and the problematic ways in which Anna Deavere Smith inserts "self" into representations of "others." Based on her 1992 one-woman stage play in which Deavere Smith performed excerpts of interviews she conducted with individuals of divergent races, ethnicities, and classes in the wake of the Rodney King verdict and subsequent riots, the artist's presence is decidedly more pronounced in the film. On film, Deavere Smith plays not only an actor playing "others," as she did onstage, but also plays "herself" as an interviewer, outsider, and culture-crossing, peacemaking arbiter. By virtue of its communal ethos, *Twilight* feels "democratic" insofar as multiple points of view, especially those of the traditionally marginalized, are given equal voice. Yet the presence of Deavere Smith's "self," particularly in the film's overtly documentary moments, serves as a jarring reminder of how much control the artist exerts on the form, content, and reception of the work. Moreover, her representation of "others" often reinforces stereotypes, which in turn promulgates the notion of identity as being stable and fixed. Deavere Smith nevertheless creates a liminal space for viewers, regardless of their race, ethnicity, and gender, to cross boundaries and stand in for her. In this way, she creates what Smith calls a "postidentity environment" where texts are "open to radically different interpretations wherein difference matters, or it doesn't" (188).

An examination of Nikki S. Lee's 1997–2001 series, *Projects,* concludes Smith's study. For *Projects,* the Korean-born Lee ingratiated herself with various subcultures "that present complexly intersected identifications" (207) by changing her appearance and engaging in their everyday activities. These groups included exotic dancers, Wall Street yuppies, lesbians, tourists, drag queens, and skateboarders, to name a few. Lee spent considerable time getting to know members of various groups before having photographs of herself taken among them. Embodying seemingly appropriate authentic physical traits and attitudes, Lee is both subject and object in the photographs. Like Deavere Smith, she flexes her autonomy and challenges her subjects' agency by determining such factors as how the artist herself appears in the photos, when and where the photos are taken, which photos are suitable for exhibition, and how the depicted cultures will be perceived (215). Smith argues that the intimacy of the photos, which evoke documentary traditions, and Lee's repeated "same but changing" presence throughout the series demonstrate "a centeredness on self that values individual identity over communal identity" (227). In this sense, *Projects* has as much to do with the politics of identity as it does with "the slippery ambivalence that defines racialization and identity-making in the United States" (231).

Enacting Others is a worthwhile, boundary-crossing endeavor in its own right. By merging art history, politics, critical theory, and diverse modes of artistic creation and expression, Smith offers a stimulating reflection on issues of identity: how it is formed and negotiated, its arbitrariness, and its constructedness. A focus on audience rightly permeates the book, as reception of the artists' work reveals as much about the period in which it occurred as it does about the present day, which Smith regards as being cloaked in "the rhetoric of post-identity and colorblindness . . . [that] seeks to erase difference" (24). Her well-researched investigation of artistic liminality and "the friction that often exists between individual and group identity, between personal agency and community empowerment, and between the private and the public spheres" (17) proves that discourses surrounding the politics of identity have been, are currently, and will continue to be as slippery and constantly shifting as her astute analysis of Antin, Lee, Piper, and Deavere Smith persuasively suggests.

—MARK SEAMON
Denison University

Shakesqueer: A Queer Companion to the Complete Works of Shakespeare. Edited by Madhavi Menon. Durham, N.C.: Duke University Press, 2011. 512 pp. + 18 illustrations. $99.95 cloth, $27.95 paper.

Madhavi Menon has edited a new collection of essays, *Shakesqueer: A Queer Companion to the Complete Works of Shakespeare,* which will prove a valuable resource for theatre historians, scholars, artists, and pedagogues. This assortment of forty-eight short essays puts queer theorists in conversation with all the extant (and a few lost) Shakespearean works. Exhaustive in scope, theoretically expansive, and critically provocative, this ambitious project explores "what is odd, eccentric, and unexpected in the canonical Shakespeare" (24). Given Menon's previous books—*Wanton Words: Rhetoric and Sexuality in English Renaissance Drama* (2004) and *Unhistorical Shakespeare: Queer Theory in Shakespearean Literature and Film* (2008)—the union of Shakespeare and queer theory in this volume does not surprise, and, as she explains in the general introduction, this collection challenges two notions: "the idea that queerness has a historical start date" and "that queerness is a synonym for embodied homosexuality" (2). Menon argues that queer theory has centered on texts composed after 1800—about the same time that sexual identity began to be named, codified, pathologized, and criminalized. In releasing her subject from the boundaries of time and sexual identity that she associates with customary queer scholarship, Menon hopes simultaneously to shake up queer theory and to queer Shakespeare. To this end, this collection focuses on three areas of common interest for Shakespeare scholars and queer theorists—language, identity, and temporality—which are destabilized, unsettled, and challenged by the essays in *Shakesqueer.* While calling for the expansion of queerness beyond erotic desire and difference does not preclude homoerotic possibility from queer pleasure (especially as evinced in many of essays in this collection, which link queerness and erotic identity), this collection follows in the critical footsteps of Lauren Berlant, Jill Dolan, David Savran, Michael Warner, and others by theorizing a more capacious idea of queerness: as oddity, non-normative, stranger, other.

The forty-eight pieces in the collection consider the entire corpus of Shakespeare's works (including the apocryphal *Cardenio* and *Love's Labour's Won*). Menon's impressive list of contributors includes luminaries of queer cultural, literary, and performance studies, foundational figures in queer Shakespeare studies, and scholars from the important second wave of queer early modern studies; in addition to the heavy hitters, Menon generously includes a significant number of papers by up-and-coming scholars. This balance of well-known and newer voices, taken alongside the predominance of non-Shakespearean queer scholars writing about Shakespeare's works, results in a collection that will appeal to readers interested in Shakespeare and sexuality studies, including theatre educators, artists, and scholars.

Shakesqueer is organized alphabetically by text title, allowing for easy access to whichever play or poem a reader desires to queer. Although the hefty number of essays makes it imprudent to recount each individual contribution, as a whole they are insightful, range from six to ten pages, and reflect wide-ranging critical approaches. Julie Crawford, for example, carefully contests marriage's implicit heterosexuality in *All's Well That Ends Well,* whereas Jeffrey Masten offers a playful reading of *Sir Thomas More* that features multiple, oftentimes incongruous, appraisals of historical bodies in performance. Steven Bruhm identifies the king's body in *All Is True (King Henry VIII)* as a "bear" ("those chubby, bearded, and hirsute gay men who constitute a significant modern subculture"), while Lynne Huffer rejects queer subjectivity via Foucault's concept of madness in *The Comedy or Errors* (28). Andrew Nicholls presents a series of drawings for *Venus and Adonis* which "take queer pleasure in the failure of heterosexual desire," while Heather Love interprets maternal ambivalence in *Macbeth* as both asynchronous and queer (415). Julian Yates reorients/disorients readers of the sonnets à la Ridley Scott's *Blade Runner,* Laurie Shannon combines the orthodoxy of Richard Hooker and close reading to queer "the cosmos" in *King Lear,* and Sharon Holland seeks lesbian desire in (and around) the Globe Theatre's all-male *Twelfth Night* (Tim Carroll, 2002). Alan Sinfield models a "queer reading position," or the active acknowledgment of "those textual cues that make sense in a queer context" in *Troilus and Cressida* (377). Kathryn Schwarz "traces a queer process [always] already at work" in *King John*, utilizing "theories of performativity and historiography . . . as parallel articulations" (164). Richard Rambus explores queerness as an expression of cross-species eroticism in *A Midsummer Night's Dream*. You get the point—and these examples only scratch the surface.

The one drawback for readers of *Theatre History Studies* might be the scarcity of essays actively engaged with performance. Because the intended audience is likely more literary than theatrical, this oversight is understandable; however, in addition to making this collection more useful for theatre educators, practitioners, and historians, performance could also assist Menon's proposal for reorienting queer theory. The conception of Shakespeare's ability to cut transversally, disturbing language, temporality, and identity, is commonly applied by theatre practitioners (more so than by literary critics). Shakespeare's plays in performance have proved exceptionally adept at simultaneously occupying multiple planes—stage productions notwithstanding, recent well-known film adaptations include *As You Like It* set in nineteenth-century Japan, a millennial high school version of *Othello*, and *The Tempest* with a female Prospero. In these and countless other examples, "Shakespeare" exists as a vestige of the historical past, performed in the present, frequently staged in period-specific way, with little regard for period-specific identities.

Additionally, the inclusion of more theatre history and performance would augment Menon's claims about Shakespeare and queerness in collaboration. I am thinking of Stefan Brecht's famous nomination of the off-off-Broadway theatre scene in the late 1960s and 1970s as "Queer Theatre," a movement that was similarly invested in sexual, political, and countercultural upheaval, and for whom Shakespeare was important, especially in the work of Jack Smith, Charles Ludlam, and John Vaccaro. Additionally, Shakespeare's plays are being presented more often in ways that support a queer conceptualization, including Neil Bartlett's work for the Royal Shakespeare Company, Rebecca Patterson's all-female productions for The Queen's Company, and almost anything by Declan Donnelan and Nick Ormerod's touring company Cheek by Jowl.

These observations are not meant to detract from the accomplishments of this collection, however. *Shakesqueer* will undoubtedly become required reading for researchers interested in the amalgamation of queer theory and Shakespeare, and it should be useful for teaching drama, theatre history, or critical theory.

—CHAD ALLEN THOMAS
The University of Alabama in Huntsville

The Theatre of Empire: Frontier Performances in America, 1750–1860. By Douglas S. Harvey. London: Pickering and Chatto, 2010. 235 pp. $99.00 cloth.

In *The Theatre of Empire: Frontier Performances in America, 1750–1860,* Douglas S. Harvey explores the ways that "frontier performance" conditioned audiences and established assumptions that ultimately served to "perpetuate, or resist, imperial expansion" (1). He argues that the "theatre of empire" was intrinsically bound up with the systematic subjugation and destruction of various "others" and that such abuses became "institutionalized" through disingenuous theatrical characterizations and their role in "sugar-coating the crimes and abuses" of an expanding empire (19). Despite the title, this is not Harvey's only project, and his introduction announces that he will contrast the theatre of empire with ceremonies of the "indigenous peoples," exploring "the entire spectrum of performance from indigenous rituals to colonial and national theatre on and near the cultural frontier of the British and Euro-American expansion" (4). *Theatre of Empire* is nothing if not ambitious, and several of his proposed topics—such as examining the transformation from one of his categories to the other—have the potential to contribute significantly to scholars' understanding of performance culture(s) in the periods he treats. Harvey's study pursues breadth over depth, however, and his evidence and methodology limit the value of *Theatre of Empire* for theatre scholars.

Harvey's analytical frame is crucial to understanding the selection and treatment of the material he presents. Building on recent work blending theories of embodiment with cognitive studies, Harvey argues that the key distinction between these types of performance and their functions inheres in the environments that shaped each. In indigenous performances "the entire cultural milieu of the performances are [*sic*] embedded in the environment of the participating bodies," whereas, for the theatre of empire, "the environment is notably absent or limited to the immediate spatial dimension that locates the performance" (8). Harvey believes that indigenous performances are structured around cultivating *relationships,* both between individuals and between the community and the natural environment; the theatre of empire, however, is concerned with *transaction* and *commodification* and alienates individuals by forcing them to interact through the lifeless medium of capital. He also draws on Bruce McConachie's usage of "simulation theory," a methodology Harvey defines as "the reasonable and intellectually honest projection of the historian's experienced judgement into past situations to overcome the limitations of objectivism and relativism"

(9). What Harvey projects is a deep compassion for the Native Americans who were displaced and eventually destroyed and a repugnance for the agents of empire and their actions, both of which inform an argument that proceeds empathetically rather than empirically.

Harvey's six main chapters traverse the titular period in roughly chronological fashion, alternating between play analysis, glosses of historical context, and descriptions of indigenous performances. In addition to plays, the "theatre" of Harvey's title includes graduation orations/recitations, popular songs, imperial spectacles, mobs, tavern brawls, circuses, dancing exhibitions, and minstrelsy. Throughout the first three chapters, he juxtaposes examples of indigenous rituals/ceremonies with "colonial" theatre (a term he prefers because it implies that the dynamics of colonial domination did not end with the Revolutionary War). He devotes considerable attention to describing indigenous performances such as the "Edge of the Woods" and "Condolence" ceremonies, which mediated contact between the Native Americans and the colonizing forces. Particular emphasis is given to Condolence ceremonies that coincided with treaty negotiations, what he calls "intercultural performed negotiations." These intriguing encounters—in which fundamentally different worldviews, languages, performance traditions, and agendas collide in the context of performance—are one of the few examples in the book that speak to the transformation from "indigenous" to "colonial," though Harvey privileges description over analysis.

The second half of *Theatre of Empire* features little discussion of indigenous performance, focusing instead on the circus, minstrelsy, and melodrama. While eighteenth-century "colonial" theatre had made explicit appeals to imperial/nationalist sentiments, "empire" in the nineteenth century employed a more subtle process of appropriation and denigration. Blackface performance, for example, initially a "screen for calling into question the social order, politics and general assumptions of the day," was soon co-opted and codified into a form that fomented racial prejudice and defended slavery, as did the numerous proslavery adaptations of *Uncle Tom's Cabin* (152). Harvey also argues that popular reform melodramas relied on a "formula that combined folktale with the bourgeois goal of worker productivity" and were part of a general effort to inculcate virtue, or at least eliminate economically unproductive behaviors in a working-class audience (168). Harvey concludes by hearkening back to his introduction, where he calls for a restoration of humanity's connection with and awareness of the natural world, and warns that "the dangers of imperial hubris are catching up with us" (178).

The utility of defining a spectrum that encompasses such profoundly different cultures and historical periods is questionable. Harvey retraces well-worn paths in American theatre history, covering familiar plays and genres, and—despite his appreciation for embodiment and the importance of lived experience—frequently chooses textual analysis over an exploration of the dynamics of theatrical reception. And, while he suggests his study is "embedded in the discourse of ritual and theatre performance," his use of performance theory tends to focus primarily on Victor Turner (4). Perhaps most problematic is Harvey's lack of objectivity, although it is a methodological choice rather than an unconscious bias. Those who share his appreciation for the indigenous worldview and echo his denunciation of all things imperial may welcome the straightforward binary he presents, although by focusing on this contrast he misses opportunities to nuance his argument.

While doing so is understandable in the context of indigenous performance in largely oral cultures, Harvey relies heavily on secondary literature and chooses not to interrogate many of the primary sources he does include. *Theatre of Empire* would also have benefited from more diligent editing, as there are numerous missing words, incorrect premiere dates and play titles, and misspelled character and author names. While this study may not fully realize Harvey's proposed project, it certainly suggests the potential of such a comparative analysis.

—AARON M. TOBIASON
University of Maryland, College Park

Rival Queens: Actresses, Performance, and the Eighteenth-Century British Theater. By Felicity Nussbaum. Philadelphia: University of Philadelphia Press, 2010. 383 pp. $55.00 cloth.

Over the last twenty years the subject of female performance and the figure of the actress have moved to the scholarly mainstream, symbolized by the publication in 2007 of *The Cambridge Companion to the Actress.* Earlier foundational works such as Elizabeth Howe's *The First English Actresses: Women and Drama, 1660–1700* (1992) are now complemented by deeply researched biographies like Claire Tomalin's absorbing, poignant *Mrs Jordan's Profession* (1994) and by studies that address both historical and modern female entertainers, as does Kirsten Pullen's *Actresses and Whores: On Stage and in Society* (2005). In *Rival Queens,* Felicity Nussbaum provocatively challenges the traditional view of the eighteenth-century British stage as the age of the actor-manager by claiming this period as "the age of *women* in the theater and especially the age of the *actress*" (6).

Nussbaum is highly regarded as a feminist scholar of the "long eighteenth century." The essays she coedited with Laura Brown in *The New Eighteenth Century* (1987) encouraged a shift toward a more theoretically informed historicism in the field, and her monographs reflect that broadening of critical scope, most recently in *The Limits of the Human: Fictions of Anomaly, Race, and Gender in the Long Eighteenth Century* (2003). *Rival Queens* is equally bold in its approach to theatre history as Nussbaum "seek[s] to enliven its empirical bent and step outside its strictures to make larger claims" (10). The volume is physically magnificent, its nine chapters interspersed with contemporary illustrations, chiefly of the eminent actresses who form its subject. Two of these images, engravings of Miss Younge in the character of Artemisia from Nicholas Rowe's *The Ambitious Step-Mother* and Mrs. Yates in the character of Calista from Rowe's *The Fair Penitent,* are juxtaposed to form an arresting pas de deux of divas on the dust jacket. The image of histrionic rivalry forms a touchstone to Nussbaum's study, which posits performing women as fearless actors in a competitive economy: "rivals to each other, as well as to managers and other actors, and also to prevailing ideas about women" (26).

One of the book's most emphatic claims is that "celebrity actresses advanced women's emergence as modern subjects who possessed new consciousness of their ability to determine their identities and reflect upon them" (12). The extended historical reach of the study, which stretches from Nell Gwyn to Sarah Siddons while focusing on the period 1700–1780, allows Nussbaum to point up the increasing artistic autonomy and economic agency exercised by actresses of the second and third generations. It is striking that of the three "star actresses" treated as case studies—Catherine Clive, Margaret Woffington, and Frances Abington—Clive and Abington separated early from their husbands, while Woffington enjoyed many affairs but remained single. Added to the often anomalous marital status of such women, the salaries they achieved at the peaks of their careers exceeded those earned by many male and most female writers, as well as the incomes of a merchant, an army officer, or a gentleman. Anne Oldfield's annual income rose from £106 at the Haymarket in 1706 to well over £500 for the 1728–29 season, while in 1752, Peg Woffington reaped an astonishing £800 at Smock Alley Theatre, more than any of her fellow male actors. The best actresses became "tough negotiators" in the professional arena, not simply on their own behalf. The redoubtable Kitty Clive, described by actor-manager Tate Wilkinson as "a mixture of combustibles" (153), campaigned in print for improved working conditions for all actors following a dispute with Drury Lane manager Charles Fleetwood in 1743.

Clive's forays into print show her manipulating her celebrity status in order to secure rights for actors as legitimate professionals, as well as defending what Nussbaum terms her "performative property" (152), most especially the parts in which she had achieved most success. Throughout *Rival Queens,* Nussbaum highlights the inaugural status of celebrity within an emergent public sphere, coinciding with the explosion of print and a growth in the market for biography and sexual scandal. Linked with the notion of outstanding actresses as celebrities is Nussbaum's representation of these women not merely as theatrical performers but as "living subjects poised at stage's edge" (21). Comediennes such as Clive and Woffington excelled in delivering epilogues directly to the audience, often *in propria persona.* Nussbaum argues further that the eighteenth-century actress's allure hinged on the public exposure of a feminine personality, synchronized with dramatic character but fed also by male and female spectators' fantasies of intimacy with a woman performer. Resembling, but crucially differing from, the illusion of selfhood we associate with the eighteenth-century novel, the resulting "interiority effect" (19) was perceived by shrewd actresses as a commodity they could trade and trade upon with their audiences.

One of the most interesting chapters of Nussbaum's study examines the performance history of Nathaniel Lee's heroic tragedy *The Rival Queens,* from its Restoration debut in 1677 through revivals and adaptations up until 1795, including Colley Cibber's *The Rival Queans* (1710), performed by men in drag. Nussbaum shows how "down-and-dirty combat scenes between actresses" (73) such as those featured in *The Rival Queens* were crucial to the ongoing stage life of this and other heroic tragedies, and she suggests that the anachronistic success of Lee's antiquated play was due in large part to the way the actresses who appeared in it "embodied fashionable and unsettling aspects of modernity" (71). The argument is ambitious and engaging, yet when Nussbaum asserts that "eighteenth-century actresses provide a key to understanding the relations between representation and reality but also between genres, sexualities, historical moments, and shifting modes of production" (65), one feels the actresses begin to wilt beneath the weight of their symbolic burden.

Any study that takes as broad a scope as Nussbaum's will have its minor errors and omissions. For the most part these do not detract from a hugely enjoyable, stimulating book. However, the chapter on "Actresses and Patrons" contains a consequential error of fact about Elizabeth Pepys, who is alleged to have "attended the theater more frequently toward the end of the seventeenth century" (137), whereas she died in 1669. As David Roberts shows in his study *The Ladies* (1989), Elizabeth's attendance at plays increased toward the end of the 1660s, in proportion with her husband's growing affluence. This misreading undermines Nussbaum's suggestion that Mrs. Pepys's theatregoing "may indicate that dramatic performances [in the Restoration] became increasingly oriented toward encouraging women's presence." The inaccuracy is unfortunate in a chapter that mounts an otherwise persuasive case for the "evolving sociability between ranks" of women (126), fostered by the actresses' modeling of social emulation.

In the introduction to *Rival Queens,* Nussbaum describes her method, using language drawn from performance studies, as articulating "the space between the archive and the repertoire," in the sense of a repertoire of embodied practices (10). Difficult as it is to conjure actors' vocal inflection and timbre, physical stance, habit of movement, innuendo, and gesture, Nussbaum succeeds wonderfully in analyzing the different sorts of "performative magic" (10) of actresses such as Oldfield, Woffington, and, in the epilogue to the book, Sarah Siddons. The archive she examines radiates from the drama in which these women performed to prologues, epilogues, after pieces, operatic spoof, lewd anecdote, histories of the stage, biographical and autobiographical writing by and about celebrated thespians, and commentary in periodical literature such as *The Tatler* and *The Theatrical Review.* Animating a dramatic repertoire that has in the past appeared jejune and lackluster—think ballad opera, farce, sentimental comedy—Nussbaum invigorates her material through an omniverousness of argument that makes the book at once exciting and risky.

—SOPHIE TOMLINSON
University of Auckland

Performing Bodies in Pain: Medieval and Post-Modern Martyrs, Mystics, and Artists. By Marla Carlson. New York: Palgrave Macmillan, 2010. xii + 228 pp. $80.00 cloth.

Somewhat paradoxically, Marla Carlson's *Performing Bodies in Pain* is a book that is both very difficult to read and so compelling that it is hard to put down. Carlson's book is not difficult because of her use of theoretical language or difficult concepts. While Carlson relies heavily on a wide variety of theorists—from cultural scholars to theorists of medicine and psychology—her book remains entirely accessible. The difficulty of *Performing Bodies in Pain* comes from how vividly Carlson writes about pain: its causes, its effects, and the ways that pain (both real and imitated) can be employed in performance. Both Carlson's vivid writing and the sensational performances she examines make her book as engaging as it is challenging.

Carlson's goal is to examine how various spectacles of pain perform cultural work. She argues that this work, despite the subjective nature of pain, is conducted not primarily through individuals but through the groups that become spectators to pain. Carlson's central argument is focused on audience reception; she writes that "dramatized pain typically serves as a means to get at the consciousness of the person who inhabits the body, thereby also serving as a call to action for the spectator" (6). Carlson's book is thus an argument against Elaine Scarry's book *The Body in Pain* (1985), which Carlson sees as arguing that "pain is uniquely private and invisible" (16). In order to support her argument for pain as a cultural spectacle, Carlson compares examples of performances from New York City in the twenty-first century with ones from late medieval France. Carlson begins each chapter with two epigraphs illustrating the nature of the performances she will examine, and alternates between beginning each chapter with the example from New York theatre and French historical performance.

In the first chapter, "Feeling Torture," Carlson examines how the state can use pain to contain marginalized peoples. She begins with a discussion of John Kani and Winston Ntshona's *The Island,* a play about cruel South African imprisonment during apartheid, juxtaposing this analysis with one of *Le geu Saint Denis,* a fifteenth-century saint play about the martyrdom of the patron saint of Paris. Carlson argues that while *The Island* is designed to lead the spectator to political action, *Le geu Saint Denis* instead inspires personal devotion.

Carlson's second chapter, "Imagining Death," explores how sympathy ("imagining the pain of another . . . includ[ing] the judgment that the suffering is not justified" [8]) relates to capital punishment. Here she begins by studying an anonymous Parisian journal written between 1405 and 1449, in which the author describes various public executions at the end of and following the Hundred Years' War. Carlson pairs this example with Martin McDonagh's play *The Pillowman,* in which a totalitarian state executes an author for murders he is believed to have committed. In this chapter, Carlson discusses how execution is "a ritual of expulsion, defining the boundaries of community" (60), but she contrasts these cultures by showing how French medieval executions simultaneously reincorporated the executed person into societal hierarchy through spectacles of pain, while modern executions use the lack of pain to exclude and dehumanize the condemned.

"Enduring Ecstasy," Carlson's third chapter, contrasts body artists' speech with the objectification of the martyred female mystic. Carlson begins with an exploration of Marina Abramović's *Seven Easy Pieces,* performed at the Solomon R. Guggenheim Museum in 2005, and moves on to discuss Jean Fouquet's illustration *Martyrdom of Saint Apollonia* (ca. 1452–60). Through these examples, Carlson examines possible intersections between the performances of femininity and pain. In contrast, the next chapter, "Whipping Up Community," goes on to explore masculine community and group identity formed through pain, first through a discussion of Giovanni del Biondo's triptych *Martyrdom of Saint Sebastian and Scenes from His Life,* and then through a discussion of male body artists, especially Ron Athey and his performance *Judas Cradle.* Here, relying heavily on David Savran's *Taking It Like a Man* (1998), Carlson explores the role of masochism and contractual relationships to the (homo)erotics of feeling pain.

In her final chapter, "Containing Chaos," Carlson compares Sarah Kane's *Blasted* (in its U.S. premiere performance at Soho Rep in 2008) to *Le mystère de Saint Sébastien* in order to explore the ways performative pain can be juxtaposed with laughter and comedy despite intense "violence that seems to turn the world upside down" (132). Using Mikhail Bakhtin's concept of the carnivalesque, Carlson shows how grotesque jokes or clownish commoners such as the villain in the French saint play can both intensify the disturbing nature of the pain we see while also "keep[ing] us . . . watching the unwatchable" (144).

In my brief description of *Performing Bodies in Pain,* I have not done justice to Carlson's intensely affecting book. Her performance criticism is meticulous and insightful, often because of unflinching descriptions of torturous performances that force the reader to imagine that pain. Her book is emotionally challenging and certainly not for the squeamish. However, *Performing Bodies in Pain* is not without several shortcomings. One Carlson acknowledges: she has not conducted archival research, but relied solely upon modern editions currently available. More problematic is the fact that while Carlson reveals illuminating ways in which the medieval and postmodern performances can speak to or against one another, some of the pairings still feel somewhat unnaturally yoked together in each chapter.

Despite these problems, *Performing Bodies in Pain* is an extraordinary book that will be of great value to scholars of pain or medieval or postmodern New York performance, and of interest to all scholars of performance. Moreover, through careful attention to historical detail, Carlson succeeds in her secondary goal of "break[ing] apart the [perceived] uniform and unified Middle Ages as a simple cultural signifier" (23). Through her analysis of the performances, she shows how, even in France alone, this period could be as complex and fragmented as our postmodern era. Carlson's historical sensitivity, superb performance criticism, and vivid writing make *Performing Bodies in Pain* compelling, and, perhaps troublingly, highly enjoyable to read.

—**DAN VENNING**
CUNY Graduate Center

Representing the Past: Essays in Performance Historiography. Edited by Charlotte M. Canning and Thomas Postlewait. Iowa City: University of Iowa Press, 2010. vii + 428 pp. $29.95 paper or e-book.

Theatre Historiography: Critical Interventions. Edited by Henry Bial and Scott Magelssen. Ann Arbor: University of Michigan Press, 2010. x + 312 pp. $28.95 paper, $85.00 cloth.

Theatre historians have been transforming their field over the past thirty years, and as Jimmy Durante often observed during his performances, in one of the most profound performative analyses and historiographical truths of all times, "Everybody wants to be in on the act." As in any maturation process, the developments in theatre history have brought opportunities, issues, and identity crises.

Our research and our classrooms, like those of most of our colleagues in the humanities and social sciences, have been reshaped by—to list only the more salient forces—postmodern insights into language and narrative, cultural studies, performance studies, pressing ethical and social justice issues, and satellite-spun webs of global communication. Among the early works in our field that spurred changes were landmark anthologies of essays representing new historiographical issues and methods. These included Thomas Postlewait and Bruce A. McConachie's *Representing the Theatrical Past* (1989), Sue-Ellen Case and Janelle Reinelt's *Performance of Power: Theatrical Discourse and Politics* (1991), and Janelle G. Reinelt and Joseph R. Roach's *Critical Theory and Performance* (1992). Important essays on historiography in *Theatre Journal* and *Theatre Survey*—including those by Postlewait, recast and offered with new work in his recent *Cambridge Introduction to Historiography* (2009)—also marked the journey. An anxious critique of some new works came in Robert D. Hume's monograph *Reconstructing Contexts: The Aims and Principles of Archeo-Historicism* (1999). Today, we and our students approach performance history aware of a variety of interpretive models and the performances of a variety of neglected peoples and cultures, historical and contemporary. We quarry the archive and also query its construction. We cross epistemological boundaries. We are also still in need of continuing conversations about theatre historiography. The two new anthologies of essays under review address the need in complementary ways.

In their introduction, Canning and Postlewait mark out five "modes of thinking" to use as we represent performances of the past: *archive, time, space, narrative,* and *identity* (16–26). In essays of exceptional quality, fifteen senior scholars engage with these in diverse ways as they work through their subjects. Each mode is illustrated by three essays—although more than one concept is sometimes in play in a given essay. The terms describe large conceptual framings, not particular interpretive strategies or subject areas, such as we find in feminist, postcolonial, or national identity studies. Those could be pursued under any one of the five rubrics and indeed are in the essays. One can find such modes in play in works in our field, emerging naturally as theatre historians ply the waters of their subjects. The careful articulation of them by Canning and Postlewait is helpful, especially today when we need to make all kinds of choices consciously from arrays of options. The five proposed are offered as especially germane to performance history, with borrowings from Louis O. Mink's *Historical Understanding* (1987). Among other modern touchstones were Marc Bloch's *The Historian's Craft* (1953) and George G. Iggers's *Historiography in the Twentieth Century: From Scientific Objectivity to the Postmodern Challenge* (1997). Of course, such fundamentals as the scrupulous weighing of evidence (or its absence) and recognizing common fallacies in reasoning will still be priorities, as should be the hard work of writing well. The volume's introduction, while prolix, instructively explains the editors' and contributors' collaborative development of the modes.

Catherine M. Cole, working with the idea of *identity,* reflects on hers as a researcher in Ghana and South Africa. Amid the shifting sands of global and national politics across two decades, her negotiations for access to documents or key people in these nations necessarily have required care, even perhaps complicity, as she encounters from gatekeepers the questions "Who are you?" and "Why are you here?" These questions raise first-order issues critical for any historian, because "knowledge about the past is always *interested*" (278). Granted, identities are never fixed, but any researcher, in any landscape, should be able to answer those questions when undertaking the production of knowledge. Under the rubric of *time,* Aparna Dharwadker explains problems in Indian theatre historiography. For one, Western historians often have tried to differentiate between East and West with a reductive binary of linear time (Western rationalistic) and cyclic time (ostensibly Hindu cosmology). Two millennia of Indian performance practices in a polyglot nation include, among other things, theatre influenced by colonialism and a modern urban drama tradition, both erased in Orientalism's dream of a pure indigenous theatre. Recovering the many Indian pasts will entail situating them within changing material circumstances. David Wiles, in the section of essays on *space,* questions the conjuring of audience experiences of the past by privileging not only pictorial representations of theatrical space but vision itself over other sensory inputs. He notes that historians often have projected onto the past notions of performance spaces that legitimate the practices of the historian's era. Considering the *archive,* Susan Bennett reveals the prominent and apparently financially successful role of Elizabeth Inchbald as critic and anthologist in the early 1800s, a role not evident in the usual narratives or archives. Bennett shows an analogous gap in the archive of prominent post–World War II British women writers. Thinking about *narrative,* Bruce McConachie shows that neuroscience's evidence for the operation of the brain's mirror neuron system in our cognitive processing lends support to R. G. Collingwood's famous account of the role of empathy in the historian's imaginative reenactment of past events. The evidence also suggests that our cognitive processes generate more narrative options than Collingwood imagined. McConachie shows empathic simulation in play in the narratives of recent theatre historians. Postlewait and Canning conceive of *narrative* very broadly; considerations of change or causality are circumscribed within it, as are play structures. The Postlewait-Canning modes and the essays that engage them will be important touchstones for discussion in the maturing of the field.

The essays in the Bial and Magelssen collection are spirited and sometimes passionate encounters with historiographical opportunities or problems. The twenty-one pieces, arranged under five broad headings, were selected to represent "the most critical issues" (8) facing theatre historians today. The essays are relatively short, accessible, and stimulating for classroom discussion. For their authors, the postmodern recognition that language and cultural formations always mediate our perceptions of the past is second nature, integral to their sensibilities. The sites of their historiographical forays include the classroom and the practical stage. Essays in part 1, "Unearthing the Past," have much in common with those under the concept of archive in Postlewait and Canning. Odai Johnson, for example, raises the buried curse tablets of Greek and Roman slaves to raise our awareness of the possible histories behind the portraits of the slaves, whom we take as a comic convention, in classical comedy. Robert B. Shimko brings William Davenant's (surprising) experience as a pirate or privateer to bear on his pre-Restoration operatic works. Heather S. Nathans tries to imagine more socially organic ways, wanting wider narrative nets, by which we might add to our knowledge of Jewish involvement in early American theatre. Under part 2, "The Stakes of Historiography," Erin B. Mee argues that in India the colonial equation of theatre with text-based, plot-driven plays by single authors erased indigenous performance-based theatre traditions. There is a classroom conversation to be had comparing this and Dharwadker's critique of Western-influenced historiography in India in Postlewait and Canning. In part 5, "Theatre History's Discipline," Judith Sebesta and Jessica Sternfield urge us to collaborate across disciplines in writing histories of musical theatre. They conclude their article on *Rent* with a dialogue between them in which their close reading of the musical onstage and in film is a model collaboration between acute theatrical and musical sensibilities. The possibilities for collaborations in cultural studies and theatre are many. In the same section, James Peck notes the array of interdisciplinary approaches that already characterizes our discipline and then suggests, using a Brechtian example, that our own theatre practices offer strategies from which we (and other disciplines) might draw.

I found Bial and Magelssen's part 4, "Performance as Historiography," especially welcome because the essays value the imaginative engagements of the historian, student, artist, and audience in representations of the past. The essays represent epistemological experiments that seem natural to a profession that understands and values the art that goes into constructing history. Magelssen suggests in his "Performance as Learner-Driven Historiography" that we can encourage the historiographic consciousness of students by helping them create performative, embodied engagements with events of the past (cf. McConachie above), including events from theatre history. They begin with information and end with reflections on their choices. Nicholas Ridout's "The Ice, a Collective History of Our Collectivity in the Theatre" shows a Latvian theatre company consciously playing with the conflicting feelings of seduction and repulsion that audiences experience watching the actors create a kind of Aryan cult, an experience analogous to the conflicted history of Latvia in World War II and the Holocaust. To turn back for a moment to the Canning and Postlewait collection, faith in the possibilities of an artist's imaginative synthesis in representing history surfaces like a dolphin in Harry J. Elam Jr.'s essay. Concerned with *identity* and *narrative,* Elam finds in Lorraine Hansberry's *Drinking Gourd* (1960) and Suzan-Lori Parks's *Venus* (1996) complex delineations of race that require us to interrogate existing narratives and identity constructions. "Play-making serves as a form of historiography," and identity "as a critical source of meaning" (283), Elam writes. Mechelle Leon, in her "Corpsing Molière: History as Fiasco" in Bial and Magelssen, considers the fascination of historians, playwrights, and filmmakers with Molière's death (or near death) onstage in his last performance of *Le malade imaginaire.* Drawing on Ridout's *Stage Fright, Animals and Other Theatrical Problems* (2006), she considers "dying" onstage, as in failing badly in a performance, as an example of phenomena that involve malfunctions of theatrical illusion. That we are fascinated with such irruptions of reality undercutting the theatre's own narrative suggests to Leon a historiographical principle: train one eye on events that trouble any representation of the past.

Most of the essays in Bial and Magelssen are successes; a few would benefit from hard-eyed critiques of their premises and implications. What the editors want us to do is talk about all of the opportunities and problems they present from the field as a work in progress (see Bial's postscript, "PS: Can we talk about this?" [276–86]).

There is a glaring absence in the two volumes, however, that should concern us if we take the combined thirty-six essays to represent our field today. Saving the pieces by Elam and Leon and one traditional one by Jonathan Chambers on death and dying on page and stage, there are no prolonged engagements in the essays in either volume with particular plays of major Western dramatists in performance (in any era), culturally, historically situated. Can we talk about this?

—GARY JAY WILLIAMS
Professor Emeritus, Drama
The Catholic University of America
Washington, D.C.

The American Stage: Writing on Theater from Washington Irving to Tony Kushner. Edited by Laurence Senelick. New York: The Library of America, 2010. xxxi + 867 pp. $40.00 cloth.

The erudite and talented actor—and, I'm happy to report, knowledgeable student of American theatre—John Lithgow, author of the foreword to Laurence Senelick's marvelous compilation of essays, reviews, parodies, and other reflections on American theatre "from Washington Irving to Tony Kushner" (or 1802–2005), suggests three ways to approach this cornucopia of delights: you can read it chronologically front to back and "you have a lively portrait of the American stage"; you can begin at the back and "you travel a unique journey back in time . . . [and] pass from the very familiar, to the vaguely remembered, to the totally forgotten"; or you can simply dip in anywhere. Lithgow does warn that it is "hard to decide what to pick and where to start" (xiv–xv).

In glancing through the content of almost one hundred pieces, I thought I knew enough not to have to read them all or read many at one sitting. I'd place the volume on my nightstand and "dip" into a few essays each evening. Furthermore, I decided to give the collection the "Wilmeth" test and look for a favorite essay chosen off the top of my head. If it was included, I could praise Senelick for his wise choices; if not, then I could note the lack of inconclusiveness in his impossible task of selectivity. So, what single item would I seek in these 850-plus pages?

In 1957, shortly after graduating from high school in Texas and before I entered college in my native state, I had the opportunity to attend summer school at Cornell University as a special student. Being intimidated by most academic choices available to me, in ignorance I turned to theatre courses (my high school drama teacher had extolled Cornell's theatre). One of my courses was Play Production taught by H. Darkes Albright, an important pioneer in academic theatre—and something of an eccentric. Early in the course Professor Albright read to the class part of an essay from *Holiday* magazine published in January 1955. It was called "The American Theatre" and was written by the playwright Arthur Miller (I was a dedicated reader of *Theater Arts* and had actually heard of him). In his seersucker suit, socks rolled down to his ankles, and pencil mustache, Albright began reading in his deep and resonant voice Miller's description of Lee J. Cobb creating the role of Willy Loman in *Death of a Salesman,* and demonstrating how "the theater can yet be one of the chief glories of mankind." I was hooked. And in retrospect (did Albright roll his socks or wear a pencil mustache?—after more than half a century I believe he did) I think I owe my life's work and passion to this moment. Senelick passed my test, for there in the center of the book is Miller's inspiring essay, and my revisiting of its content brought back a lifetime of memories.

At that moment I decided I could not follow Lithgow's suggestion of reading from back to front—or even dip into the book at random. No, I had to begin at the beginning (after reading with pleasure Senelick's vivid potted history of American theatre, full of his wit and unique turn of a phrase) and travel to the end. And I urge others to do so as well!

Without The Library of America, founded in 1979 and designed to help "preserve our nation's literary heritage by publishing, and keeping in print, authoritative editions of America's best and most significant writing," Senelick's extensive compilation likely could not exist in this time of shrinking publication in our discipline and rising cost in publishing. *The American Stage* is number 203 in this series and quite unlike most of the other volumes, which tend to focus on one author or one genre. Senelick had the challenge of selecting from roughly 250 years of history pieces that represented important moments, or individuals, or attitudes, or analyses of plays or productions that signal landmarks, notable change, or simply a vivid glimpse into the past. Senelick, a master of good writing, a devotee of language and style in prose exposition, and always striving for clarity in his own writing—and that of others—critiques contemporary serious academic writing on theatre in his introduction. He writes that many academics (note: not all) "who take the theatre as their field of interest are content to address fellow specialists in an argot impenetrable to the uninitiated" (xxix). He also notes the loss of great critical minds who have few opportunities today to write thoughtful pieces on the theatre. Print has lost much of its authority to the Internet; to true critics of the past (as contrasted to daily reviewers today) "the rich hoard of past writing stands as an articulate testament to the importance of playgoing, play-acting, and playwriting to past generations and to the thinking present" (xxix). With these ideas articulated, it is fairly easy to see the criteria that guided Senelick to make his choices: "My intention was to put together an assortment of first-hand written responses to the theatrical experience that display insight, wit, or strong feeling" (xxix).

Senelick admits that he has not created a documentary history of the American theatre (although with his authoritative, often witty, succinct, and contextualized introductions to each selection, he certainly offers effective background and transitions for each piece). Perhaps not a documentary history, this volume nevertheless belongs to a tradition of overviews that date back at least to 1934 and *The American Theatre as Seen by Its Critics, 1752–1934*, edited by the early historian of American drama Montrose J. Moses and the productive (and I believe undervalued) critic John Mason Brown (represented in this volume by a 1949 essay). Composed wholly of print reviews, this remains a worthy collection, from whence Senelick has, not surprisingly, made a number of obvious selections.

In 1957, Barnard Hewitt, a pioneer in the study of American theatre, did attempt to compile, with his own narrative providing a historical structure for the individual documents (and essays, not limited to reviews), a work that essentially provided one of the first American theatre texts *(Theatre U.S.A., 1668 to 1957)*. Finally, in 1996, Barry Witham edited a volume devoted to *Theatre in the United States: A Documentary History* (this was volume 1, 1750–1915; a second planned volume has yet to appear). More than the first two, Witham's volume *is* a documentary history, utilizing a wide variety of documents in telling its story.

So how does Senelick differ from these three? As noted above, the choices made by him are almost all beautifully articulated, representative of the best writing on American theatre to date. Readers will not be disappointed in what they find as they move through the volume. Most of the great critics are here: Washington Irving, Edgar Allan Poe, Walt Whitman, Alan Dale, William Winter, Stark Young, Alexander Woollcott, James G. Huneker, Robert Benchley, Gilbert Seldes, George Jean Nathan, Brooks Atkinson, Morton Eustis, Mary McCarthy, Harold Clurman, John Mason Brown, Eric Bentley, Walter Kerr, John Simon, John Lahr, and Frank Rich. (As one moves toward the end of the compilation, fewer and fewer critics are cited, a fact that makes it own comment about the present state of serious critical writing.)

But this is *not* a book of just criticism; other outstanding writers and unexpected surprises are just as prominent as the critics. In addition to writers whom one might well expect (William Dunlap, Frances Trollope, de Tocqueville, Olive Logan, William Gillette, Hallie Flanagan, Elia Kazan, William Goldman, John Houseman, Anne Bogart, and other practitioners), Senelick has included writings on American theatre from literary greats such as Mark Twain, Henry James, Willa Cather, Ezra Pound, Dorothy Parker, Ring Lardner, Edmund Wilson, Alain Locke, Hamlin Garland, Thomas Wolfe, Tennessee Williams, Gore Vidal, Lorraine Hansberry, Edward Albee, Luis Valdez, Spalding Gray, Charles Ludlam, Wendy Wasserstein, David Mamet, and Tony Kushner, among others.

As Senelick openly confesses, one could easily argue for other choices—either in addition to those included or in place of them—and his selections as a whole could be attacked for their sins of omission. But such an exercise would be petty, a waste of energy, and ultimately counterproductive. For this compilation is based on judicious choices—informed, drawn from options immensely larger than what we find here, and ultimately quite satisfying. The coverage is balanced, the criteria clear, and the joy of discovery marks virtually every page. Few in our discipline could have accomplished this task with such appreciation, objectivity, and wholehearted dedication. Thank you, Laurence Senelick!

My advice: obtain a copy of *The American Stage,* read it often, take pleasure in your discoveries and learn from them, glory in the wit and entertainment here, and be grateful for the tireless effort it required to produce this stunning collection.

—DON B. WILMETH
Brown University, emeritus

BOOKS RECEIVED

Anderson, Joseph L. *Enter a Samurai: Kawakami Otojirõ and Japanese Theatre in the West.* Vols. 1 and 2. Tucson: Wheatmark, 2011.

Bernstein, Robin. *Racial Innocence: Performing American Childhood from Slavery to Civil Rights.* New York: New York University Press, 2011.

Chazin-Bennahum, Judith. *René Blum and the Ballets Russes: In Search of a Lost Life.* New York: Oxford University Press, 2011.

Estok, Simon. *Ecocriticism and Shakespeare: Reading Ecophobia.* New York: Palgrave MacMillan, 2011.

Garebian, Keith. *The Making of Cabaret.* 2nd ed. New York: Oxford University Press, 2011.

Hart, Jonathan. *Shakespeare and His Contemporaries.* New York: Palgrave MacMillan, 2011.

Holdsworth, Nadine. *Joan Littlewood's Theatre.* New York: Cambridge University Press, 2011.

Knapp, James A. *Image Ethics in Shakespeare and Spenser.* New York: Palgrave MacMillan, 2011.

O'Quinn, Daniel. *Entertaining Crisis in the Atlantic Imperium, 1770–1790.* Baltimore: Johns Hopkins University Press, 2011.

Ramirez, Elizabeth C., and Catherine Casiano, eds. *La Voz Latina: Contemporary Plays and Performance Pieces by Latinas.* Urbana: University of Illinois Press, 2011.

Schneider, Rebecca. *Performing Remains: Art and War in Times of Theatrical Reenactment.* New York: Routledge, 2011.

Storm, William. *Irony and the Modern Theatre.* New York: Cambridge University Press, 2011.

Sullivan, Jill A. *The Politics of the Pantomime: Regional Identity in the Theatre, 1860–1900.* Hertfordshire: University of Hertfordshire Press, 2011.

Thompson, Ayanna. *Passing Strange: Shakespeare, Race, and Contemporary America.* New York: Oxford University Press, 2011.

Wiles, David. *Theatre and Citizenship: The History of a Practice.* London: Cambridge University Press, 2011.

CONTRIBUTORS

PENNY FARFAN is a Professor of Drama at the University of Calgary. She is the author of *Women, Modernism, and Performance* (2004) as well as many articles and book chapters, including "Women's Modernism and Performance" in *The Cambridge Companion to Modernist Women Writers* (2010). She coedited (with Kate Kelly) a special issue of *South Central Review* on "Staging Modernism" (2008) and she is the currently the editor of *Theatre Journal.*

VICTOR HOLTCAMP is an Assistant Professor of Theatre at the University of South Carolina in Columbia. He has published in a variety of journals and has given papers at national and international conferences. Research areas include Shakespearean studies, acting pedagogy, and the intersections of culture, industry, and theatre.

LISA JACKSON-SCHEBETTA is an Assistant Professor in Theatre Arts at the University of Pittsburgh. Her current book project examines U.S.-based English- and Spanish-language theatre in relation to the Spanish Civil War. She holds a Ph.D. in Theatre History, Criticism, and Theory from the University of Washington and an M.F.A. in Theatre Pedagogy from Virginia Commonwealth University.

RICHARD L. POOLE, Chair/Professor of Theatre and Speech Communication at Briar Cliff University, is a Fulbright Scholar who has written and lectured extensively on Midwestern rural theatre. His essays have appeared in *Theatre History Studies*, *The Guide to United States Popular Culture*, *The Tamkang Review* (Taiwan), and the *Cambridge Guide to American Theatre* (2nd ed.). He is coauthor (with Dr. George Glenn) of *The Opera Houses of Iowa* (1992).

BILL RAUCH was named Artistic Director of the Oregon Shakespeare Festival in 2007. Prior to his appointment, he completed a twenty-year journey as cofounder and artistic director of the Cornerstone Theater Company. He has directed at the Lincoln Center Theater, the Guthrie Theater, and the Mark Taper Forum. He is an Associate Artist at Yale Repertory Theatre and South Coast Repertory and is the recipient of the 2009 Margo Jones Medal.

THOMAS ROBSON is an Assistant Professor of Theatre and Dance at Millikin University, where he teaches courses in theatre history, dramatic literature, and directing. His research focuses on turn-of-the-century African-American theatre and drama, with additional work on American musical theatre and American film. His work has previously appeared in the performance journal *Ecumenica* and the film journal *Jump Cut*.

MARLIS SCHWEITZER is an Associate Professor of Theatre Studies at York University, where she teaches courses on performance and commodity culture, theatre research methodologies, and nineteenth-century popular entertainment. She is the author of *When Broadway Was the Runway: Theater, Fashion, and American Culture* (2009) and has published articles in *Theatre Journal, Theatre Survey, TDR, Theatre Research International,* and *Theatre Research in Canada.* Her current research focuses on tracking the transnational trade in theatrical commodities between Europe and North America in the nineteenth and early twentieth centuries.

VIRGINIA SCOTT is a Professor Emerita of Theater at the University of Massachusetts at Amherst. Her most recent book is *Women on the Stage in Early Modern France* (2010).

CHRISTINE WOODWORTH is an Assistant Professor in the Department of Theatre and a cross-appointed faculty member in the Women's and Gender Studies Program at the University of North Carolina at Greensboro. She teaches theatre history and feminist theatre and serves as departmental dramaturge. Her articles and reviews have appeared in *Theatre Symposium, Theatre Annual, Text and Presentation, Theatre Topics, Theatre Journal,* and TLA's *Broadside* as well as several essay collections.

www.ingramcontent.com/pod-product-compliance
Lightning Source LLC
LaVergne TN
LVHW091920120926
847717LV00046B/161